Protecting Privacy in Video Surveillance

Andrew Senior

Editor

Protecting Privacy in Video Surveillance

 Springer

Editor
Andrew Senior
Google Research, New York
USA
a.senior@ieee.org

ISBN 978-1-84882-300-6   e-ISBN 978-1-84882-301-3
DOI 10.1007/978-1-84882-301-3
Springer Dordrecht Heidelberg London New York

British Library Cataloguing in Publication Data
A catalogue record for this book is available from the British Library

Library of Congress Control Number: 2009922088

Printed on acid-free paper

Springer is part of Springer Science+Business Media (www.springer.com)

Foreword

Fueled by growing asymmetric/terrorist threats, deployments of surveillance systems have been exploding in the 21st century. Research has also continued to increase the power of surveillance, so that today's computers can watch hundreds of video feeds and automatically detect a growing range of activities. Proponents see expanding surveillance as a necessary element of improving security, with the associated loss in privacy being a natural if unpleasant choice faced by society trying to improve security. To the surprise of many, a 2007 federal court ruled that the New York Police must stop the routine videotaping of people at public gatherings unless there is an indication that unlawful activity may occur. Is the continuing shift to a surveillance society a technological inevitability, or will the public backlash further limit video surveillance?

Big Brother, the ever-present but never seen dictator in George Orwell's *Nineteen Eighty-Four*, has been rated as one of the top 100 villains of all time and one of the top 5 most influential people that never lived. For many the phrase "Big Brother" has become a catch-phrase for the potential for abuse in a surveillance society. On the other hand, a "Big Brother" can also be someone that looks out for others, either a literal family member or maybe a mentor in a volunteer program.

The diametric interpretations of "Big Brother", are homologous with the larger issue in surveillance. Video surveillance can be protective and beneficial to society or, if misused, it can be intrusive and used to stifle liberty. While policies can help balance security and privacy, a fundamental research direction that needs to be explored, with significant progress presented within this book, challenges the assumption that there is an inherent trade-off between security and privacy.

The chapters in this book make important contributions in how to develop technological solutions that simultaneously improve privacy while still supporting, or even improving, the security systems seeking to use the video surveillance data. The researchers present multiple win-win solutions. To the researchers whose work is presented herein, thank you and keep up the good work. This is important work that will benefit society for decades to come.

There are at least three major groups that should read this book. If you are a researcher working in video surveillance, detection or tracking, or a researcher in social issues in privacy, this is a must-read. The techniques and ideas presented could transform your future research helping you see how to solve both security and privacy problems. The final group that needs to read this book are technological advisors to policy makers, where it's important to recognize that there are effective alternatives to invasive video surveillance. When there was a forced choice between security and privacy, the greater good may have lead to an erosion of privacy. However, with the technology described herein, that erosion is no longer justified. Policies need to change to keep up with technological advances.

It's a honor to write a Foreword for this book. This is an important topic, and is a collection of the best work drawn from an international cast of preeminent researchers. As a co-organizer of the first IEEE Workshop on Privacy Research in Vision, with many of the chapter authors presenting at that workshop, it is great to see the work continue and grow. I hope this is just the first of many books on this topic – and maybe the next one will include a chapter by you.

El Pomar Professor of Innovation and Security,   Terrance Boult
University of Colorado at Colorado Springs Chair,   April 2009
IEEE Technical Committee on Pattern
Analysis and Machine Intelligence

Preface

Privacy protection is an increasing concern in modern life, as more and more information on individuals is stored electronically, and as it becomes easier to access and distribute that information. One area where data collection has grown tremendously in recent years is video surveillance. In the wake of London bombings in the 1990s and the terrorist attacks of September 11th 2001, there has been a rush to deploy video surveillance. At the same time prices of hardware have fallen, and the capabilities of systems have grown dramatically as they have changed from simple analogue installations to sophisticated, "intelligent" automatic surveillance systems.

The ubiquity of surveillance cameras linked with the power to automatically analyse the video has driven fears about the loss of privacy. The increase in video surveillance with the potential to aggregate information over thousands of cameras and many other networked information sources, such as health, financial, social security and police databases, as envisioned in the "Total Information Awareness" programme, coupled with an erosion of civil liberties, raises the spectre of much greater threats to privacy that many have compared to those imagined by Orwell in "1984".

In recent years, people have started to look for ways that technology can be used to protect privacy in the face of this increasing video surveillance. Researchers have begun to explore how a collection of technologies from computer vision to cryptography can limit the distribution and access to privacy intrusive video; others have begun to explore mechanisms protocols for the assertion of privacy rights; while others are investigating the effectiveness and acceptability of the proposed technologies.

Audience

This book brings together some of the most important current work in video surveillance privacy protection, showing the state-of-the-art today and the breadth of the field. The book is targeted primarily at researchers, graduate students and developers in the field of automatic video surveillance, particularly those interested in the areas of computer vision and cryptography. It will also be of interest to those with a broader interest in privacy and video surveillance, from fields such as social effects, law and public policy. This book is intended to serve as a valuable resource for video surveillance companies, data protection offices and privacy organisations.

Organisation

The first chapter gives an overview of automatic video surveillance systems as a grounding for those unfamiliar with the field. Subsequent chapters present research from teams around the world, both in academia and industry. Each chapter has a bibliography which collectively references all the important work in this field.

Cheung et al. describe a system for the analysis and secure management of privacy containing streams. Senior explores the design and performance analysis of systems that modify video to hide private data. Avidan et al. explore the use of cryptographic protocols to limit access to private data while still being able to run complex analytical algorithms. Schiff et al. describe a system in which the desire for privacy is asserted by the wearing of a visual marker, and Brassil describes a mechanism by which a wireless Privacy-Enabling Device allows an individual to control access to surveillance video in which they appear. Chen et al. show conditions under which face obscuration is not sufficient to guarantee privacy, and Gross et al. show a system to provably mask facial identity with minimal impact on the usability of the surveillance video. Babaguchi et al. investigate the level of privacy protection a system provides, and its dependency on the relationship between the watcher and the watched. Hayes et al. present studies on the deployment of video systems with privacy controls. Truong et al. present the BlindSpot system that can prevent the capture of images, asserting privacy not just against surveillance systems, but also against uncontrolled hand-held cameras.

Video surveillance is rapidly expanding and the development of privacy protection mechanisms is in its infancy. These authors are beginning to explore the technical and social issues around these advanced technologies and to see how they can be brought into real-world surveillance systems.

Acknowledgments

I gratefully acknowledge the support of my colleagues in the IBM T.J.Watson Research Center's Exploratory Computer Vision group during our work together on the IBM Smart Surveillance System and the development of privacy protection ideas together: Sharath Pankanti, Lisa Brown, Arun Hampapur, Ying-Li Tian, Ruud Bolle, Jonathan Connell, Rogerio Feris, Chiao-Fe Shu. I would like to thank the staff at Springer for their encouragement, and finally my wife Christy for her support throughout this project.

The WITNESS project

Royalties from this book will be donated to the WITNESS project (witness.org) which uses video and online technologies to open the eyes of the world to human rights violations.

New York *Andrew Senior*

Contents

Contributors

Shai Avidan Adobe Systems Inc., Newton, MA, USA, avidan@adobe.com

Noboru Babaguchi Deparment of Communication Engineering, Osaka University, Suita, Osaka 565-0871, Japan, babaguchi@comm.eng.osaka-u.ac.jp

Simon Baker Microsoft Research, Microsoft Corporation, Redmond, WA 98052, USA, sbaker@microsoft.com

Jack Brassil HP Laboratories, Princeton, NJ 08540, USA, jtb@hpl.hp.com

Yi Chang School of Computer Science, Carnegie Mellon University, Pittsburgh, PA 15213, USA, changyi@cs.cmu.edu

Datong Chen School of Computer Science, Carnegie Mellon University, Pittsburgh, PA 15213, USA, datong@cs.cmu.edu

S.-C.S. Cheung Center for Visualization and Virtual Environments, University of Kentucky, Lexington, KY 40507, USA, cheung@engr.uky.edu

Jeffrey Cohn Department of Psychology, University of Pittsburgh, Pittsburgh, PA, USA, jeffcohn@pitt.edu

Ariel Elbaz Columbia University, New York, NY, USA, arielbaz@cs.columbia.edu

Ken Goldberg Faculty of Departments of EECS and IEOR, University of California, Berkeley, CA, USA, goldberg@berkeley.edu

Ralph Gross Data Privacy Lab, School of Computer Science,Carnegie Mellon University, Pittsburgh, PA, USA, rgross@cs.cmu.edu

Gillian R. Hayes Department of Informatics, Donald Bren School of Information and Computer Science, University of California, Irvine, CA 92697-3440, USA, gillianrh@ics.uci.edu

Takashi Koshimizu Graduate School of Engineering, Osaka University, Suita, Osaka 565-0871, Japan

Tal Malkin Columbia University, New York, NY, USA, tal@cs.columbia.edu

Marci Meingast Department of EECS, University of California, Berkeley, CA, USA, marci@eecs.berkeley.edu

Ryan Moriarty University of California, LA, USA, ryan@cs.ucla.edu

Deirdre K. Mulligan Faculty of the School of Information, University of California, Berkeley, CA, USA, dmulligan@law.berkeley.edu

T. Nguyen School of Electrical Engineering and Computer Science, Oregon State University, Corvallis, OR 97331, USA

J.K. Paruchuri Center for Visualization and Virtual Environments, University of Kentucky, Lexington, KY 40507, USA

Shwetak N. Patel Computer Science and Engineering and Electrical Engineering, University of Washington Seattle, WA 98195, USA, shwetak@cs.washington.edu

Shankar Sastry Faculty of the Department of EECS, University of California, Berkeley, CA, USA, sastry@eecs.berkeley.edu

Jeremy Schiff Department of EECS, University of California, Berkeley, CA, USA, jschiff@eecs.berkeley.edu

Andrew Senior Google Research, New York, USA, a.senior@ieee.org

Jay W. Summet College of Computing & GVU, Center Georgia Institute of Technology Atlanta, GA 30332, USA summetj@cc.gatech.edu

Latanya Sweeney Data Privacy Lab, School of Computer Science,Carnegie Mellon University, Pittsburgh, PA, USA, latanyag@cs.cmu.edu

Tomoji Toriyama Advanced Telecommunications Research Institute International, Kyoto, Japan

Fernando de la Torre Robotics Institute, Carnegie Mellon University, Pittsburgh, PA, USA, ftorre@cs.cmu.edu

Khai N. Truong Department of Computer Science, University of Toronto, Toronto, ON M5S 2W8, Canada, khai@cs.toronto.edu

Ichiro Umata National Institute of Information and Communications Technology, Koganei, Tokyo 184-8795, Japan

M.V. Venkatesh Center for Visualization and Virtual Environments, University of Kentucky, Lexington, KY 40507, USA

Rong Yan School of Computer Science, Carnegie Mellon University, Pittsburgh, PA 15213, USA, yanrong@cs.cmu.edu

Jie Yang School of Computer Science, Carnegie Mellon University, Pittsburgh, PA 15213, USA, yang@cs.cmu.edu

J. Zhao Center for Visualization and Virtual Environments, University of Kentucky, Lexington, KY 40507, USA

An Introduction to Automatic Video Surveillance

Andrew Senior

Abstract We present a brief summary of the elements in an automatic video surveillance system, from imaging system to metadata. Surveillance system architectures are described, followed by the steps in video analysis, from preprocessing to object detection, tracking, classification and behaviour analysis.

1 Introduction

Video surveillance is a rapidly growing industry. Driven by low-hardware costs, heightened security fears and increased capabilities; video surveillance equipment is being deployed ever more widely, and with ever greater storage and ability for recall. The increasing sophistication of video analysis software, and integration with other sensors, have given rise to better scene analysis, and better abilities to search for and retrieve relevant pieces of surveillance data. These capabilities of "understanding" the video that permit us to distinguish "interesting" from "uninteresting" video, also allow some distinction between "privacy intrusive" and "privacy neutral" video data that can be the basis for protecting privacy in video surveillance systems. This chapter describes the common capabilities of automated video surveillance systems (e.g. [3, 11, 17, 26, 34]) and outlines some of the techniques used, to provide a general introduction to the foundations on which the subsequent chapters are based. Readers familiar with automatic video analysis techniques may want to skip to the remaining chapters of the book.

1.1 Domains

Video surveillance is a broad term for the remote observation of locations using video cameras. The video cameras capture the appearance of a scene (usually in the visible spectrum) electronically and the video is transmitted to another location

A. Senior (✉)
Google Research, New York, NY, USA
e-mail: a.senior@ieee.org

A. Senior (ed.), *Protecting Privacy in Video Surveillance*,
DOI 10.1007/978-1-84882-301-3_1, © Springer-Verlag London Limited 2009

Fig. 1 A simple, traditional CCTV system with monitors connected directly to analogue cameras, and no understanding of the video

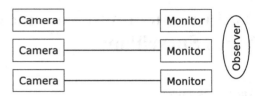

to be observed by a human, analysed by a computer, or stored for later observation or analysis. Video surveillance has progressed from simple closed-circuit television (CCTV) systems, as shown in Fig. 1, that simply allowed an operator to observe from a different location (unobtrusively and from many viewpoints at once) to automatic systems that analyse and store video from hundreds of cameras and other sensors, detecting events of interest automatically, and allowing the search and browsing of data through sophisticated user interfaces.

Video surveillance has found applications in many fields, primarily the detection of intrusion into secure premises and the detection of theft or other criminal activities. Increasingly though, video surveillance technologies are also being used to gather data on the presence and actions of people for other purposes such as designing museum layouts, monitoring traffic or controlling heating and air-conditioning.

Current research is presented in workshops such as Visual Surveillance (VS); Performance Evaluation of Tracking and Surveillance (PETS); and Advanced Video and Signal-based Surveillance (AVSS). Commercial systems are presented at tradeshows such as ISC West & East.

2 Architectures

In this section, we outline common architectures for surveillance systems. Figure 1 shows a simple, directly monitored, CCTV system. Analogue video is being replaced by digital video which can be multiplexed via Internet Protocol over standard networks. Storage is increasingly on digital video recorders (DVRs) or on video content management systems. Figure 2 shows a more complex, centralized system where video from the cameras is stored at a central server which also distributes video for analysis, and to the user through a computer interface. Video analysis is carried out by computers (using conventional or embedded processors) and results in the extraction of salient information (metadata) which is stored in a database for searching and retrieval.

More sophisticated distributed architectures can be designed where video storage and/or processing are carried out at the camera (See Fig. 3), reducing bandwidth requirements by eliminating the need to transmit video except when requested for viewing by the user, or copied for redundancy. Metadata is stored in a database, potentially also distributed, and the system can be accessed from multiple locations.

A key aspect of a surveillance system is physical, electronic and digital security. To prevent attacks and eavesdropping, all the cameras and cables must be secured,

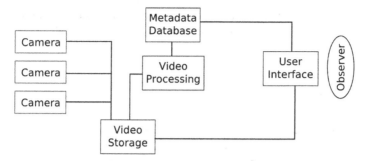

Fig. 2 A centralized architecture with a video management system that stores digital video as well as supplying it to video processing and for display on the user interface. A database stores and allows searching of the video based on automatically extracted metadata

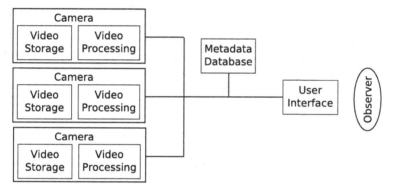

Fig. 3 A decentralized architecture with video processing and storage at the camera. Metadata is aggregated in a database for searching

and digital signals need to be encrypted. Furthermore, systems need full IT security to prevent unauthorized access to video feeds and stored data.

2.1 Sensors

The most important sensor in a video surveillance system is the video camera. A wide range of devices is now available, in contrast to the black-and-white, low-resolution, analogue cameras that were common a few years ago. Cameras can stream high-resolution digital colour images, with enhanced dynamic range, large zoom factors and in some cases automatic foveation to track moving targets. Cameras with active and passive infrared are also becoming common, and costs of all cameras have tumbled.

Even a simple CCTV system may incorporate other sensors, for instance recording door opening, pressure pads or beam-breaker triggers. More sophisticated surveillance systems can incorporate many different kinds of sensors and integrate their information to allow complex searches. Of particular note are biometric sensors and RFID tag readers that allow the identification of individuals observed with the video cameras.

3 Video Analysis

Figure 4 shows a typical sequence of video analysis operations in an automatic video surveillance system. Each operation is described in more detail in the following sections. Video from the camera is sent to the processing unit (which may be on the same chip as the image sensor, or many miles apart, connected with a network) and may first be processed (Section 3.1) to prepare it for the subsequent algorithms. Object detection (Section 3.2) finds areas of interest in the video, and tracking (Section 3.3) associates these over time into records corresponding to a single object (e.g. person or vehicle). These records can be analysed further (Section 3.4) to determine the object type or identity (Section 3.4.1) and to analyse behaviour (Section 3.4.2), particularly to generate alerts when behaviours of interest are observed. In each of the following sections we present some typical examples, though there is a great variety of techniques and systems being developed.

Fig. 4 Basic sequence of processing operations for video analysis

3.1 Preprocessing

Preprocessing consists of low-level and preliminary operations on the video. These will depend very much on the type of video to be processed, but might include decompression, automatic gain and white-balance compensation as well as smoothing, enhancement and noise reduction [6] to improve the quality of the image and reduce errors in subsequent operations. Image stabilization can also be carried out here to correct for small camera movements.

3.2 Object Detection

Object detection is the fundamental process at the core of automatic video analysis. Algorithms are used to detect objects of interest for further processing. Detection algorithms vary according to the situation, but in most cases moving objects are of interest, and static parts of the scene are not, so object detection is recast as the detection of motion. In many surveillance situations, there is often very little activity, so moving objects are detected in only a fraction of the video. If pan-tilt-zoom (PTZ) cameras are used, then the whole image will change when the camera moves, so techniques such as trained object detectors (below) must be used, but the vast majority of video surveillance analysis software assumes that the cameras are static.

Motion detection is most commonly carried out using a class of algorithms known as "background subtraction". These algorithms construct a background model of the usual appearance of the scene when no moving object is present. Then, as live video frames are processed, they are compared to the background model and differences are flagged as moving objects. Many systems carry out this analysis independently on each pixel of the image [8, 13], and a common approach today is based on the work of Stauffer and Grimson [27] where each pixel is modelled by multiple Gaussian distributions which represent the observed variations in colour of the pixel in the red–green–blue colour space. Observations that do not match the Gaussian(s) most frequently observed in the recent past are considered foreground. Background modelling algorithms need to be able to handle variations in the input, particularly lighting changes, weather conditions and slow-moving or stopping objects. Much contemporary literature describes variations on this approach, for instance considering groups of pixels or texture, shadow removal or techniques to deal with water surfaces [10, 20, 30].

Regions of the image that are flagged as different to the background are cleaned with image-processing operations, such as morphology and connected components, and then passed on for further analysis. Object detection alone may be sufficient for simpler applications, for instance in surveillance of a secure area where there should be no activity at all, or for minimizing video storage space by only capturing video at low-frame rates except when there is activity in a scene. However, many surveillance systems group together detections with tracking.

Many authors use trained object detectors to detect objects of a particular category against a complex, possibly moving, background. These object detectors, trained on databases of pedestrians [18], vehicles [1] or on faces (See Section 3.4.3), generally detect instances of the object class in question in individual frames and these detections must be tracked over time, as in the next section.

3.3 Tracking

Background subtraction detects objects independently in each frame. Tracking attempts to aggregate multiple observations of a particular object into a track – a record encapsulating the object's appearance and movement over time. Tracking gives structure to the observations and enables the object's behaviour to be analysed, for instance detecting when a particular object crosses a line.

At a simple level, tracking is a data-association problem, where new observations must be assigned to tracks which represent the previous observations of a set of objects. In sparse scenes, the assignment is easy, since successive observations of an object will be close to one another, but as objects cross in front of one another (*occlude* each other), or the density increases so that objects are always overlapping, the problem becomes much more complicated, and more sophisticated algorithms are required to resolve the occlusions, splitting foreground regions into areas representing different people. A range of techniques exist to handle these problems, including those which attempt to localise a particular tracked object such as template trackers [12, 25], histogram-based trackers like Mean Shift [5] and those using contours [2]. To solve complex assignment problems, formulations such as JPDAF [19], BraMBLe [14] or particle filtering [14] have been applied.

Tracking across multiple cameras leads to further complications. If the cameras' views overlap, then the areas of overlap can be learned [28] and the object "handed off" from one camera to another while continuously in view, leading to a single track across multiple cameras. When the cameras are non-overlapping then temporal techniques can learn how objects move from one camera to another, though it becomes more difficult to provide a reliable association between tracks in the different cameras [9, 15]. Longer-term association of multiple tracks of a given individual requires some kind of identification, such as a biometric or a weaker identifier such as clothing colour, size or shape.

Multi-camera systems benefit from using 3D information if the cameras are calibrated, either manually or automatically. Understanding of the expected size and appearance of people and other objects on a known ground plane allows the use of more complex model-based tracking algorithms [29, 35].

3.4 Object Analysis

After tracking, multiple observations over time are associated with a single track corresponding to a single physical object (or possibly a group of objects moving together), and the accumulated information can be analysed to extract further characteristics of the object, such as speed, size, colour, type, identity and trajectory. The track is the fundamental record type of a surveillance indexing system with which these various attributes can be associated for searching.

Speed and size can be stored in image-based units (pixels), unless there is calibration information available, in which case these can be converted to real-world units, and the object's path can be expressed in real-world coordinates. Colour may be represented in a variety of ways, such as an average histogram. For purposes such as matching across different cameras, the difficult problem of correcting for camera and lighting characteristics must be solved [16].

3.4.1 Classification & Identification

In many surveillance situations, objects of multiple types can be observed and object type provides a valuable criterion for searches and automatic analysis. A surveillance system will generally have a predefined set of categories to distinguish, discriminating between people and vehicles (for instance, using periodic motion [7]) or between different vehicle types (e.g. car *vs.* bus), or even different vehicle models [36]. With rich enough data, the object may be identified – for instance by reading the license plate, or recognizing a person's face or gait, or another biometric, possibly captured through a separate sensor and associated with the tracked object.

3.4.2 Behaviour Analysis

Finally the object's behaviour can be analysed, varying from simple rules, such as detecting if the object entered a certain area of a camera's field of view, or crossed a virtual tripwire, to analysis of whether a particular action was carried out, for instance detecting abandoned luggage [31], or even acts of aggression. Behaviour, particularly the object's trajectory [21], can also be compared to established patterns of activity to characterise the behaviour as similar to one of a set of previously observed "normal behaviours", or as an unusual behaviour, which may be indicative of a security threat.

Generic behaviours may be checked for continuously on all feeds automatically, or specific event may need to be defined by a human operator (such as drawing a region of interest or the timing of a sequence of events). Similarly, the outcome of an event being detected might be configurable in a system, from being silently recorded in a database as a criterion for future searching, to the automatic ringing of an alarm.

3.4.3 Face Processing

Surveillance systems are usually deployed where they can be used to observe people, and one of the main purposes of surveillance systems is to capture images that can be used to identify people whose behaviour is being observed. The face images can be stored for use by a human operator, but increasingly face recognition software [22] is being coupled with surveillance systems and used to automatically recognize people. In addition to being used for identification, faces convey emotion, gestures and speech and display information about age, race, gender which, being subject to prejudice are also privacy-sensitive. All of these factors can be analysed automatically by computer algorithms [4, 23, 33].

Faces are usually found in video by the repeated application of a face detector at multiple locations in an image. Each region of an image is tested, with the detector determining if the region looks like a face or not, based on the texture and colour of the region. Many current face detectors are based on the work of Viola and Jones [32]. Faces once detected can be tracked in a variety of ways using the techniques of Section 3.3.

3.5 User Interface

After all these steps, the database is populated with rich metadata referring to all the activity detected in the scene. The database can be searched using a complex set of criteria with simple SQL commands, or through a web services interface. Generic or customized user interfaces can communicate to this server back end to allow a user to search for events of a particular description, see statistical summaries of the activity, and use the events to cue the original video for detailed examination. Rich, domain-specific visualizations and searches can be provided, linking surveillance information with other data such as store transaction records [24].

4 Conclusions

This chapter has given a short overview of the typical features of automated video surveillance systems, and provided reference for further study. The field is developing rapidly with active research and development in all aspects of systems.

References

1. Alonso, D., Salgado, L., Nieto, M.: Robust vehicle detection through multidimensional classification for on board video based systems. In: Proceedings of International Conference on Image Processing, vol. 4, pp. 321–324 (2007)
2. Baumberg, A.: Learning deformable models for tracking human motion. Ph.D. thesis, Leeds University (1995)
3. Black, J., Ellis, T.: Multi camera image tracking. Image and Vision Computing (2005)
4. Cohen, I., Sebe, N., Chen, L., Garg, A., Huang, T.: Facial expression recognition from video sequences: Temporal and static modeling. Computer Vision and Image Understanding **91**(1–2), 160–187 (2003)
5. Comaniciu, D., Ramesh, V., Meer, P.: Real-time tracking of non-rigid objects using mean shift. In: CVPR, vol. 2, pp. 142–149. IEEE (2000)
6. Connell, J., Senior, A., Hampapur, A., Tian, Y.L., Brown, L., Pankanti, S.: Detection and tracking in the IBM PeopleVision system. In: IEEE ICME (2004)
7. Cutler, R., Davis, L.S.: Robust real-time periodic motion detection, analysis, and applications. IEEE Transactions on Pattern Analysis and Machine Intelligence **22**(8), 781–796 (2000)
8. Elgammal, A., Harwood, D., Davis, L.: Non-parametric model for background subtraction. In: European Conference on Computer Vision (2000)
9. Ellis, T., Makris, D., Black, J.: Learning a multi-camera topology. In: J. Ferryman (ed.) PETS/Visual Surveillance, pp. 165–171. IEEE (2003)
10. Eng, H., Wang, J., Kam, A., Yau, W.: Novel region based modeling for human detection within high dynamic aquatic environment. In: Proceedings of Computer Vision and Pattern Recognition (2004)
11. Hampapur, A., Brown, L., Connell, J., Ekin, A., Lu, M., Merkl, H., Pankanti, S., Senior, A., Tian, Y.: Multi-scale tracking for smart video surveillance. IEEE Transactions on Signal Processing (2005)
12. Haritaoğlu, I., Harwood, D., Davis, L.S.: W^4: Real-time surveillance of people and their activities. IEEE Trans. Pattern Analysis and Machine Intelligence **22**(8), 809–830 (2000)
13. Horprasert, T., Harwood, D., Davis, L.S.: A statistical approach for real-time robust background subtraction and shadow detection. Tech. rep., University of Maryland, College Park (2001)
14. Isard, M., MacCormick, J.: BraMBLe: A Bayesian multiple-blob tracker. In: International Conference on Computer Vision, vol. 2, pp. 34–41 (2001)
15. Javed, O., Rasheed, Z., Shafique, K., Shah, M.: Tracking across multiple cameras with disjoint views. In: International Conference on Computer Vision (2003)
16. Javed, O., Shafique, K., Shah, M.: Appearance modeling for tracking in multiple non-overlapping cameras. In: Proceedings of Computer Vision and Pattern Recognition. IEEE (2005)

17. Javed, O., Shah, M.: Automated Multi-camera surveillance: Algorithms and practice, The International Series in Video Computing, vol. 10, Springer (2008)
18. Jones, M., Viola, P., Snow, D.: Detecting pedestrians using patterns of motion and appearance. In: International Conference on Computer Vision, pp. 734–741 (2003)
19. Kang, J., Cohen, I., Medioni, G.: Tracking people in crowded scenes across multiple cameras. In: Asian Conference on Computer Vision (2004)
20. Li, L., Huang, W., Gu, I., Tian, Q.: Statistical modeling of complex backgrounds for foreground object detection. Transaction on Image Processing 13(11) (2004)
21. Morris, B.T., Trivedi, M.M.: A survey of vision-based trajectory learning and analysis for surveillance. IEEE Transactions on Circuits and Systems for Video Technology 18(8), 1114–1127 (2008)
22. Phillips, P., Scruggs, W., O'Toole, A., Flynn, P., Bowyer, K., Schott, C., Sharpe, M.: FRVT 2006 and ICE 2006 large-scale results. Tech. Rep. NISTIR 7408, NIST, Gaithersburg, MD 20899 (2006)
23. Ramanathan, N., Chellappa, R.: Recognizing faces across age progression. In: R. Hammoud, M. Abidi, B. Abidi (eds.) Multi-Biometric Systems for Identity Recognition: Theory and Experiments. Springer-Verlag (2006)
24. Senior, A., Brown, L., Shu, C.F., Tian, Y.L., Lu, M., Zhai, Y., Hampapur, A.: Visual person searches for retail loss detection: Application and evaluation. In: International Conference on Vision Systems (2007)
25. Senior, A., Hampapur, A., Tian, Y.L., Brown, L., Pankanti, S., Bolle, R.: Appearance models for occlusion handling. In: International Workshop on Performance Evaluation of Tracking and Surveillance (2001)
26. Siebel, N., Maybank, S.: The ADVISOR visual surveillance system, prague. In: ECCV Workshop on Applications of Computer Vision (2004)
27. Stauffer, C., Grimson, W.E.L.: Adaptive background mixture models for real-time tracking. In: Proceedings of IEEE Computer Society Conference on Computer Vision and Pattern Recognition, Fort Collins, CO, June 23–25, pp. 246–252 (1999)
28. Stauffer, C., Tieu, K.: Automated multi-camera planar tracking correspondence modeling. In: Proceedings of Computer Vision and Pattern Recognition, vol. I, pp. 259–266 (2003)
29. Tan, T., Baker, K.: Efficient image gradient-based vehicle localisation. IEEE Trans. Image Processing 9(8), 1343–1356 (2000)
30. Tian, Y.L., Hampapur, A.: Robust salient motion detection with complex background for real-time video surveillance. In: Workshop on Machine Vision. IEEE (2005)
31. Venetianer, P., Zhang, Z., Yin, W., Lipton, A.: Stationary target detection using the ObjectVideo surveillance system. In: Advanced Video and Signal-based Surveillance (2007)
32. Viola, P., Jones, M.: Robust real-time object detection. International Journal of Computer Vision (2001)
33. Yang, M.H., Moghaddam, B.: Gender classification with support vector machines. In: 4th IEEE International Conference on Automatic Face and Gesture Recognition, pp. 306–311 (2000)
34. Zhang, Z., Venetianer, P., Lipton, A.: A robust human detection and tracking system using a human-model-based camera calibration. In: Visual Surveillance (2008)
35. Zhao, T., Nevatia, R., Lv, F.: Segmentation and tracking of multiple humans in complex situations. In: Proceedings of Computer Vision and Pattern Recognition (2001)
36. Zheng, M., Gotoh, T., Shiohara, M.: A hierarchical algorithm for vehicle model type recognition on time-sequence road images. In: Intelligent Transportation Systems Conference, pp. 542–547 (2006)

Protecting and Managing Privacy Information in Video Surveillance Systems

S.-C.S. Cheung, M.V. Venkatesh, J.K. Paruchuri, J. Zhao and T. Nguyen

Abstract Recent widespread deployment and increased sophistication of video surveillance systems have raised apprehension of their threat to individuals' right of privacy. Privacy protection technologies developed thus far have focused mainly on different visual obfuscation techniques but no comprehensive solution has yet been proposed. We describe a prototype system for privacy-protected video surveillance that advances the state-of-the-art in three different areas: First, after identifying the individuals whose privacy needs to be protected, a fast and effective video inpainting algorithm is applied to erase individuals' images as a means of privacy protection. Second, to authenticate this modification, a novel rate-distortion optimized data-hiding scheme is used to embed the extracted private information into the modified video. While keeping the modified video standard-compliant, our data hiding scheme allows the original data to be retrieved with proper authentication. Third, we view the original video as a private property of the individuals in it and develop a secure infrastructure similar to a Digital Rights Management system that allows individuals to selectively grant access to their privacy information.

1 Introduction

Rapid technological advances have ushered in dramatic improvements in techniques for collecting, storing and sharing personal information among government agencies and private sectors. Even though the advantages brought forth by these methods cannot be disputed, the general public are becoming increasingly wary about the erosion of their rights of privacy [2]. While new legislature and policy changes are needed to provide a collective protection of personal privacy, technologies are playing an equally pivotal role in safeguarding private information [14]. From encrypting online financial transactions to anonymizing email traffic [13], from automated

S.-C.S. Cheung (✉)
Center for Visualization and Virtual Environments, University of Kentucky,
Lexington, KY 40507, USA
e-mail: cheung@engr.uky.edu

A. Senior (ed.), *Protecting Privacy in Video Surveillance*,
DOI 10.1007/978-1-84882-301-3_2, © Springer-Verlag London Limited 2009

negotiation of privacy preference [11] to privacy protection in data mining [24], a wide range of cryptographic techniques and security systems have been deployed to protect sensitive personal information.

While these techniques work well for textual and categorical information, they cannot be directly used for privacy protection of imagery data. The most relevant example is video surveillance. Video surveillance systems are the most pervasive and commonly used imagery systems in large cooperations today. Sensitive information including identities of individuals, activities, routes and association are routinely monitored by machines and human agents alike. While such information about distrusted visitors is important for security, misuse of private information about trusted employees can severely hamper their morale and may even lead to unnecessary litigation. As such, we need privacy protection schemes that can protect selected individuals without degrading the visual quality needed for security. Data encryption or scrambling schemes are not applicable as the protected video is no longer viewable. Simple image blurring, while appropriate to protect individuals' identities in television broadcast, modifies the surveillance videos in an irreversible fashion, making them unsuitable for use as evidence in the court of law.

Since video surveillance poses unique privacy challenges, it is important to first define the overall goals of privacy protection. We postulate here the five essential attributes of a privacy protection system for video surveillance. In a typical digital video surveillance system, the surveillance video is stored as individual segments of fixed duration, each with unique ID that signifies the time and the camera from which it is captured. We call an individual *a user* if the system has a way to uniquely identify this individual in a video segment, using a RFID tag for example, and there is a need to protect his/her visual privacy. The imagery about a user in a video segment is referred to as *private information*. A *protected video* segment means that all the privacy information has been removed. A *client* refers to a party who is interested in viewing the privacy information of a user. Given these definitions, a privacy protection system should satisfy these five goals:

Privacy Without the proper authorization, a protected video and the associated data should provide no information on whether a particular user is in the scene.

Usability A protected video should be free from visible artifacts introduced by video processing. This criterion enables the protected video for further legitimate computer vision tasks.

Security Raw data should only be present at the sensors and at the computing units that possess the appropriate permission.

Accessibility A user can provide or prohibit a client's access to his/her imageries in a protected video segment captured at a specific time by a specific camera.

Scalability The architecture should be scalable to many cameras and should contain no single point of failure.

In this chapter, we present an end-to-end design of a privacy-protecting video surveillance system that possesses these five essential features. Our proposed design advances the state-of-the-art visual privacy enhancement technologies in the following aspects:

1. To provide complete privacy protection, we apply video inpainting algorithm to erase privacy information from video. This modification process not only offers effective privacy protection but also maintains the apparent nature of the video making it usable for further data processing.
2. To authenticate this video modification task, a novel rate-distortion optimized data-hiding scheme is used to embed the identified private information into the modified video. The data hiding process allows the embedded data to be retrieved with proper authentication. This retrieved information along with the inpainted video can be used to recover the original data.
3. To provide complete control of privacy information, we view the embedded information as private property of the users and develop a secure infrastructure similar to a Digital Right Management system that allows users to selectively grant access to their privacy information.

The rest of the chapter is organized as follows: in Section 2, we provide a comprehensive review on existing methods to locate visual privacy information, to obfuscate video and to manage privacy data. In Section 3, we describe the design of our proposed system and demonstrate its performance. Finally in Section 4, we identify the open problems in privacy protection for video surveillance and suggest potential approaches towards solving them.

2 Related Works

There are three major aspects to privacy protection in video surveillance systems. The first task is to identify the privacy information needed to be preserved. The next step is to determine a suitable video modification technique that can be used to protect privacy. Finally, a privacy data management needs to be devised to securely preserve and manage the privacy information. Here we provide an overview of existing methods to address these issues and discuss the motivation behind our approach.

2.1 Privacy Information Identification

The first step in the privacy protection system is to identify individuals whose privacy needs to be protected. While face recognition is obviously the least intrusive technique, its performance is highly questionable in typical surveillance environments with low-resolution cameras, non-cooperative subjects and uncontrolled illumination [31]. Specialized visual markers are sometimes used to enhance recognition. In [36], Schiff et al. have these individuals wearing yellow hard hats for identification. An Adaboost classifier is used to identify the specific color of a hard hat. The face associated with the hat is subsequently blocked for privacy protection. While the colored hats may minimize occlusion and provide a visual cue for tracking and recognition, its prominent presence may be singled out in certain environments. A much smaller colored tag worn on the chest was used in our earlier work [50]. To combat mutual and self occlusion, we develop multiple camera planning algorithms to optimally place cameras in arbitrary-shaped environments in order to triangulate the location of these tags.

Non-visual modality can also be used but they require additional hardware for detection. Megherbi et al. exploit a variety of features including color, position, and acoustic parameters in a probabilistic frame to track and identify individuals [26]. Kumar et al. present a low-cost surveillance system employing multimodality information, including video, infrared (IR), and audio signals, for monitoring small areas and detecting alarming events [23]. Shakshuki et al. have also incorporated Global Positioning System (GPS) to aid the tracking of objects [38]. The drawback of these systems is that audio information and GPS signals are not suitable for use in indoor facilities with complicated topology.

Indoor wireless identification technologies such as RFID systems offer better signal propagation characteristics when operating indoors. Nevertheless, the design of a real-time indoor wireless human tracking system remains a difficult task [41] – traditional high-frequency wireless tracking technologies like ultra-high frequency (UHF) and ultra-wideband (UWB) systems do not work well at significant ranges in highly reflective environments. Conversely, more accurate short-range tracking technologies, like IR or ultrasonics, require an uneconomically dense network of sensors for complete coverage. In our system, we have chosen to use a wireless tracking system based on a technology Near-Field Electromagnetic Ranging (NFER®). NFER exploits the properties of medium- and low-frequency signals within about a half wavelength of a transmitter. Typical operating frequencies are within the AM broadcast band (530–1710 kHz). The low frequencies used by NFER are more penetrating and less prone to multipath than microwave frequencies. These near-field relationships are more fully described in a patent [35] and elsewhere [34]. In our system, each user wears an active RFID tag that broadcasts a RF signal of unique frequency. After triangulating the correspondence between the RF signals received at three antennas, the 2D spatial location of each active tag can then be continuously tracked in real-time. This location information, along with the visual information from the camera network is combined to identify those individuals whose privacy needs to be protected.

It should be pointed out that there are privacy protection schemes that do not require identification of privacy information. For example, the PrivacyCam surveillance system developed at IBM protects privacy by revealing only the relevant information such as object tracks or suspicious activities [37]. While this may be a sensible approach for some applications, such a system is limited by the types of events it can detect and may have problems balancing privacy protection with the particular needs of a security officer.

2.2 Privacy Information Obfuscation

Once privacy information in the video has been identified, we need to obfuscate them for privacy protection. There are a large variety of such video obfuscation techniques, ranging from the use of black boxes or large pixels (pixelation) in [2, 8, 36, 44] to complete object replacement or removal in [28, 43, 46, 48]. Black boxes or pixelation has been argued of not being able to fully protecting a person's identity [28]. Moreover, these kinds of perturbations to multimedia signals destroy the nature of the signals, limiting their utility for most practical purposes. Object replacement techniques are geared towards replacing sensitive information such as human faces or bodies with generic faces [28] or stick figures [43] for privacy protection. Such techniques require precise position and pose tracking which are beyond the reach of current surveillance technologies. Cryptographical techniques such as secure multi-party computation have also been proposed to protect privacy of multimedia data [1, 18]. Sensitive information is encrypted or transformed in a different domain such that the data is no longer recognizable but certain image processing operations can still be performed. While these techniques provide strong security guarantee, they are computationally intensive and at the current stage, they support only a limited set of image processing operations.

We believe that complete object removal proposed in [9, 46] provides a more reasonable and efficient solution for full privacy protection, while preserving a natural-looking video amenable to further vision processing. This is especially true for surveillance video of transient traffic at hallways or entrances where people have limited interaction with the environment. The main challenge with this approach lies in recreating occluded objects and motion after the removal of private information. We can accomplish this task through video inpainting which is an image-processing technique used to fill in missing regions in a seamless manner. Here we briefly review existing video inpainting and outline our contributions in this area.

Early work in video inpainting focused primarily on repairing small regions caused by error in transmission or damaged medium and are not suitable to complete large holes due to the removal of visual objects [3, 4]. In [45], the authors introduce the Space–Time video completion scheme which attempts to fill the hole by sampling spatio-temporal patches from the existing video. The exhaustive search strategy used to find the appropriate patches makes it very computationally intensive. Patwardhan et al. extend the idea of prioritizing structures in image inpainting in [12] to video [30]. Inpainting techniques that make use of the motion information along with texture synthesis and color re-sampling have been proposed in [39, 49]. These schemes rely on local motion estimates which are sensitive to noise and have difficulty in replicating large motion. Other object-based video inpainting such as [20] and [21] relies on user-assisted or computationally intensive object segmentation procedures which are difficult to deploy in existing surveillance camera networks.

Our approach advocates the use of semantic objects rather than patches for video inpainting and hence provides significant computational advantage by avoiding exhaustive search [42]. We use Dynamic Programming (DP) to holistically inpaint foreground objects with object templates that minimizes a sliding-window dissimilarity cost function. This technique can effectively handle large regions of occlusions, inpaint objects that are completely missing for several frames, inpaint moving objects with complex motion, changing pose and perspective making it an effective alternative for video modification tasks in privacy protection applications. We will briefly describe our approach in Section 3.2 with more detailed analysis and performance analysis available in [42].

2.3 Privacy Data Management

A major shortcoming in most of the existing privacy protection systems is that once the modifications are done on the video for the purpose of privacy protection, the original video can no longer be retrieved. Consider a video surveillance network in a hospital. While perturbing or obfuscating the surveillance video may conceal the identity of patients, the process also destroys the authenticity of the signal. Even with the consensus from the protected patients, law enforcement and arbitrators will no longer have access to the original data for investigation. Thus, a privacy protection system must provide mechanism to enable users to selectively grant access to their private information. This is in fact the fundamental premise behind the Fair Information Practices [40, Chapter 6]. In the near future, the use of cameras will become more prevalent. Dense pervasive camera networks are utilized not only for surveillance but also for other types of applications such as interactive virtual environment and immersive teleconferencing. Without jeopardizing the security of the organization, a flexible privacy data control system will become indispensable to handle a complex privacy policy with large number of individuals to protect and different data requests to fulfill.

To tackle the management of privacy information, Lioudakis et al. recently introduce a framework which advocates the presence of a trusted middleware agent referred to as Discreet Box [25]. The Discreet Box acts as a three-way mediator among the law, the users, and the service providers. This centralized unit acts as a communication point between various parties and enforces the privacy regulations. Fidaleo et al. describe a secure sharing scheme in which the surveillance data is stored in a centralized server core [17]. A privacy buffer zone, adjoining the central core, manages the access to this secure area by filtering appropriate personally identifiable information thereby protecting the data. Both approaches adopt a centralized management of privacy information making them vulnerable to concerted attacks. In contrast to these techniques, we propose a flexible software agent architecture that allows individual users to make the final decision on *every access* to their privacy data. This is reminiscent to a Data Right Management (DRM) system where the content owner can control the access of his/her content after proper payment is received [47]. Through a trusted mediator agent in our system, the user and the client agents can anonymously exchange data request, credential, and authorization. We believe that our management system offers a much stronger form of privacy protection as the user no longer needs to trust, adhere, or register his/her privacy preferences with a server. Details of this architecture will be described in Section 3.1.

To address the issue of preserving the privacy information, the simplest solution is to store separately a copy of the original surveillance video. The presence of a separate copy becomes an easy target for illegal tampering and removal, making it very challenging to maintain the security and integrity of the entire system. An alternative approach is to scramble the privacy information in such a way that the scrambling process can be reversed using a secret key [5, 15]. There are a number of drawbacks of such a technique. First, similar to pixelation or blocking, scrambling is unable to fully protect the privacy of the objects. Second, it introduces artifacts that may affect the performance of subsequent image processing steps. Lastly, the coupling of scrambling and data preservation prevents other obfuscation schemes like object replacement or removal to be used.

On the other hand, we advocate the use of data hiding or steganography for preserving privacy information [29, 33, 48]. Using video data hiding, the privacy information is hidden in the compressed bit stream of the modified video and can be extracted when proper authorization can be established. The data hiding algorithm is completely independent from the modification process and as such, can be used with any modification technique. Data hiding has been used in various applications such as copyright protection, authentication, fingerprinting, and error concealment. Each application imposes different set of constraints in terms of capacity, perceptibility, and robustness [10]. Privacy data preservation certainly demands large embedding capacity as we are hiding an entire video bitstream in the modified video. As stated in Section 1, perceptual quality of the embedded video is also of great importance. Robustness refers to the survivability of the hidden data under various processing operations. While it is a key requirement for applications like copyright protection and authentication, it is of less concern to a well-managed video surveillance system targeted to serve a single organization. In Section 3.3, we describe a new approach of optimally placing hidden information in the Discrete Cosine Transform (DCT) domain that simultaneously minimizes both the perceptual distortion and output bit rate. Our scheme works for both high-capacity irreversible embedding with QIM [7] and histogram-based reversible embedding [6], which will be discussed in details as well.

3 Description of System and Algorithm Design

A high-level description of our proposed system is shown in Fig. 1. Green (shaded) boxes are secured processing units within which raw privacy data or decryption keys are used. All the processing units are connected through an open local area network, and as such, all privacy information must be encrypted before transmission and the identities of all involved units must be validated. Gray arrows show the flow of the compressed video and black arrows show the control information such as RFID data and key information.

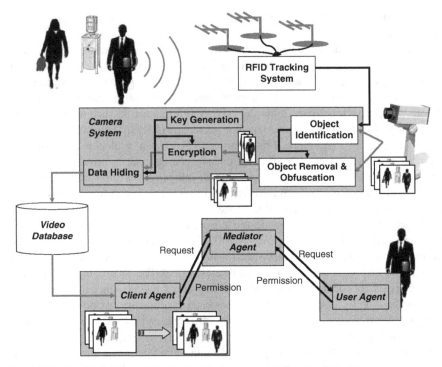

Fig. 1 High-level description of the proposed privacy-protecting video surveillance system

Every trusted user in the environment carries an active RFID tag. The RFID System senses the presence of various active RFID tags broadcasting in different RF frequencies and triangulates them to compute their ground plane 2D coordinates in real time. It then consults the mapping between the tag ID and the user ID before creating an IP packet that contains the user ID, his/her ground plane 2D coordinates and the corresponding time-stamp. In order for the time-stamp to be meaningful to other systems, all units are synchronized using the Network Timing Protocol (NTP) [27]. NTP is an Internet Protocol for synchronizing multiple computers within 10 ms, which is less than the capturing period of both the RFID and the camera systems. To protect the information flow, the RFID system and all the camera systems are grouped into an IP multicast tree [32] with identities of systems authenticated and packets encrypted using IPsec [22]. The advantage of using IP multicast is that adding a new camera system amounts to subscribing to the multicast address of the RFID system. There is no need for the RFID system to keep track of the network status as the multicast protocol automatically handles the subscription and the routing of information. IPsec provides a transparent network layer support to authenticate each processing unit and to encrypt the IP packets in the open network.

In each camera system, surveillance video is first fed into the Object Identification and Tracking unit. The object tracking and segmentation algorithm used in the camera system is based on our earlier work in [9, 42]. Background subtraction and shadow removal are first applied to extract foreground moving blobs from the video. Object segmentation is then performed during object occlusion using a real-time constant-velocity tracker followed by a maximum-likelihood segmentation based on color, texture, shape, and motion. Once the segmentation is complete, we need to identify the persons with the RFID tags. The object identification unit visually tracks all moving objects in the scene and correlates them with the received RFID coordinates according to the prior joint calibration of the RFID system and cameras. This is accomplished via a simple homography that maps between the ground plane and the image plane of the camera. This homography translates the 2D coordinates provided by the RFID system to the image coordinates of the junction point between the user and the ground plane. Our assumption here is that this junction point is visible at least once during the entire object track, thus allowing us to discern the visual objects corresponding to the individuals carrying the RFID tags.

Image objects corresponding to individuals carrying the RFID tags are then extracted from the video, each padded with black background to make a rectangular frame and compressed using a H.263 encoder [19]. The compressed bitstreams are encrypted along with other auxiliary information later used by the privacy data management system. The empty regions left behind by the removal of objects are perceptually filled in the Video Inpainting Unit described in Section 3.2. The resulting protected video forms the cover work for hiding the encrypted compressed bitstreams using a perceptual-based rate-distortion optimized data hiding scheme described in Section 3.3. The data hiding scheme is combined with a H.263 encoder which produces a standard-compliant bitstream of the protected video to be stored in the database. The protected video can be accessed without any restriction as all the privacy information is encrypted and hidden in the bitstream. To retrieve this privacy information, we rely on the privacy data management system to relay request and permission among the client, the user, and a trusted mediator software agent. In the following section, we provide the details of our privacy data management system.

3.1 Privacy Data Management

The goal of privacy data management is to allow individual users to control accessibility of their privacy data. This is reminiscent of a Digital Rights Management (DRM) system where the content owner can control the access of his/her content after proper payment is received. Our system is more streamlined than a typical DRM system as we have control over the entire data flow from production to consumption – for example, encrypted privacy information can be directly hidden in the protected video and no extra component is needed to manage privacy information. We use a combination of an asymmetric public-key cipher (1024-bit RSA) and a symmetric cipher (128-bit AES) to deliver a flexible and simple privacy data management system. RSA is used to provide flexible encryption of control and key information while AES is computationally efficient for encrypting video data. Each user u and client c publish their public keys PK_u and PK_c while keeping the secret keys SK_u and SK_c to themselves. As a client has no way of knowing the presence of a user in a particular video, there is a special *mediator m* to assist the client in requesting permission from the user. The mediator also has a pair of public and secret keys PK_m and SK_m.

Suppose there are N users u_i with $i = 1, 2, \ldots, N$ who appear in a video segment. We denote the protected video segment as V and the extracted video stream corresponding to user u_i as V_{u_i}. The Camera System prepares the following list of data to be embedded in V:

1. N AES-encrypted video streams $AES(V_{u_i}; K_i)$ for $i = 1, 2, \ldots, N$, each using a randomly generated 128-bit key K_i.
2. An encrypted table of contents $RSA(TOC; PK_m)$ using the mediator's public key PK_m. For each encrypted video stream V_{u_i}, the table of contents TOC contains the following three data fields: (a) the ID of user u_i; (b) the size of the encrypted bitstream, and (c) the RSA-encrypted AES key $RSA(K_i; PK_{u_i})$ using the public key of the user. (d) other types of meta-information about the user in the scene such as the trajectory of the user or the specific events involved the user can also be included. Such information helps the mediator to identify the video streams that match the queries from client. On the other hand, this field can be empty if the privacy policy of the user forbids the release of such information.

The process of retrieving privacy information is illustrated in Fig. 2. When a client wants to retrieve the privacy data from a video segment, the corresponding client agent retrieves the hidden data from the video and extracts the encrypted table of contents. The client agent then sends the encrypted table of contents and the specific query of interest to the mediator agent. Since the table of contents is encrypted with the mediator's public key PK_m, the mediator agent can decrypt it using the corresponding secret key SK_m. However, the mediator cannot authorize the direct access to the video as it does not have the decryption key for any of the embedded video streams. The mediator agent must forward the request to those users that match the client's query for proper authorization. The request data packet for user u_j contains the encrypted AES key $RSA(K_j; PK_{u_j})$ and all the information about the requesting client c. If the user agent of u_j agrees with the request, it decrypts the AES key using its secret key SK_{u_j} and encrypts it using the client's public key PK_c before sending it back to the mediator. The mediator finally forwards all the encrypted keys back to the client which decrypts the corresponding video streams using the AES keys.

The above key distribution essentially implements a one-time pad for the encryption of each private video stream. As such, the decryption of one particular stream does not enable the client to decode any other video streams. The three-agent architecture allows the user to modify his/her private policy at will without first announcing it to everyone on the system. While the mediator agent is needed in every transaction, it contains no state information and thus can be replicated for load balancing. Furthermore, to prevent overloading the network, no video data is ever exchanged among agents. Finally, it is assumed that proper authentication is performed for each transaction to authenticate the identity of each party and the integrity of the data.

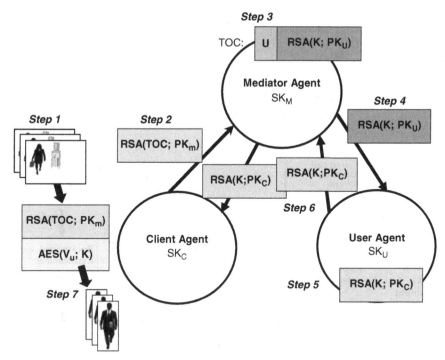

Fig. 2 Flow of privacy information: (1) Client extracts hidden data; (2) Encrypted TOC forwarded to mediator; (3) Mediator decrypts TOC; (4) Mediator forwards encrypted video key to User; (5) User decrypts key and re-encrypts it with Client's public key; (6) Encrypted video key forwarded to Client; (7) Client decrypts video stream depicting user

3.2 Video Inpainting for Privacy Protection

In this section, we briefly describe the proposed video inpainting module used in our Camera System. The removal of the privacy object leaves behind an empty region or a spatial-temporal "hole" in the video. Our inpainting module, with its high-level schematic shown in Fig. 3, is used to fill this hole in a perceptually consistent manner. This module contains multiple inpainting algorithms to handle different portions of the hole. The hole may contain static background that is occluded by the moving privacy object. If this static background had been previously observed, its appearance would have been stored as a background image that can be used to fill that portion of the hole. If this background was always occluded, our system would interpolate it based on the observed pixel values in the background image in its surroundings [12]. Finally, the privacy object may also occlude other moving objects that do not require any privacy protection. Even though we do not know the precise pose of these moving objects during occlusion, we assume that the period of occlusion is brief and the movement of these objects can be recreated via a two-stage process that we shall explain next.

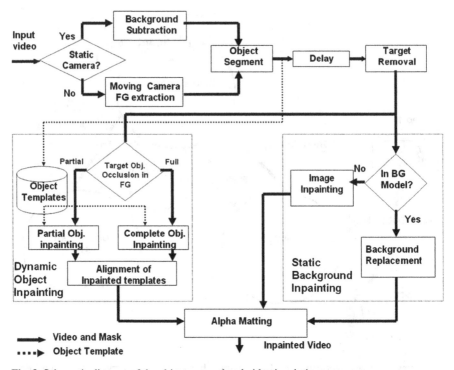

Fig. 3 Schematic diagram of the object removal and video inpainting system

In the first stage, we classify the frames containing the hole as either partially occluded or completely occluded as shown in Fig. 4. This is accomplished by comparing the size of the templates in the hole with the median size of templates in the database. The reason for handling these two cases separately is that the availability of partially occluded objects allow direct spatial registration with the stored templates, while completely occluded objects must rely on registration done before entering and after exiting the hole.

In the second stage, we perform a template search over the available object templates captured throughout the entire video segment. The partial objects are first completed with the appropriate object templates by minimizing a dissimilarity

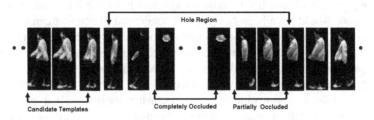

Fig. 4 Classification of the input frames into partially and completely occluded frames

measure defined over a temporal window. Between a window of partially occluded objects and a window of object templates from the database, we define the dissimilarity measure as the Sum of the Squared Differences (SSD) in their overlapping region plus a penalty based on the area of the non-overlapping region. The partially occluded frame is then inpainted by the object template that minimizes the window-based dissimilarity measure. Once the partially occluded objects are inpainted, we are left with completely occluded ones. They are inpainted by a DP based dissimilarity minimization process, but the matching cost is given by the dissimilarity between the available candidates in the database and the previously completed objects before and after the hole. The completed foreground and background regions are fused together using simple alpha matting. Figure 5 shows the result of applying our video inpainting algorithm to remove two people whose privacy needs to be protected.

In many circumstances, the trajectory of the person is not parallel to the camera plane. This can happen, for example, when we use ceiling-mounted cameras or when the person is walking at an angle with respect to the camera position. Under this condition, the object undergoes a change in appearance as it moves towards or away from the camera. To handle such cases, we perform a normalization procedure

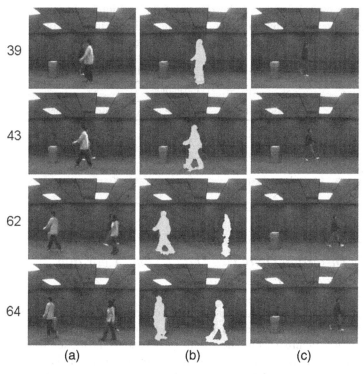

Fig. 5 (a) The *first column* shows the original input sequence along with the frame number. (b) The *second column* shows the results of the tracking and foreground segmentation. (c) The *third column* shows the inpainted result in which the individuals in the foreground are erased to protect their privacy. Notice that the moving person in the back is inpainted faithfully

to rectify the foreground templates so that the motion trajectory is parallel to the camera plane. Under calibrated cameras, it is fairly straightforward to perform the metric rectification for normalizing the foreground volume. Otherwise, as explained in [42], we use features extracted from the moving person to compute the required geometrical constraints for metric rectification. After rectification, we perform our object-based video inpainting to complete the hole.

Our algorithm offers several advantages over existing state-of-the-art methods in the following aspects: First, using image objects allows us to handle large holes including cases where the occluded object is completely missing for several frames. Second, using object templates for inpainting provides significant speed up over existing patch-based schemes. Third, the use of a temporal window-based matching scheme generates natural object movements inside the hole and provides smooth transitions at hole boundaries without resorting to any a prior motion model. Finally, our proposed scheme also provides a unified framework to address videos from both static and moving cameras and to handle moving objects with varying pose and changing perspective. We have tested the performance of our algorithm under varying conditions and the timing information for inpainting along with the time taken in the pre-processing stage for segmentation are presented in Table 1. The results of the inpainting along with the original video sequences referred in the table are available in our project website at http://vis.uky.edu/mialab/VideoInpainting.html.

Table 1 Execution time on a Xeon 2.1 GHz machine with 4 GB of memory

| Video | Segment length | Inpainting | |
		3-frame window (min)	5-frame window (min)
Three person (Fig. 5)	30 s	7.4	10.2
One board	40 s	3.5	8.3
Moving camera	3 min	2.6	4.8
Spinning person	35 s	12.6	18.2
Perspective	35 s	3.6	7.1
Jumping girl	30 s	6.4	11.4

3.3 Rate Distortion Optimized Data Hiding Algorithm for Privacy Data Preservation

In this section, we describe a rate-distortion optimized data hiding algorithm to embed the encrypted compressed bitstreams of the privacy information in the inpainted video. Figure 6 shows the overall design and its interaction with the H.263 compression algorithm. We apply our design to both reversible and irreversible data hiding. Reversible data hiding allows us to completely undo the effect of the hidden data and recover the compressed inpainted video. Irreversible data hiding will modify the compressed inpainted video though mostly in an imperceptible manner. Reversibility is sometimes needed in order to demonstrate the authenticity of the

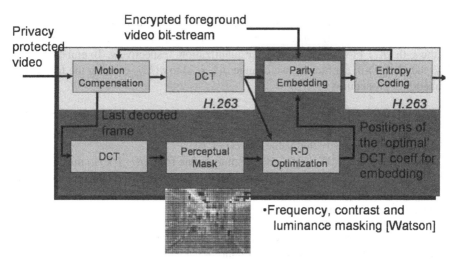

Fig. 6 Schematic diagram of the data hiding and video compression system

surveillance video – for example, the compressed inpainted video may have been digitally signed and the reversible data hiding scheme can ensure that the incorporation of the data hiding process will not destroy the signature. On the other hand, reversible data hiding has worse compression efficiency and data hiding capacity than its irreversible counterpart. As such irreversible data hiding is preferred if small imperceptible changes in the inpainted video can be tolerated.

To understand this difference between reversible and irreversible data hiding, we note that motion compensation, a key component of the H.263 video compression, cannot be used in the case of reversible embedding because the feedback loop in motion compensation will have to incorporate the hidden data in the residual frame, making the compensation process irreversible. In our implementation of the reversible data hiding, we simply turn off the motion compensation, resulting in a compression scheme similar to Motion JPEG (M-JPEG). The embedding process is performed at frame level so that the decoder can reconstruct the privacy information as soon as the compressed bitstream of the same frame has arrived. Data is hidden by modifying the luminance DCT coefficients which typically occupy the largest portion of the bit stream. To minimize the impact on the quality, the coefficients will be modified, if at all, by incrementing or decrementing one unit. After the embedding process, these coefficients will be entropy-coded. In most cases, the DCT coefficients remain very small in magnitude and they will be coded together with the runlengths using a Huffman table. In very rare occasions, the modified DCT coefficients may become large and fixed-length coding will be used as dictated by the H.263 standard.

In the following section, we describe two types of embedding approaches namely Irreversible and Reversible data hiding. The former approach offers higher embedding capacity when compared to the latter but at the expense of irreversible distortion at the decoder.

We first start with the irreversible data embedding where the modification to the cover video cannot be undone. Let $c(i, j, k)$ and $q(i, j, k)$ be the (i, j)-th coefficient of the k-th DCT block before and after quantization, respectively. To embed a bit x into the (i, j, k)-th coefficient, we change $q(i, j, k)$ to $\tilde{q}(i, j, k)$ using the following embedding procedure:

1. If x is 0 and $q(i, j, k)$ is even, add or subtract one from $q(i, j, k)$ to make it odd. The decision of increment or decrement is chosen to minimize the difference between the reconstructed value and $c(i, j, k)$.
2. If x is 1 and $q(i, j, k)$ is odd, add or subtract one from $q(i, j, k)$ to make it even. The decision of increment or decrement is chosen to minimize the difference between the reconstructed value and $c(i, j, k)$.
3. $q(i, j, k)$ remains unchanged otherwise.

Following the above procedure, each DCT coefficient can embed at most one bit. Decoding can be accomplished using Equation (1):

$$x = (\tilde{q}(i, j, k) + 1) \bmod 2 \tag{1}$$

For the reversible embedding process, we exploit the fact that DCT coefficients follow a Laplacian distribution concentrated around zero with empty bins towards either ends of the distribution [6]. Due to the high data concentration at the zero bin, we can embed high-volume of hidden data at the zero coefficients by shifting the bins with values larger (or smaller) than zero to the right (or left). Let $L = \lceil M_k/Z \rceil$ where Z is the number of zero coefficients and M_k is the number of bits to be embedded in the DCT block. We modify each DCT coefficients $q(i, j, k)$ into $\tilde{q}(i, j, k)$ using the following procedure until all the M_k bits of privacy data are embedded.

1. If $q(i, j, k)$ is zero, extract L bits from the privacy data buffer and set $\tilde{q}(i, j, k) = q(i, j, k) + 2^{L-1} - V$ where V is the unsigned decimal value of these L privacy data bits.
2. If $q(i, j, k)$ is negative, no embedding is done in this coefficient and $\tilde{q}(i, j, k) = q(i, j, k) - 2^{L-1} - 1$.
3. If $q(i, j, k)$ is positive, no embedding is done in this coefficient but $\tilde{q}(i, j, k) = q(i, j, k) + 2^{L-1}$.

Similarly, at the decoder the level of embedding L is calculated first and then data extraction and distortion reversal is done using the following procedure.

1. If $-2^{L-1} < \tilde{q}(i, j, k) \leq 2^{L-1}$, L hidden bits can be obtained as the binary equivalent of the decimal number $2^{L-1} - \tilde{q}(i, j, k)$ and $q(i, j, k) = 0$.
2. If $\tilde{q}(i, j, k) \leq -2^{L-1}$, no hidden bit in this coefficient and $q(i, j, k) = \tilde{q}(i, j, k) + 2^{L-1} - 1$.
3. If $\tilde{q}(i, j, k) > 2^{L-1}$, no bit is hidden in this coefficient and $q(i, j, k) = \tilde{q}(i, j, k) - 2^{L-1}$.

Since only zero bins are actually used for data hiding, the embedding capacity is quite limited and hence it might be required to hide more than one bit at a coefficient in certain DCT blocks. Though the distortion due to this embedding is reversible at a frame level for an authorized decoder, the distortion induced is higher than the irreversible approach for a regular decoder.

To identify the embedding locations that cause the minimal disturbance to visual quality, we need a distortion metric in our optimization framework. Common distortion measures like mean square does not work for our goal of finding the optimal DCT coefficients to embed data bits: Given the number of bits to be embedded, the mean square distortion will always be the same regardless of which DCT coefficients are used as DCT is an orthogonal transform. Instead, we adopt the DCT perceptual model described in [10]. Considering the luminance and contrast masking of human visual system as described in [10], we calculate the final perceptual mask $s(i, j, k)$ that indicates the maximum permissible alteration to the (i, j)th coefficient of the kth 8×8 DCT block of an image. With this perceptual mask, we can compute a perceptual distortion value for each DCT coefficient in the current frame as:

$$D(i, j, k) = \frac{QP}{s(i, j, k)} \qquad (2)$$

where QP is the quantization parameter used for that coefficient.

In our joint data hiding and compression framework, we aim at minimizing the output bit rate R and the perceptual distortion D caused by embedding M bits into the DCT coefficients. By using a user-specified control parameter δ, we combine the rate and distortion into a single cost function as follows:

$$C = (1 - \delta) \cdot N_F \cdot D + \delta \cdot R \qquad (3)$$

N_F is used to normalize the dynamic range of D and R. δ is selected based on the particular application which may favor the least amount of distortion by setting δ close to zero, or the least amount of bit rate increase by setting δ close to one. In order to avoid any overhead in communicating the embedding positions to the decoder, both of these approaches compute the optimal positions based on the previously decoded DCT frame so that the process can be repeated at the decoder.

The cost function in Equation (3) depends on which DCT coefficients used for the embedding. Thus, our optimization problem becomes

$$\min_{\Gamma} C(\Gamma) \text{ subject to } M = N \qquad (4)$$

where M is the variable that denotes the number of bits to be embedded, N is the target number of bits to be embedded, C is the cost function as described in Equation (3) and Γ is a possible selection of N DCT coefficients for embedding the data. Using Lagrangian Multiplier, this constrained optimization is equivalent to the following unconstrained optimization:

$$\min_{\Gamma} \Theta(\Gamma, \lambda) \text{ with } \Theta(\Gamma, \lambda) = C(\Gamma) + \lambda \cdot (M - N) \tag{5}$$

We can further simplify Equation (5) by decomposing it into the sum of similar quantities from each DCT block k:

$$\Theta(\Gamma, \lambda) = \sum_k C_k(\Gamma_k) + \lambda \cdot \left(\sum_k M_k - N \right) \tag{6}$$

To prepare for the above optimization, we need to first generate the curves between the cost and the number of embedded bits for all the DCT blocks. The cost function, as described in Equation (3) consists of both the distortion and the rate. The distortion is calculated using an L_4 norm pooling of distorted coefficients obtained from Equation (2). Rate increase is considerably more difficult as it depends on the run-length patterns. Embedding at the same coefficient may result in different rate increase depending on the order of embedding. While one can resort to DP techniques to compute the optimal curve, the computation time is prohibiting and we approximate the rate increase function using a greedy approach by embedding at the minimum cost position at each step. As the decoder does not know the actual bit to be embedded, the worst case scenario is assumed – both the distortion and the rate increase are computed by embedding the bit value at each step that leads to a bigger increase in cost. Once the cost curves are generated for all the DCT blocks, we can minimize the Lagrangian cost $\Theta(\Gamma, \lambda)$ for any fixed value of λ to find the distribution of embedding bits. λ value is chosen using the binary search such that the total bits over all the DCT blocks is just greater than or equal to the target embedding requirement. At this optimal slope, we get the number of bits to be embedded as the value of N which minimizes the unconstrained equation.

Figure 7 shows a sample frame of the hall monitor test sequence using irreversible embedding with different δ. The presence of hidden data is not visible for both $\delta = 0$ and $\delta = 0.5$ and becomes marginally visible at $\delta = 1$. Table 2 shows the bit rates for the hall monitor sequence at different δ values for both irreversible embedding using H.263 and reversible embedding using M-JPEG. The baseline for measurement is using separate files for storage – for H.263, the baseline is the sum of 119.15 kbps for the inpainted video and 81 kbps for the privacy information, making it a total of 200.15 kbps. For M-JPEG, the baseline is the sum of 2493 kbps for the inpainted video and 807 kbps for the privacy information or a total of 3300 kbps. The distortion is the pooled perceptual distortion measured based on the output from a standard compliant decoder with no knowledge of the data hidden inside. While the irreversible embedding causes less perceptual distortion than the reversible embedding, it has higher relative increase in bit rate as well. The bit-rate increase also changes with QP. Fixing $\delta = 0.5$, Table 3 shows the bit rates of the inpainted video (R_o), the privacy information (R_p), and the inpainted video with privacy information embedded (R_e) at different QP's for the reversible embedding. Operating at higher quality (or lower QP) induces a lower relative increase in bit rate, and irreversible embedding shows a similar trend as well.

Fig. 7 234th frame of Hall Monitor Sequence after data hiding for QP $= 10$. *Top Left*: No Watermark; *Top Right*: $\delta = 0$; *Bottom Left*: $\delta = 0.5$; *Bottom Right*: $\delta = 1$

Table 2 Bit rates and perceptual distortion of Hall Monitor Sequence (QP=10)

	Non reversible embedding		Reversible embedding	
δ	Rate increase	Distortion	Rate increase	Distortion
Separate files	0 (%)	0	0 (%)	0
0	63.8	21.65	44.2	127
0.5	50.9	27	41.1	135
1	43.4	102	16.9	255

Table 3 Bit rates of reversible embedding at different QP's

QP	R_o(kbps)	R_p(kbps)	R_e(kbps)	% increase
20	1560	710	3607	58.9
15	1885	744	3845	46.2
10	2493	807	4656	41.1
5	4018	960	6281	26.2

4 Challenges and Opportunities in Privacy Protection

In this chapter, we describe a comprehensive solution of protecting privacy in a multi-camera video surveillance system. Selected individuals are identified with a real-time human tracking RFID system. The RFID system relays the information to each camera which tracks, segments, identifies and removes visual objects that correspond to individuals with RFID tags. To repair the remainder of the video, we employ an object-based video inpainting algorithm to fill in the empty regions and create the protected video. The original visual objects are encrypted and embedded into the compressed protected video using a rate-distortion optimal data hiding algorithm. Using a privacy data management system that comprises of three software agents, users can grant access to these privacy information to authenticated clients under a secure and anonymous setting.

Privacy protection in video surveillance is a new area with its requirements still heavily debated. It is a truly interdisciplinary topic that requires inputs from privacy advocates, legal experts, technologists, and the general public. The most pressing challenge facing the construction of such a system is the reliability of various components. RFID failures, less-than-perfect segmentation or inpainting even in a single video frame may expose the identity of a person and defeat the entire purpose of privacy protection. While our experiments indicate that these techniques perform well in controlled laboratory settings, their performances under different lighting conditions or in environments with reflective surfaces are questionable. While it might take years for these techniques to mature and be robust enough for privacy protection, it is possible to build a baseline system that simply blocks off all moving objects as a safety measure. As such, there is a spectrum of privacy protecting systems that trade off functionality with robustness and a careful study of their performance is an important step to move forward.

Acknowledgments The authors at University of Kentucky would like to acknowledge the support of Department of Justice under the grant 2004-IJ-CK-K055.

References

1. S. Avidan and B. Moshe. Blind vision. In *Proceedings of the 9th European Conference on Computer Vision*, pages 1–13, 2006.
2. A.M. Berger. *Privacy Mode for Acquisition Cameras and Camcorders*. Sony Corporation, US patent 6,067,399 edition, May 23 2000.
3. M. Bertalmio, A.L. Bertozzi, and G. Sapiro. Navier-stokes, fluid dynamics, and image and video inpainting. In *Proceedings of International Conference on Computer Vision and Pattern Recognition*, volume I, pages 355–362, Hawaii, 2001.
4. M. Bertalmio, G. Sapiro, V. Caselles, and C. Ballester. Image inpainting. In *Proceedings of ACM Conference on Computer Graphics (SIGGRAPH)*, pages 417–424, New Orleans, USA, July 2000.
5. T.E. Boult. Pico: Privacy through invertible cryptographic obscuration. In *Proceedings of Computer Vision for Interactive and Intelligent Environments: The Dr. Bradley D. Carter Workshop Series*. University of Kentucky, 2005.

6. C.C. Chang, W.L. Tai, and M.H. Lin. A reversible data hiding scheme with modified side match vector quantization. In *Proceedings of the International Conference on Advanced Information Networking and Applications*, volume 1, pages 947–952, 2005.

7. B. Chen and G.W. Wornell. Quantization index modulation: A class of provably good methods for digital watermarking and information embedding. In *ISIT: Proceedings IEEE International Symposium on Information Theory*, 2000.

8. D. Chen, Y. Chang, R. Yan, and J. Yang. Tools for protecting the privacy of specific individuals in video. *EURASIP Journal on Advances in Signal Processing*, 2007, Article ID 75427, 9 pages, 2007. doi:10.1155/2007/75427.

9. S.-C. Cheung, J. Zhao, and M.V. Venkatesh. Efficient object-based video inpainting. In *Proceedings of IEEE International Conference on Image Processing, ICIP 2006*, pages 705–708, 2006.

10. I.J. Cox, M.L. Miller, and J.A. Bloom. *Digital Watermarking*. Morgan Kaufmann Publishers, 2002.

11. L. Cranor, M. Langheinrich, M. Marchiori, M.P. Marshall, and J. Reagle. The platform for privacy preferences 1.0 (p3p1.0) specification. Technical report, World Wide Web Consortium (W3C), http://www.w3.org/TR/P3P/, 2002.

12. A. Criminisi, P. Perez, and K. Toyama. Region filling and object removal by exemplar-based inpainting. *IEEE Transactions on Image Processing*, 13(9):1200–1212, September 2004.

13. C. Diaz. *Anonymity and Privacy in Electronic Services*. PhD thesis, Katholieke Universiteit Leuven, 2005.

14. W. Diffie and S. Landau. *Privacy on the Line: The Politics of Wiretapping and Encryption*, The MIT Press, 1998.

15. F. Dufaux and T. Ebrahimi. Scrambling for video surveillance with privacy. *2006 Conference on Computer Vision and Pattern Recognition Workshop (CVPRW'06)*, page 160, 2006.

16. Electronic Privacy Information Center, http://www.epic.org/privacy/survey. *Public Opinion on Privacy*, May 2006.

17. D.-A. Fidaleo, H.-A. Nguyen, and M. Trivedi. The networked sensor tapestry (NEST): A privacy enhanced software architecture for interactive analysis of data in video-sensor networks. In *VSSN '04: Proceedings of the ACM 2nd international workshop on Video surveillance & sensor networks*, pages 46–53, New York, USA, ACM Press, 2004.

18. N. Hu and S.-C. Cheung. Secure image filtering. In *Proceedings of IEEE International Conference on Image Processing (ICIP 2006)*, pages 1553–1556, October 2006.

19. ITU-T Recommendation H.263 Version 2. *Video Coding for Low Bitrate Communication Version 2*, 1998.

20. J. Jia, Y.W. Tai, T.P. Wu, and C.K. Tang. Video repairing under variable illumination using cyclic motions. *IEEE Transactions on Pattern Analysis and Machine Intelligence (PAMI)*, 1:364–371, July 2006.

21. Y. T. Jia, S.M. Hu, and R.R. Martin. Video completion using tracking and fragment merging. In *Proceedings of Pacific Graphics*, volume 21, pages 601–610, 2005.

22. S. Kent and K. Seo. Security architecture for the internet protocol. Technical report, IETF RFC 4301, December 2005.

23. P. Kumar and A. Mittal. A multimodal audio visible and infrared surveillance system (maviss). In *International Conference of Intelligent Sensing and Information Processing*, 2005.

24. Y. Lindell and B. Pinkas. Privacy preserving data mining. *Journal of Cryptology*, 15(3): 177–206, 2002.

25. G.V. Lioudakis, E.A. Koutsoloukas, N.L. Dellas, N. Tselikas, S. Kapellaki, G.N. Prezerakos, D.I. Kaklamani, and I.S. Venieris. A middleware architecture for privacy protection. *Computer Networks: The International Journal of Computer and Telecommunications Networking*, 51(16):4679–4696, November 2007.

26. N. Megherbi, S. Ambellousi, O. Colot, and F. Cabestaing. Joint audio-video people tracking using belief theory. In *Proceedings of IEEE Conference on Advanced Video and Signal Based Surveillance*, 2005.

27. D.L. Mills. Network time protocol (version 3) specification, implementation and analysis. Technical report, IETF, 1992.
28. E.N. Newton, L. Sweeney, and B. Main. Preserving privacy by de-identifying face images. *IEEE transactions on Knowledge and Data Engineering*, 17(2):232–243, February 2005.
29. J.K. Paruchuri and S.-C. Cheung. Joint optimization of data hiding and video compression. In *To appear in IEEE International Symposium on Circuists and Systems (ISCAS 2008)*, 2008.
30. K.A. Patwardhan, G. Sapiro, and M. Bertalmio. Video inpainting under constrained camera motion. *IEEE Transactions on Image Processing*, 16(2):545–553, February 2007.
31. P.J. Phillips, W.T. Scruggs, A.J.O Toole, P.J. Flynn, K.W. Bowyer, C.L. Schott, and M. Sharpe. FRVT 2006 and ICE 2006 large-scale results. Technical Report NISTRI 7408, National Institute of Standards and Technology, Marge, 2007.
32. B. Quinn and K. Almeroth. IP multicast applications: Challenges and solutions. Technical report, IETF RFC 3170, September 2001.
33. J.K. Paruchuri, S.-C. Cheung and T. Nguyen. Managing privacy information in pervasive camera networks. In *Proceedings of IEEE International Conference on Image Processing, ICIP 2008*, 2008.
34. H. Schantz. Near field phase behavior. In *Proceedings of IEEE APS Conference*, 2005.
35. H. Schantz and R. Depierre. System and method for near-field electromagnetic ranging. Technical Report 6,963,301, U.S. Patent, 2005.
36. J. Schiff, M. Meingast, D. Mulligan, S. Sastry, and K. Goldberg. Respectful cameras: Detecting visual markers in real-time to address privacy concerns. In *International Conference on Intelligent Robots and Systems (IROS)*, 2007.
37. A. Senior, S. Pankanti, A. Hampapur, Y.-L. Tian, L. Brown, and A. Ekin. Blinkering surveillance: Enabling video privacy through computer vision. *Security and Privacy*, 3:50–57, 2005.
38. E. Shakshuki and Y. Wang. Using agent-based approach to tracking moving objects. In *Proceedings of 17th International Conference on Advance Information Networking and Application*, 2003.
39. T. Shiratori, Y. Matsushita, S.B. Kang, and X. Tang. Video completion by motion field transfer. In *Proceedings of IEEE Conference on Computer Vision and Pattern Recognition (CVPR)*, volume 1, pages 411–418, June 2006.
40. D. J. Solove. *The Digital Person: Technology and Privacy in the Information Age*. New York University Press, 2004.
41. SPAWAR System Center. *Correctional Officer Duress Systems: Selection Guide*, November 2003.
42. M. Vijay Venkatesh, S.-C. Cheung, and J. Zhao. Efficient object-based video inpainting. *Pattern Recognition Letters : Special issue on Video-based Object and Event Analysis*, 2008.
43. H. Wactlar, S. Stevens, and T. Ng. *Enabling Personal Privacy Protection Preferences in Collaborative Video Observation*. NSF Award Abstract 0534625, http://www.nsf.gov/awardsearch/showAward.do?awardNumber=0534625.
44. J. Wada, K. Kaiyama, K. Ikoma, and H. Kogane. *Monitor Camera System and Method of Displaying Picture from Monitor Camera Thereof*. Matsushita Electric Industrial Co. Ltd., European Patent, ep 1 081 955 a2 edition, April 2001.
45. Y. Wexler, E. Shechtman, and M. Irani. Space-time completion of video. *IEEE Transactions on Pattern Analysis and Machine Intelligence*, 29(3):463–476, 2007.
46. J. Wickramasuri, M. Datt, S. Mehrotra, and N. Venkatasubramanian. Privacy protecting data collection in media spaces. *ACM Multimedia*, pages 48–55, October 2004.
47. W. Zeng, H. Yu, and C.-Y. Lin. *Multimedia Security Technologies for Digital Rights Management*. Academic Press, 2006.
48. W. Zhang, S.-C. Cheung, and M. Chen. Hiding privacy information in video surveillance system. In *Proceedings of the 12th IEEE International Conference on Image Processing*, Genova, Italy, September 2005.

49. Y. Zhang, J. Xiao, and M. Shah. Motion layer based object removal in videos. In *Proceedings of the Seventh IEEE Workshops on Application of Computer Vision*, volume 1, pages 516–521, 2005.
50. J. Zhao and S.-C. Cheung. Multi-camera surveillance with visual tagging and generic camera placement. In *Proceedings of ACM/IEEE International Conference on Distributed Smart Cameras*, September 2007.

Privacy Protection in a Video Surveillance System

Andrew Senior

Abstract This chapter presents mechanisms for privacy protection in a distributed, multicamera surveillance system. The design choices and alternatives for providing privacy protection while delivering meaningful surveillance data for security and retail environments are described, followed by performance metrics to evaluate the effectiveness of privacy protection measures and experiments to evaluate these in retail store video. This chapter concludes with a discussion including five principles for data presentation of privacy protection systems.

1 Introduction

Video surveillance has become a ubiquitous feature of modern life. Everywhere, video cameras are watching our movements – on the street, in stations, in shops and in the workplace. At the same time, automatically processing surveillance video has become feasible and, given the number of video feeds to be monitored, necessary. The parallel growth in deployment of information technology in all domains, and the increased networking of the computers that store our personal information has led to increasing fears about our privacy, as every week new accounts emerge about millions of government or corporate records being stolen or inadvertently made publicly available.

Video surveillance has always aroused privacy fears, but increasing automation, the growing capabilities of computer algorithms and the potential for linking to many other electronic sources of information have driven increased concerns about the potential effects of video surveillance to invade our privacy. Video surveillance is privacy intrusive because it allows the observation of certain information that is considered privacy intrusive. Privacy-intrusive information may involve a person's identity or characteristics (age, race, gender). Video surveillance in public places

A. Senior (✉)
Google Research, New York, NY, USA
e-mail: a.senior@ieee.org

A. Senior (ed.), *Protecting Privacy in Video Surveillance*,
DOI 10.1007/978-1-84882-301-3_3, © Springer-Verlag London Limited 2009

is generally permitted because there is no expectation of privacy in public, similarly in the work place an employee may be considered to have no expectation of privacy from their employer. Nevertheless, the increased capabilities of automatic surveillance systems give "superhuman" powers of information extraction and accumulation that can exceed the traditional expectations when in a public space. A system with face recognition [1] could easily build, for each of a large group of known people, a searchable database of all the times each of them passes through any one of its cameras, something that would demand infeasible resources if done manually.

At the same time, it has been noted that automated processing technologies may be able to limit the intrusiveness of video surveillance both by reducing the need for people to watch the video and by automatically hiding certain information in such video and limiting access to different types of information obtained from the video [5, 27]. Recent advances in video analysis have enabled the separation of surveillance video into separate streams of information, containing, for instance, the slowly varying background; the appearance of pedestrians and vehicles; the faces of the pedestrians; license plates; and the movements of each object. The system can determine which of these streams a user should be shown, and thus present much usable information without revealing other, potentially privacy-intrusive data. While several authors have begun to describe systems that implement such privacy protection, little work has been carried out to evaluate their effectiveness in the task.

This chapter builds on previous work in this area, which is described in Section 2 and describes some of the privacy protection methods that have been tested in conjunction with the IBM Smart Surveillance System, discussing some of the design options for deploying privacy in such a system, and focusing on video redaction (Section 5). Section 6 describes techniques for how such a system's performance may be analysed. Some experiments on the effectiveness of one implementation of privacy protection algorithms are described in Section 7. The final section discusses the implications of performance failures in such a privacy protection scheme.

2 Previous Work

With the dramatic growth of interest in automatic surveillance algorithms, researchers have begun to explore techniques to protect privacy in surveillance video, investigating different aspects of the problem.

Several authors have developed systems that redact surveillance video for privacy protection [4, 8, 10, 13, 17, 20, 24, 26, 31], with most assuming a simple blanking-out, blurring, pixellation, filling in with background [29] or scrambling [11]. Neustaedter et al. evaluated the effectiveness of scene blurring for privacy in home-based video conferencing [22], and other authors have applied similar techniques for privacy protection in other domains [12, 28]. Chen et al. [6] showed that that certain identification tasks can still be carried out with redacted data and Newton et al. [23] have shown that blurring and pixellation may be insufficient to prevent the use of automatic face recognition systems. Coutaz et al. [9] described hiding facial expressions in media spaces with a "socially correct" Eigenspacefilter that preserves certain qualities of facial appearance while hiding others, and Newton et al. [23] and Gross et al. [14, 15] have also used face models to prevent identification while preserving facial expressions.

Koshimizu et al. [19] have evaluated people's reactions to different types of redaction, while Hayes and Abowd [16] have begun to investigate attitudes to privacy in deployed video archiving systems.

Other authors have explored how radio frequency identification (RFID) tags or other devices can be used to apply privacy policies to particular individuals or groups [2, 25, 30]. Others have investigated the need to design a security infrastructure to handle the different encrypted data streams that might be produced by a surveillance system [7, 31].

3 Threats to Privacy

The goal of privacy protection is to prevent access to information that intrudes on an individual's privacy, but specifying exactly what information is sensitive is difficult. We limit ourselves to considering the actions of people (including driving vehicles) in front of the camera, though certainly other visual information (e.g. documents, the presence of an object) can compromise privacy in certain circumstances. In particular we focus on preventing the identification of individuals – the major threat to individual privacy. In Table 1 we list a number of factors that play a role in the threat to privacy posed by an automatic video surveillance system.

The location of the system is certainly one factor. In high-security environments, no privacy protection may be necessary, but in one's home no level of video obfuscation may be considered acceptable. The person with access to the information also determines the level of privacy intrusiveness, as shown by [18]. A person from

Table 1 Factors affecting video surveillance privacy protection

Scenario	Observer	Familiarity	Role of subject
High security	Law enforcement	Familiar	Member of general public
Low security	System managers	Unfamiliar	Employee
e.g. workplace	System operators		Wearer of privacy tag
Public space	Authorized accessors		Intruder
Private space	Public		
	Hackers		
	Person observed		

Effort	Data type	Tools
Passive	Raw video	Summary
Opportunistic	Redacted video	Video review
Deliberate	Raw extracted data	Freeze-frame
Sophisticated.	Anonymized data	Search
	Linked to an identity	

any of the categories of Table 1 may be familiar with an individual observed by the system, increasing the risk of information being viewed as sensitive, but an unfamiliar person is still subject to voyeurism and prejudiced treatment. In each category the availability of each type of data must be limited as far as possible, consistent with the person's need to access information. The person seen by the camera also plays a role, being observed with some kind of informed consent (e.g. an employee); with active consent and the carrying of a privacy token [2, 25]; passively as a member of the public; or indeed as an intruder.

In preventing privacy breaches from a surveillance system, we must review the information that can be leaked, the access points to that information within the system, and the availability to different groups of people. Raw video contains much privacy-intrusive information, but much effort is required to get that data. A keyframe may convey much less information, but if well-chosen presents that information more succinctly. An index with powerful search facilities can easily direct a user to a particular clip of video. The power to intrude on privacy is greatly enhanced if the system has the capability to identify individuals. In principle all the information stored in a networked digital system is vulnerable to hacking, but preventing such breaches is a matter of conventional information and physical security.

4 Guaranteeing Video Privacy

Video information processing systems, including the system outlined here, are error prone. Perfect performance cannot be guaranteed, even under fairly benign operating conditions, and the system makes two types of errors when separating video into streams: missed detection (of an event or object) and false alarm. We can trade these errors off against one another, choosing an *operating point* with high sensitivity that has few missed detections, but many false alarms, or one with low sensitivity that has few false alarms, but more often fails to detect real events when they occur.

The problems of imperfect video processing capability can be minimized by selecting the appropriate system operating point. The *costs* of missed detection and false alarm are significantly different, and differ in privacy protection from those for a surveillance system. Given the sensitive nature of the information, it is likely that a single missed detection may reveal personal information over extended periods of time. For example, failing to detect, and thus obscure, a face in a single frame of video could allow identity information to be displayed and thus compromise the anonymity of days of aggregated track information associated with the supposedly anonymous individual. On the other hand, an occasional false alarm (e.g. obscuring something that isn't a face) may have a limited impact on the effectiveness of the installation. The operating point can be part of the access-control structure – higher authority allows the reduction of the false alarm rate at a higher risk of compromising privacy. Additional measures such as limiting access to freeze-frame or data export functions can also overcome the risks associated with occasional failures in the system.

Even with perfect detection, anonymity cannot be guaranteed. Contextual information may be enough to uniquely identify a person even when all identifying characteristics are obscured in the video. Obscuring biometrics (face, gait) and weak identifiers (height, pace length, clothing colour) will nevertheless reduce the potential for privacy intrusion. These privacy-protection algorithms, even when operating imperfectly, will serve the purpose of making it harder, if not impossible, to run automatic algorithms to extract privacy-intrusive information, and making abuses by human operators more difficult or costly.

4.1 Increasing Public Acceptance

The techniques described in this chapter can be considered as an optional addition to a surveillance system – one that will cost more and risk impinging on the effectiveness of the surveillance offered, while the privacy-protection benefits accrue to third parties. We must then ask the question of why anybody would accept this extra burden, and how the tragedy of the commons can be overcome. A principal reason is likely to be through legislation. In future, it may be required by law that CCTV systems impose privacy protection of the form that we describe. Existing legislation in some jurisdictions may already require the deployment of these techniques as soon as they become feasible and commercially available. Without legislation, it may still be that companies and institutions deploying CCTV choose, or are pressured (by the public, shareholders or customers), to "do the right thing" and include privacy-protecting technology in their surveillance systems. Liability for infringement of privacy may encourage such a movement.

Even when privacy protection methods are mandated, compliance and enforcement are still open to question. McCahill and Norris [21] estimated that nearly 80% of CCTV systems in London's business space did not comply with current data protection legislation, which specifies privacy protection controls such as preventing unauthorized people from viewing CCTV monitors. Legislating public access to surveillance systems as proposed by Brin [3] is one solution, but that still begs the question of whether there are additional video feeds that are not available for public scrutiny. A potential solution is certification and registration of systems, perhaps along the lines of the TRUSTe system that evolved for internet privacy. Vendors of video systems might invite certification of their privacy-protection system by some independent body. For purpose-built devices with a dedicated camera sensor (like PrivacyCam [27]) this would suffice. Individual surveillance installations could also be certified for compliance with installation and operating procedures, with a certification of the privacy protection offered by the surveillance site prominently displayed on the equipment and CCTV advisory notices. Such notices might include a site (or even camera) identification number and the URL or SMS number of the surveillance privacy registrar where the site can be looked up to confirm the certification of the surveillance system. Consumer complaints would invoke investigations by the registrar, and conscientious companies could invite voluntary inspections.

5 Video Privacy by Redaction

In a privacy-protecting surveillance system, there are several design choices that must be made, involving the flow of protected and unprotected data; data protection methods; access control; and auditing. Following our model [27], this chapter is focused on privacy protection by the redaction of images. That is, it is assumed that automatic processing determines regions in the image that may contain sensitive information, and that privacy protection is implemented by methods such as blurring, pixellating or obscuring some or all of these sensitive regions, or their complements. As shown in Section 2, there is new work being carried out in evaluating the effectiveness and desirability of these different redaction methods. We remain agnostic to the method – given a region of an image, any of these methods can easily be applied and a particular system may well allow several methods for different circumstances.

When redacted information is to be presented to the user, one fundamental question is what redaction is necessary and when the redaction is to occur. In some scenarios (such as the PrivacyCam), the system may need to guarantee that redaction happens at the earliest stage, and that unredacted data is never accessible. Only one level of redaction at a time is possible when such a system is a drop-in replacement for an analogue camera. However, for a general surveillance system, it may be necessary to present both redacted and unredacted data to end users according to the task and their rights, and to allow different types and extents of redaction according to the circumstances.

In a distributed surveillance system, such as that shown in Fig. 1, there are three principal locations through which the data must pass: the video processor, database and browser (or end-user application), each of which can be a reasonable choice for the redaction to take place:

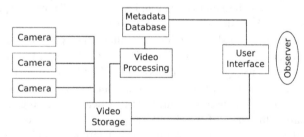

Fig. 1 Possible architecture for a video surveillance system

5.1 Browser

Here the unredacted data is delivered to the client and client software carries out the redaction and presents the redacted information to the user. This scenario means that redacted data does not need to be stored and transmitted but metadata for redaction does need to be transferred with the raw data. Since the browser is the part of a system most exposed to attack, transmitting the unredacted data there is not secure.

5.2 Content Management

The content management system can redact the information when requested for viewing, which will minimise storage requirements and allow complete flexibility, but involve additional processing (with the same keyframe perhaps being redacted multiple times), latency and imposes image modification requirements on the database system.

5.3 Video Analytics

The video analytics system has access to the richest information about the video activity and content, and thus can have the finest control over the redaction, but committing at encoding time allows for no post-hoc flexibility. In the other two scenarios for instance, a set of people and objects could be chosen and obscured on-the-fly. Sending redacted and raw frames to the database imposes bandwidth and storage requirements.

5.4 Double Redaction

Perhaps the most flexible and secure method is double redaction, in which privacy protection is applied at the earliest possible stage, and privacy-protected data flows through the system by default. Separate streams containing the private data can be transmitted in parallel to the database and to authorized end users, allowing the inversion of the privacy protection in controlled circumstances. The operating point of the detection system can even be changed continuously at display time according to a user's rights, to obscure all possible detections, or only those above a certain confidence. Figure 2 shows an example of such a double redaction scheme, with two levels of redaction.

Fig. 2 Double redaction: Video is decomposed into information streams which protect privacy and are recombined when needed by a sufficiently authorized user. Information is not duplicated and sensitive information is only transmitted when authorized. Optionally an unmodified (but encrypted) copy of the video may need to be securely stored to meet requirements for evidence

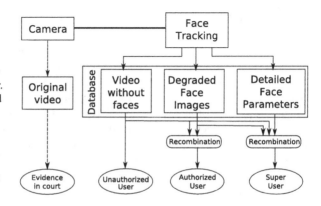

In the system that we describe below, protection happens at the video analytics module, with redacted and raw data being stored in the database, with the latter only being served to the browsers of authorized users. In each of these methods, we assume that all data flows and storage are encrypted to prevent simple eavesdropping and hacking from bypassing the privacy protection.

6 Performance Evaluation

For privacy protection to become a viable technology for implementation in real surveillance systems, we must begin to measure the performance and effectiveness of systems that claim to protect privacy, especially if privacy protection is to be widely deployed or demanded by regulation.

In our system, we have been most concerned with face obscuration, as the key to protecting individual identity, as well as hiding, to some extent, other personal attributes such as race, gender and age. It is clear that in the observation of familiar individuals or with sufficient contextual information, identification can be made based on other factors, such as clothing or gait, but face obscuration is a sufficient and widely accepted method of privacy protection in many circumstances.

We must then ask the question of when face (or full body) obscuration is sufficient to protect privacy. We make the assumption that if ever a face is displayed without redaction then the privacy protection has failed, in that an operator would plausibly be able to uniquely identify an individual based on even a single frame of video seen "in the clear".

Here, we focus on the algorithmic performance of our system and consider those failures where errors in detection of activity lead to failures to correctly redact the video. Naturally other kinds of errors can occur in a complete system, such as failure to specify a privacy policy correctly, or to implement a specified policy. If redaction does take place, we assume that an appropriate method has been chosen that renders the face and thus person (pace Chen et al. [6]) unidentifiable.

7 Experiments

Experiments were carried out on recorded video of real customers in a retail store during normal operation. For privacy reasons, the store required face obscuration of all data before publication. Video was acquired at the entrance of the store, with customers moving towards and away from the camera, and at the returns desk where the camera faced the customers, looking obliquely over the heads of staff, as shown in Fig. 3. Privacy protection is considered to have failed if an individual's face appears unredacted in the data available to the system end user. All experiments assumed a simple policy requiring all faces to be obscured, rather than a more complex policy where staff, say, or (non-)bearers of RFID tags were excluded from privacy protection requirements.

Fig. 3 *Left*: A keyframe from the retail store returns desk, with two customers' faces automatically obscured. *Right*: the corresponding close-up keyframe

The entrance video was processed with a generic appearance-based "object" tracker enabled. This generates keyframes with all detected objects blurred (blurring covers the entire bounding box of the person with an additional margin of 3 pixels), and video where all pixels of detected objects are obscured by a "silhouette" filled with a uniformly coloured region. The effectiveness of the system in protecting privacy was evaluated based on the information to be presented to the user, considering first the keyframes that are presented in a summary of all activity in a given camera. One keyframe is generated for each detected moving object. To protect privacy of the individuals being viewed, the image area occupied by any person currently in the image must be redacted. Figure 4 shows a set of such keyframes. In each case the object that the keyframe represents is blurred, surrounded by a bright box, and its trajectory is displayed. Other objects in the scene are also blurred, and surrounded by a darker box. The individual in the top right keyframe is stationary, and is thus poorly detected, so the redaction bounding box fails to completely cover their face. The performance of the privacy protection is measured by the number of individuals whose face is visible in the keyframes, as shown in Table 2.

Fig. 4 Keyframes from the store entrance showing customers blurred out. At *top right* a customer who is stationary is incompletely blurred while in the keyframe for another tracked customer

Table 2 Effectiveness for the store entrance keyframes. The one failure is that shown in Fig. 4

Keyframes	Number with any face visible
100	1

Table 3 Effectiveness for the store entrance video clips

Tracks	Number not always obscured
29	1

A second experiment involves viewing the redacted video. In this experiment, privacy protection is deemed to have failed if an individual's face is visible in any frame of the video. Table 3 shows the results of this experiment on 10 min of entrance video (distinct from that used for the keyframe test above). The returns desk video was processed with a face-tracking algorithm that detects frontal and profile faces and uses correlation-based tracking to maintain track when detection fails. A track is created for each person detected, recording the location of the face over the period for which it is visible. This location can be used to obscure the face during video playback.

Each track is represented by a keyframe (Fig. 3, left) showing the entire scene, conveying the position and activity of the person, together with their relationship to other people in the scene. When such keyframes are browsed with privacy protection enabled, the faces of all the people in the scene are obscured. In this case, a failure of tracking or detection can cause the inadvertent revelation of facial appearance under two circumstances: (1) the tracker fails to track correctly the person being tracked, so the face obscuration is misplaced and the face is visible; (2) another person in the scene is not detected or is mistracked and thus is not correctly obscured.

A second keyframe (Fig. 3) is created by cropping out the "best" (greatest area, frontal) face detected for the track. Such keyframes are used to represent the track when being browsed through the GUI, and can be blurred to allow only minimal information about the person to be visible, though generally a face keyframe is intended for identification and privacy protection is not required. There is little chance of a failure of privacy protection, since the image is cropped to show only the face, and a false positive would lead to a non-face being shown.

The face tracker is evaluated by counting the number of faces that are visible in the whole-scene keyframes of customers at the returns desk. Table 4 shows the results of the face-tracking experiment.

Table 4 Face obscuration effectiveness for the returns counter. Each keyframe is triggered by one main subject but may contain other customers who could be revealed in the keyframe

Main subject		Other subjects		False
Keyframes	Failures	Number	Failures	alarms
475	0	96	59	17

8 Discussion

It can be seen from the above experiments that each redaction system (based on blob tracking or face tracking) has the potential to fail and allow the presentation of privacy-sensitive information to a user of the system. The blob-tracking system is more effective, because it is dependent on the simpler, more reliable feature of background subtraction differences, rather than the complex and more fallible face detector. The tracking-based redaction can fail when objects (or parts of objects) stop and become absorbed into the background. It is possible to overcome many such failures of background subtraction by controlling the adaptation of moving objects, but ultimately the foreground/background distinction is ill-defined and some errors will always be possible.

The face detector is sensitive to variations in lighting, pose, personal appearance (sunglasses, beards, hats, etc.) and will always be prone to make some errors. By using a tracker to "fill-in" between detections, frames where the face is not detected can still be redacted. Extrapolation to the frames where a person enters the scene would also be possible, but the problem remains that some faces, particularly those that are partially obscured or looking down/away may never be detected, albeit that those faces are less likely to be identifiable.

In both algorithms, thresholds control the sensitivity of detection (of foreground pixels and faces, as well as the persistence of tracks) and the sensitivities used in these experiments are those defined for normal surveillance operations, not privacy protection. False alarms in privacy protection have little cost, whereas in general surveillance false alarms dilute results, and waste operator time, processor power and storage. Laxer thresholds can be used when generating the privacy-protecting views, at the expense of complexity in the system, but it remains true that the background subtraction method will be more reliable than the face detection method, so even in views where face-based tracking is desired, the most conservative privacy protection should be based on motion, with mechanisms to handle objects that become static for a while. In the worst case, some areas (such as the edge of the image where detection is unreliable, or areas where faces occur most frequently) might be obscured by default when the penalty for doing so is not high.

It can also be seen that restricting the amount of data available to the user is fundamental in maintaining the effectiveness of privacy protection. Doubling the number of keyframes available will double the likelihood of a face being improperly exposed. Allowing the user to watch redacted video, rather than individual keyframes will again increase the chances of a lapse of privacy protection. Constraining how the available data is accessed is also important – preventing freeze-frame and rewind in video viewing will limit the risk of a lapse, as well as presenting keyframes one at a time rather than presenting many to be browsed freely – the costs in usability of such strategies will depend on the application.

Finally one can present data only when a detector has fired. Thus, rather than allowing the user to watch all the redacted video from a camera, which might include segments where the detector failed, the user can be presented only with segments known to contain people, and thus for which we know redaction has taken place, albeit that the redaction may be incomplete.

Thus we arrive at five principles for presenting data in a privacy protection system, that can be applied whatever design choices about data type, access (video vs. stills vs. statistics; which information is to be presented or redacted), redaction method, privacy and access control policies are made:

- Use the most reliable detection method available for privacy protection.
- Bias operating point towards false-alarms for privacy protection.
- Limit the quantity of information available.
- Limit access to that information.
- Only present data where the detection mechanism has triggered.

9 Conclusions and Future Work

As we have seen, privacy protection by redaction is based on computer vision techniques that are not accurate enough to allow guarantees of privacy, but as part of a carefully designed system it can make gathering privacy-intrusive information a more difficult task. Even error-prone privacy protection techniques can transform a surveillance system from a tool for privacy intrusion into one where abuse of privacy is a technically challenging and time-consuming task. In particular, removing the passive exposure of operators to privacy information, even if the redaction is only partially effective, may reduce much of the prejudicial and voyeuristic uses of surveillance.

Video surveillance privacy protection technology is in its infancy but shows much promise for the future. More future work needs to be done to design real-world systems incorporating privacy protection features in a way that maintains the usefulness for the primary surveillance task, and to set up mechanisms to ensure that privacy protection features are deployed and used. Future research must cover security protocols, detection and tracking algorithms, video redaction techniques and usability studies. Future research needs to consider the accuracy of the underlying methods used and to measure their effectiveness in protecting privacy, as examined in this chapter.

References

1. Bowyer, K.: Face recognition technology and the security versus privacy tradeoff. Technology and Society, pp. 9–20 (2004)
2. Brassil, J.: Using mobile communications to assert privacy from video surveillance. In: 19th IEEE International Parallel and Distributed Processing Symposium, p. 290a (2005)
3. Brin, D.: The Transparent Society: Will Technology Force Us to Choose Between Privacy and Freedom. Perseus Publishing (1999)
4. Cavallaro, A.: Adding privacy constraints to video-based applications. In: European Workshop on the Integration of Knowledge, Semantics and Digital Media Technology (2004)
5. Cavallaro, A.: Privacy in video surveillance. Signal Processing Magazine, pp. 166–168 (2007)
6. Chen, D., Chang, Y., Yan, R., Yang, J.: Tools for protecting the privacy of specific individuals in video. EURASIP Journal on Applied Signal Processing, p. 107 (2007)
7. Cheung, S., Paruchuri, J., Nguyen, T.: Managing privacy data in pervasive camera networks. In: Proceedings of International Conference on Image Processing (2008)
8. Chinomi, K., Nitta, N., Ito, Y., Babaguchi, N.: PriSurv: Privacy protected video surveillance system using adaptive visual abstraction. In: International Multimedia Modelling Conference, pp. 144–154 (2008)

9. Coutaz, J., Bérard, F., Carraux, E., Astier, W., Crowley, J.: CoMedi: Using computer vision to support awareness and privacy in mediaspaces. In: CHI, pp. 13–14. ACM Press (1999)
10. Dufaux, F., Ebrahimi, T.: Smart video surveillance system preserving privacy. In: SPIE Image and Video Communication and Processing (2005)
11. Dufaux, F., Ebrahimi, T.: Scrambling for video surveillance with privacy. In: Proceedings of Computer Vision and Pattern Recognition, p. 160 (2006)
12. Fan, J., Hacid, M.S., Bertino, E.: A novel approach for privacy preserving video sharing. In: CIKM. ACM (2005)
13. Fidaleo, D., Nguyen, H.A., Trivedi, M.: The networked sensor tapestry (NeST): A privacy enhanced software architecture for interactive analysis of data in video-sensor networks. In: ACM International Workshop on Video Surveillance and Sensor Networks (2004)
14. Gross, R., Airoldi, E., Malin, B., Sweeney, L.: Integrating utility into face de-identification. In: Workshop on Privacy Enhancing Technologies. CMU (2005)
15. Gross, R., Sweeney, L., de la Torre, F., Baker, S.: Model-based face de-identification. In: Workshop on Privacy Research in Vision. IEEE (2006)
16. Hayes, G., Abowd, G.: Tensions in designing capture technologies for an evidence-based care community. In: CHI (2006)
17. Kitahara, I., Kogure, K., Hagita, N.: Stealth vision for protecting privacy. In: Proceedings of the International Conference on Pattern Recognition, vol. 4 (2004)
18. Koshimizu, T., Toriyama, T., Babaguchi, N.: Factors on the sense of privacy in video surveillance. In: Proceedings of the 3rd ACM workshop on Continuous archival and retrival of personal experences, pp. 35–44. ACM (2006). http://doi.acm.org/10.1145/1178657.1178665
19. Koshimizu, T., Toriyama, T., Noboru, B.: Factors on the sense of privacy in video surveillance. In: 3rd ACM Workshop on Continuous Archival and Retrival of Personal Experiences, pp. 35–44 (2006)
20. Martínez-Ponte, I., Desurmont, X., Meesen, J., Delaigle, J.F.: Robust human face hiding ensuring privacy. In: International Workshop on Image Analysis for Multimedia Interactive Services (WIAMIS) (2005)
21. McCahill, M., Norris, C.: CCTV. Perpetuity Press (2003)
22. Neustaedter, C., Greenberg, S., Boyle, M.: Blur filtration fails to preserve privacy for home-based video conferencing. In: ACM Transactions on Computer Human Interactions (2006)
23. Newton, E., Sweeney, L., Malin, B.: Preserving privacy by de-identifying facial images. Tech. Rep. CMU-CS-03-119, Carnegie Mellon University, School of Computer Science, Pittsburgh (2003)
24. Pankanti, S., Senior, A., Brown, L., Hampapur, A., Tian, Y.L., Bolle, R.: Work in progress: PeopleVision: Privacy protection in visual surveillance. IEEE Pervasive Computing 2(1), 96 (2003)
25. Schiff, J., Meingast, M., Mulligan, D., Sastry, S., Goldberg, K.: Respectful cameras: Detecting visual markers in real-time to address privacy concerns. In: International Conference on Intelligent Robots and Systems (2007)
26. Senior, A., Pankanti, S., Hampapur, A., Brown, L., Tian, Y.L., Ekin, A.: Blinkering surveillance: Enabling video privacy through computer vision. Tech. Rep. RC22886, IBM T.J.Watson Research Center, NY 10598 (2003)
27. Senior, A., Pankanti, S., Hampapur, A., Brown, L., Tian, Y.L., Ekin, A.: Enabling video privacy through computer vision. IEEE Security and Privacy 3(5), 50–57 (2004)
28. Tansuriyavong, S., Hanaki, S.: Privacy protection by concealing persons in circumstantial video image. In: Workshop on Perceptive User Interfaces, pp. 1–4. ACM (2001)
29. Teng, C.Y., Wang, K.C., Chu, H.H.: Privacy-aware camera: Automating the removal of accidental passers from unintentional cameras. Submitted to Location Awareness Workshop 2nd International Workshop on Location- and Context-Awareness (LoCA 2006)
30. Wickramasuriya, J., Alhazzazi, M., Datt, M., Mehrotra, S., Venkatasubramanian, N.: Privacy-protecting video surveillance. In: SPIE Real-Time Imaging IX, vol. 5671, pp. 64–75 (2005)
31. Zhang, W., Cheung, S.C., Chen, M.: Hiding privacy information in video surveillance system. In: Proceedings of International Conference on Image Processing (2005)

Oblivious Image Matching

Shai Avidan, Ariel Elbaz, Tal Malkin and Ryan Moriarty

Abstract Video surveillance is an intrusive operation that violates privacy. It is therefore desirable to devise surveillance protocols that minimize or even eliminate privacy intrusion. A principled way of doing so is to resort to Secure Multi-Party methods, that are provably secure, and adapt them to various vision algorithms. In this chapter, we describe an Oblivious Image Matching protocol which is a secure protocol for image matching. Image matching is a generalization of detection and recognition tasks since detection can be viewed as matching a particular image to a given object class (i.e., does this image contain a face?) while recognition can be viewed as matching an image of a particular instance of a class to another image of the same instance (i.e., does this image contain a *particular* car?). And instead of applying the Oblivious Image Matching to the entire image one can apply it to various sub-images, thus solving the localization problem (i.e., where is the gun in the image?). A leading approach to object detection and recognition is the bag-of-features approach, where each object is reduced to a set of features and matching objects is reduced to matching their corresponding sets of features. Oblivious Image Matching uses a secure fuzzy match of string and sets as its building block. In the proposed protocol, two parties, Alice and Bob, wish to match their images, without leaking additional information. We use a novel cryptographic protocol for fuzzy matching and adopt it to the bag-of-features approach. Fuzzy matching compares two sets (or strings) and declares them to match if a certain percentage of their elements match. To apply fuzzy matching to images, we represent images as a set of visual words that can be fed to the secure fuzzy matching protocol. The fusion of a novel cryptographic protocol and recent advances in computer vision results in a secure and efficient protocol for image matching. Experiments on real images are presented.

S. Avidan (✉)
Adobe Systems Inc., Newton, MA, USA,
avidan@adobe.com

A. Senior (ed.), *Protecting Privacy in Video Surveillance*,
DOI 10.1007/978-1-84882-301-3_4, © Springer-Verlag London Limited 2009

1 Introduction

Video surveillance is becoming ubiquitous with the growing availability of low-cost cameras, high-bandwidth networks, and increasing computing power. This, in turn, leads to a growing concern for privacy as it is unclear who collects, maintains, and mines these huge video databases. The problem is further complicated when data must be shared across parties. For example, a law enforcement agency might want to use the surveillance video of a private company to help solve a crime. Or two different government agencies might have to collaborate to gather information on potential suspects. Such scenarios are common and are currently solved simply by transferring the entire video from one party to the other thus increasing the risk of privacy invasion. Privacy preserving video surveillance algorithms can play a positive role in balancing the right for privacy and the greater good by supplying the various parties with the information they need, and nothing more, while protecting the privacy of individuals.

Video surveillance can be reduced to a couple of basic questions such as detection, recognition, and localization. In detection one needs to verify if a generic object appears in the image. For example, the system must alert the user if a car (regardless of make, model, and color) appears in the image. In other cases a particular instance must be detected. For example, in case of a robbery the police might know the specific make and model of the car and would like to mine the video to find images in which this particular car appears, or in a surveillance network one camera might want to verify if a particular object of interest appeared before in the field of view of another camera so that its trajectory can be established. Yet in other cases one is interested in locating an object. That is, where exactly does a particular object appear in the image? All these questions are special cases of the image matching problem which is at the core of computer vision research.

There has been great progress in the field of object detection and recognition in recent years and in particular the bag of features approach emerged as one of the leading techniques. It was borrowed from the text analysis community where a text document is treated as a bag of words and similarity between text documents is measured by the similarity between their bags of words. This technique, with the proper modifications, is now used for image and object matching. In a nutshell, the method works as follows. First, in an offline process a large collection of images is used to construct a dictionary of visual words. In run time, each image is reduced to a bag of visual words, or features, and two images are matched by matching their corresponding bags-of-features. In case one is interested in detecting an object in one image in another image, then only features that appear within the bounding box of the object are matched to all sub-windows of the other image. And in case one is interested in matching a query image to a video sequence, then the process must be repeated for every frame in the video.

In what follows we assume that there are two parties involved in the process. One party, Alice, holds the query image and the other party, Bob, holding the surveillance video. And both would like to match their images without leaking or learning additional information about the other party. Object detection, recognition, and localization can all be reduced to this framework. Our goal is not to describe a specific privacy preserving video surveillance application but instead investigate the theoretical properties that such a system must have.

Oblivious Image Matching is a novel secure image matching protocol that allows two parties to find if they have images of the same object, without revealing any additional information. This is a special case of the general secure multi-party computation field that allows two parties to achieve a common goal without revealing their data to each other. It is known that there are general solutions to this problem, but they are slow and we use domain-specific knowledge to accelerate them.

At the heart of our method is a novel secure fuzzy matching protocol that allows two parties to compute a fuzzy match between two sets (or strings), each owned by one of the parties. The two sets are said to match if a certain fraction of their elements match. Given this basic building block, we build a secure image-matching system that can match two images and declare if they are of the same object or not, without leaking any additional information to any of the parties.

2 Background and Preliminaries

We give a short review of the relevant method in computer vision, followed by the necessary background in cryptography.

2.1 Computer Vision

Video surveillance can be regarded as a visual search problem where the goal is to rapidly and accurately locate objects in video despite changes in camera viewpoint, lighting, and partial occlusions. The bag-of-word approach to visual search represents an image as a collection of interest points, each described by a feature descriptor such as SIFT [Low04]. This approach, known as probabilistic Latent Semantic Analysis (pLSA) [Hof99] and its hierarchical Bayesian form, Latent Dirichlet Allocation (LDA) [BNJ03] was imported, with great success from the textual analysis community [SZ03]. There is now a plethora of papers that differ in the way interest points are extracted from an image, as well as in the feature descriptors used to describe each interest point, see [SZ08] for a review of the method, as well as [MS04] for a comparison of various feature descriptors.

In their seminal work [SZ03] presented a system for locating objects in video. First, a large collection of training images is used to create a dictionary of SIFT features. Then, each frame in the video sequence is reduced to a bag of SIFT features that are stored in an inverted file table. The query image that is specified by the user is also reduced to a bag of SIFT features that are then used to index the inverted file table and find the video frames that match the query image. This work was applied with great success to full length feature films and not surveillance video, but the underlying principles are similar.

Here we focus on the approach taken by [SZ03] but using other interest point detectors or different feature descriptors can be used as well. In addition, they have a spatial consistency step to improve retrieval results, a step that we do not take here.

This is because some later work [NS06] reported comparable results *without* using this step.

In the vision field, the work most closely related to ours is that of Avidan et al. [AB06] that proposed a method for secure face detection. However, their method is limited to stump-based AdaBoost type classifiers of the sort used for face detection, where as ours is general and can be used for general image, and object, matching.

2.2 Cryptography

We start with a quick review of the necessary cryptographic background. The interested reader is referred to [Gol04] and references within for a primer on cryptography. A cryptographically oriented version of this work can be found in [AEMM07].

Secure two-party protocols (as well as multi-party protocols) are measured against an ideal model, in which both parties submit their input to a trusted third party who performs the computation and returns the results, without leaking any intermediate information to either party. The goal of secure protocols is to do away with the trusted third party, while still preserving the privacy and ensuring that each party learns only its prescribed output from the protocol and nothing more. Yao [Yao82] was the first to define the problem and solved it for the two-party case, where two parties are interested in evaluating a given function that takes private input from each party. As a concrete example consider the millionaire problem: Two parties want to find which one has a larger number, without revealing anything else about the numbers themselves. Yao solved the problem by reducing it to privately evaluating a Boolean circuit, and showing how each gate can be evaluated securely (under standard cryptographic assumptions). The communication and complexity of the secure protocol is linear in the size of the circuit. A large body of work on secure two-party and multi-party computation emerged in the last two decades. More recently, much effort was made to reduce the communication and complexity of the protocols by relying on the specific characteristics of the problem at hand.

Throughout this chapter, we assume that the parties are semi-honest (also known as honest-but-curious) meaning that they will follow the agreed upon protocol but try to infer as much information from it as possible. This is a standard model in the cryptographic literature.[1]

Of particular interest here are two, well known, cryptographic tools named Homomorphic Encryption and Private Information Retrieval (PIR), which we explain shortly below.

---

[1] Our protocols can be changed to work in a malicious environment by using cryptographic techniques such as the general (and typically not efficient) zero knowledge, or more efficient specific techniques for the matching problem, which we do not include here.

2.2.1 Public Key Homomorphic Encryption Schemes

In cryptography, one denotes by *plaintext* the unencrypted message and by *ciphertext* the encrypted one and a central theme in cryptography is to develop encryption techniques that allow users to operate directly on the encrypted data, even without knowing the secret key. One such tool is Homomorphic Encryption which is defined as follows:

Definition 1. *Semantically Secure Public Key Encryption Scheme* A public key encryption scheme consists of three algorithms (G, E, D), all of which are efficiently computable, such that given a security parameter k

1. $G(1^k)$ (called the key generator) generates a pair of keys (pk, sk).
2. For any message m and any $c \in E_{pk}m$, $D_{sk}(c) = m$ (except with negligible error probability).
3. Without access to the private key, it is hard to distinguish between the encryptions of any two different messages. That is, for any efficient algorithm A, $|Pr[A(E_{pk}(m_0)) = 1] - Pr[A(E_{pk}(m_1)) = 1]|$ is negligible (even if A knows in advance the messages m_0, m_1).

We say that an encryption scheme (G, E, D) is additively homomorphic if $D(E(x_1) + E(x_2)) = D(E(x_1)) + D(E(x_2))$, and also $D(c \cdot E(x)) = c \cdot D(E(x))$ for constant c (where the addition operation $+$ is in the respective domain).

It is well known that homomorphic encryption can be used for secure polynomial evaluation where two parties wish to evaluate the polynomial $P(x)$ where one party, Bob, has the polynomial P and the other party, Alice, has x. Bob can send the encrypted coefficients $E(a_0), E(a_1), \dots, E(a_d)$ to Alice, which can multiply them by $1, x, x^2, \dots, x^d$ (respectively) and obtain the *encrypted* value of $P(x)$. Alice then sends the result to Bob who decrypts it and sends it back to Alice. Thus, both parties learn the value of $P(x)$, without learning anything else in the process.

2.2.2 Private Information Retrieval

Private Information Retrieval (introduced by Chor et al. [CGKS95]) comes to protect a client's privacy when querying a database. We model the client's secret input as an index i into an n-bit string B held by the server, and want a communication-efficient protocol that enables the client to learn B_i without the server learning i. A trivial and *not* efficient solution is to have the server send all of B to the client. Perhaps surprisingly, there are efficient PIR protocols that require communicating only $polylog(n)$ bits (where the index i is represented by $\log n$ bits).

The first PIR protocol that achieved $polylog(n)$ communication complexity (using two rounds) is that of Cachin, Micali, and Stadler [CMS99]. In this protocol, the client runs in time $k \log n$ (where k is a security parameter), and the server runs in time $O(nk^c)$ for some c. (note, the server always "looks" at all his input bits; this must be the case, or else the server can tell which bits were surely not required by the client).

3 Oblivious Image Matching

We first present the non-secure version of our image-matching computation, followed by a description of our secure protocol for oblivious image matching.

3.1 Image Matching (Without Security)

Inspired by the work of [SZ03] we say that two images match, if a certain percentage of their interest points match, and we say that a pair of interest points match if a certain percentage of their SIFT attributes match. Recall that a SIFT descriptor consists of a $128D$ feature vector that corresponds to sixteen 8-bin histograms in small regions around the interest point. Thus, we can treat each 8-bin histogram as a letter in some large alphabet and view SIFT as a 16 character long string from now on. We will elaborate on that later on. This motivates the following definitions, specifying our image-matching functionality for which we design a secure protocol (oblivious image matching) in the next subsection, and which we use for our experiments in the next section.

3.1.1 Match Definitions

Let $\mathcal{X} = \{\overline{X}_1, \ldots, \overline{X}_n\}$ and $\mathcal{Y} = \{\overline{Y}_1, \ldots, \overline{Y}_m\}$ be sets of d-dimensional vectors over alphabet Σ;

1. We say that there is a *fuzzy match* between two vectors $\overline{X}_i, \overline{Y}_j$ if at least t of the coordinates are equal; that is

$$\overline{X}_i \sim_t \overline{Y}_j \text{ iff } \#\{(\overline{X}_i)_k = (\overline{Y}_j)_k\} \geq t$$

2. We say that the vector $\overline{X}_i$ *fuzzy matches* the set $\mathcal{Y}$ if there exists some $\overline{Y}_j \in \mathcal{Y}$ such that $\overline{X}_i$ fuzzy matches $\mathcal{Y}_j{}^2$; that is

$$\overline{X}_i \sim_t \mathcal{Y} \text{ if } \exists \overline{Y}_j \in \mathcal{Y} \text{ s.t. } \overline{X}_i \sim_t \overline{Y}_j$$

3. We say that the sets $\mathcal{X}$, $\mathcal{Y}$ *image match* if there are at least T vectors $\overline{X}_i \in \mathcal{X}$ that fuzzy-match the set $\mathcal{Y}$; that is

$$\mathcal{X} \approx_{t,T} \mathcal{Y} \text{ if } \#\{i | \overline{X}_i \sim_t \mathcal{Y}\} \geq T$$

Note that a fuzzy match $\overline{X}_i, \overline{Y}_j$ matches between strings (where the order of each component matters), while at the outer level, an image match $\mathcal{X} \approx_{t,T} \mathcal{Y}$ matches between sets (where the order does not matter). As discussed above, the former

---

[2] An alternative definition requires that there is *exactly* one $\overline{Y}_j$ such that $\overline{X}_i \sim_t \overline{Y}_j$. We make use of both versions in the experimental section.

applies to SIFT descriptors (when viewed as strings), while the latter applies to sets of interest points.

3.2 Oblivious Image Matching

We now need to compute the image matching problem securely, without leaking any additional information. The straight-forward solution is to compare $\overline{X}_i$ to $\overline{Y}_j$, and to repeat that for all $i = 1 \ldots n$ and $j = 1 \ldots m$. The number of comparisons required is $O(n \cdot m \cdot d \cdot \log \Sigma)$. Thus we can expect the complexity of the general algorithm, according to Yao, to be $O(nmd \log \Sigma)$. Observe that this complexity is both for communication and computation. Instead, we describe below a protocol that significantly improves this efficiency, while maintaining the provable cryptographic security.

3.2.1 High-Level Description

Our protocol proceeds in three main steps. In the first step, Alice and Bob construct a 2D table that establishes matches between the feature points of Alice and the feature points of Bob. That is, by the end of this stage Bob should hold a 2D table $S_{n \times m}$ where $S(i, j)$ holds the *encrypted* number of attributes that match between the SIFT descriptor of Alice's ith interest point and the SIFT descriptor of Bob's jth interest point. In the second step, Alice and Bob need to figure out, for each row (i.e., for each of Alice's interest points), if there is one, or more, feature points in Bob's image that fuzzy match it. And, in the last step, they need to count the number of such rows and see if it is above some threshold.[3] All operations must be done in a secure fashion so no intermediate information is revealed to the other party.

3.2.2 Basic Oblivious Image Matching Protocol

In what follow we give the full Oblivious Image Matching protocol for secure image matching that uses, as a building block the secure fuzzy matching protocol. The protocol relies completely on Homomorphic Encryption and after we describe it we show we can improve the communication complexity by using PIR.

As a pre-processing stage, we assume that both Alice and Bob have access to an algorithm that can take an image, detect interest points in the image, represent each such interest point with a SIFT descriptor and have a deterministic way of converting the SIFT descriptor into a string. Hence, each image was reduced to a set of strings that must be fuzzy matched.

---

[3] Our protocol can be adjusted to other variants of fuzzy matching, e.g., trying to compute how many elements fuzzy match, or which elements fuzzy match (note that this is the original formulation of the problem proposed in [FNP04]). This may be of independent interest for other cryptographic applications in the vision or data mining domains.

In what follows we will assume that all values are always encrypted by one of the parties, unless otherwise stated. Due to the power of Homomorphic Encryption we can still operate on them as if they are not encrypted.

1. **Alice constructs a 3D table** $Q(i, j, k)$ of size $n \times |\Sigma| \times d$ where:

$$Q(i, j, k) = \begin{cases} E(1) & (\overline{X}_i)_k = \sigma_j \\ E(0) & otherwise \end{cases}$$

That is, $Q(i, j, k)$ holds an encryption of the value one, if the kth character of the ith string is the letter σ_j in the alphabet Σ. Otherwise, $Q(i, j, k) = 0$. *Alice then sends these* $nd|\Sigma|$ *values to Bob.*

2. **Bob constructs an** $n \times m$ **table** $S(i, j)$ where

$$S(i, j) = \sum_{k=0}^{d} Q(i, (\overline{Y}_j)_k, j)$$

Observe that $S(i, j)$ is a cyphertext encrypted with Alice's public key, so Bob is oblivious to the actual value. $S(i, j)$ is exactly the number of matching characters between $\overline{X}_i$ and $\overline{Y}_j$.

Bob holds $n \times m$ encrypted values, and he's only interested in those where the plaintext has value at least the threshold t. The plaintexts are in the range $[0..d]$, and we will say that the values $[t, t + 1, \ldots, d]$ are "good," while the values $[0, 1, \ldots, t - 1]$ are "bad."

3. **Bob selects** nm **random values** $r_{i,j} \in_R [0..d]$ and uses the homomorphic properties of the encryption to shift $S'(i, j) = S(i, j) + r_{i,j} \pmod{d + 1}$.
   Bob sends the encrypted values S' **to Alice.**

4. **Alice receives the** $n \times m$ **matrix** S' **and decrypts it.** Note that for $S'(i, j)$, the values $[t + r_{i,j}, t + 1 + r_{i,j}, \ldots, d + r_{i,j}] \pmod{d + 1}$ are "good," whereas the other $d - t + 1$ values are "bad." Denote $GOOD(i, j)$ the set of "good" values for (i, j). Bob knows which values are in $GOOD(i, j)$ and which are not. Now, *for each instance of* (i, j) *Bob creates the index vector* $1_{GOOD(i,j)} \in \{0, 1\}^{d+1}$ and encrypts it with his public key.

   Alice only needs the component of the index vector that matches the value $S'(i, j)$ she received from Bob. *Bob sends Alice the entire encrypted index vector* and Alice can simply ignore the encryptions corresponding to values that do not match her $S'(i, j)$.[4]

   By now, all Alice learn is an encryption of zero, if $S(i, j) < t$, and encryption of one otherwise, so Alice now holds an $n \times m$ matrix where there is one at entry (i, j) if and only if $\overline{X}_i$ matches $\overline{Y}_j$, and zero otherwise. Denote this matrix $\hat{S}$.

---

[4] Alice might learn more information about other values of Bob, but since these are cyphertexts of semantically secure encryption, this does not give her any advantage.

5. **Alice uses the homomorphic properties of the encryption to sum up the values for each row of the matrix,** $R_i = \sum_{j=1}^{m} \hat{S}(i, j)$. We have that $R_i \in [0..m]$, and if $R_i \geq 1$ then there was a match for row i, which means that there was at least one element $\overline{Y}_j$ that matched $\overline{X}_i$. [5] To single out these elements, Alice and Bob repeat the same technique as in steps 3 and 4 except with their roles reversed; *For each row* $i \in [1..n]$ *Alice chooses* $r_i' \in_R [0..m]$ and uses the homomorphic properties of the encryption to shift $R_i' = R_i + r_i' \pmod{m + 1}$. *Alice sends* $\{R_i'\}_{i=1}^{n}$ *to Bob.*

6. **Bob receives n values R_i' and decrypts them.** The good values for R_i' are $[r_i' + 1, .., r_i' + m] \pmod{d + 1}$ and the only bad value is $r_i' + 0$. Denote the set of good values by $GOOD(i)$.

   Alice encrypts the index vectors $\{1_{GOOD(i)}\}_{i=1}^{n}$ and sends them to Bob. Bob picks from each vector $1_{GOOD(i)}$ the R_i'-th value, which is an encryption (using Alice's key) of 1 if and only if $R(i) \geq 1$. Denote this cyphertext R_i''.

   Bob sums up $\tilde{R} = \sum_{i=1}^{n} R_i''$, where the plaintext of $\tilde{R}$ is the number of objects $\overline{X}_i$ that fuzzy-matched some $\overline{Y}_j$ object.

7. **Bob takes the result $\tilde{R}$, chooses $r_i' \in_R [0..n]$ and sends to Alice the following** $n - T + 1$ **values** $((\tilde{R} - T)r_T'', \ldots, (\tilde{R} - n)r_n'')$. Alice decrypts these values, and if she finds any of them to be zero, she learns that $T \leq R \leq n$. Otherwise, Alice sees random numbers and concludes that there were less than T matches.

3.2.3 Improving the Communication Complexity Using PIR

In order to improve the communication complexity in steps 1, 4, and 6 we can use PIR. Recall that PIR enables a party to select a value at a certain index without the other party that holds the indices knowing which value was selected. Thus instead of Alice sending all $nd|\Sigma|$ values in step 1, Bob can use PIR to select only the encryptions that match his values $(\overline{Y}_j)_k$, reducing the communication complexity of step 1 to $O(nd \log^{k_1} |\Sigma|)$. Recall that while PIR have very small communication complexity, they guarantee that Alice does not learn which encryptions Bob chose. This can be done similarly in steps 4 and 6.

3.3 Communication Complexity

The communication complexity between Alice and Bob is dominated by step 1, in which Alice sends Bob $nd|\Sigma|$ cyphertexts, and by step 4 in which Bob sends Alice nmd cyphertexts, thus $O(nd(|\Sigma| + m))$ bits. If we use the PIR improvement, this goes down to $O(n(d \log^{k_1} |\Sigma| + m \log^{k_1} d))$.

---

[5] We can also easily handle the case where we want to only consider *single* matches, by considering only $R_i = 1$.

The running time of Alice in this protocol is $O(nd(|\Sigma| + m))$, and if we use PIR this goes down slightly to $O(n(|\Sigma|d + m \log^{k_1} d))$. The running time of Bob is $O(nd(m + |\Sigma|))$, and using PIR this goes down slightly to $O(nd(m + \log^{k_1} |\Sigma|))$.

The straight-forward solution, without regarding security, is to compare $\overline{X}_i$ to $\overline{Y}_j$, and to repeat that for all $i = 1 \ldots n$ and $j = 1 \ldots m$. The number of comparisons required is $O(n \cdot m \cdot d \cdot \log \Sigma)$. A general result in cryptography, due to Yao, shows that we can, in a generic way, turn this into a secure two-party protocol with communication complexity of $O(nmd \log |\Sigma|)$.

4 Experiments

Our goal, in these experiments, is to establish that it is possible to match scenes or generic objects viewed from different viewpoints and under varying viewing conditions in a secure and robust fashion. To this end, we simulated a non-secure version of the Oblivious Image Matching protocol in MATLAB and found that it can indeed be used for *secure* image and object matching. However, it is not as accurate as existing, non-secure techniques that are used in the vision literature. This is because Oblivious Image Matching has to balance vision, security, and efficiency constraints. It does that by achieving the best efficiency known, under strict cryptographically secure assumptions, at the cost of hurting some of the accuracy associated with a vision algorithm. The alternative would be to make state-of-the-art vision algorithms secure using the general Yao construction, which would result in inefficient, and hence not very useful, secure protocols.

4.1 Preprocessing

We have collected approximately $100, 000$ interest points, from the Caltech 100 image data set [FFFP04]. We use the Harris-affine detector [MS04] to detect them and the SIFT descriptor [Low04] to describe them. Recall that a SIFT descriptor consists of a $128D$ feature vector that corresponds to sixteen 8-bin histograms in small regions around the interest point. Then, we clustered each of the sixteen histograms independently into 32 clusters. This gives a position-dependent alphabet of size 32. Every $128D$ vector is mapped to a 16 characters long string. In the following, we assume that both parties have access to the clusters and so each party can transform his/her SIFT descriptor to a 16 character long string.

We performed three types of experiments. The first experiment was on a data set of 10 stereo pairs. The second experiment was done on a more challenging set of 9 pairs of images of different objects. The last experiment was done on the affine covariant data set of Mikolajczyk et al. [MS05] to measure the robustness of the representation and the fuzzy matching technique to changes in viewpoint, blur, illumination, rotation and zoom, and JPEG compression.

4.2 Oblivious Image Matching

In the first experiment we use an easy data set of 10 well-known stereo image pairs. We set the threshold t to 0.7 (i.e., at least 12 out of the 16 characters must match), allowed for one-to-many matches (i.e., Alice's feature point is allowed to match multiple feature points in Bob's image) and then compared all images against each other. Results are reported in Fig. 1. The actual images appear next to the confusion matrix. There is a total of 10 pairs and each image is compared against the remaining 19 images. As is evident from the block structure of the matrix, the Oblivious Image Matching protocol does a nice job of finding a significantly higher number of matches within a stereo pair than that found outside the pair.

In the second experiment, we use a more challenging set of 9 pairs of images of different objects, taken from the CALTECH toys dataset. In this case, we match the first image of every pair with all the second images of every pair. We empirically set the fuzzy matching threshold t to 0.8 (i.e., at least 13 out of the 16 characters must match) and, again, allowed for one-to-many matches. Results are reported in Fig. 2. Each entry in the confusion matrix encodes the number of matching interest points found. In this case, we compare each of the images to the left of the confusion

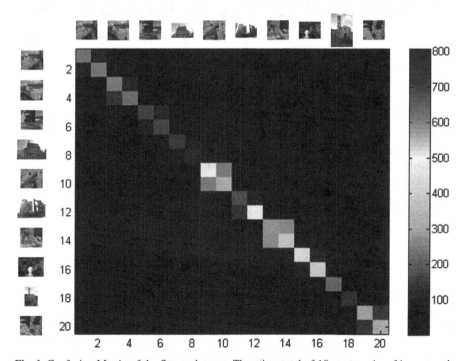

Fig. 1 Confusion Matrix of the Stereo data set. There is a total of 10 stereo pairs of images and every image is compared against the remaining 19. As can be seen from the diagonal structure of the matrix, Oblivious Image Matching does a good job of finding a significantly higher number of matching point between an image pair, as opposed to other images

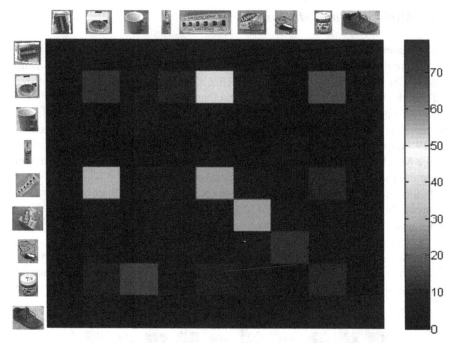

Fig. 2 Confusion Matrix of the Toys data set. In this case each image to the *left* of the confusion matrix is matched to the images above the confusion matrix. Also, each image above is matched against all images to the *left* of the confusion matrix. Again, the Oblivious Image Matching protocol shows that in most cases images of the object can be found securely

matrix to all the images above the confusion matrix. The correct match was found in the 7 out of the 9 pairs. Oblivious Image Matching failed on the first and fourth pairs. Note however that in four cases (pairs 1, 3, 4, 9) the number of matches found was fairly low (below 10 matches) which means that the system should probably discard such a match. The low number of matches is due to the fact that a fairly tight threshold was chosen – having at least 13 out of the 16 characters match. Lowering the threshold will increase the number of false matches.

4.3 Oblivious Image Matching Robustness

The Mikolajczyk–Schmid data set consists of 8 sets of images, containing 6 images each. These sets measure robustness to blur, viewpoint change, zoom and rotation, illumination change, and JPEG compression. We extracted feature points from each image and converted their SIFT descriptor to a 16 character long string, using a 32 alphabet. Then we computed the number of one-to-one matches between the first image in every set to the rest of the images in the set, where the fuzzy matching threshold t was set to 0.7 (i.e., at least 12 out of the 16 character must match). Then, we used the supplied homographies to verify that indeed the correct matches

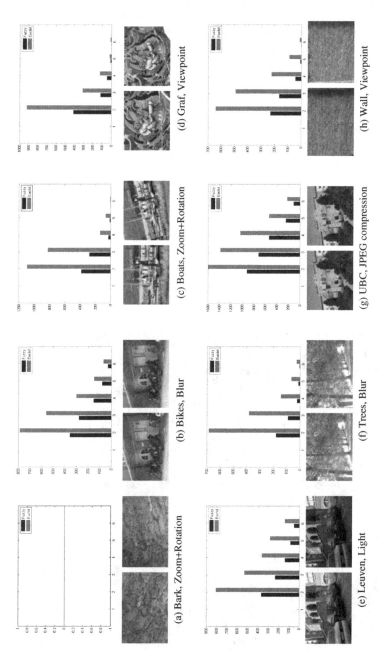

Fig. 3 Fuzzy Matching Stability. Comparing Oblivious Image Matching (*dark gray*) with ratio-test in L2 space (*light gray*). For each sub-figure we give a histogram of matches, as well as the first and second images in the set. In all cases, we compare the first image to the remaining 5 images, within its set. The *y*-axis shows the number of matches. For clarity, we also give the name of the set in the Mikolajczyk-Schmid data set, as well as the image transformation being examined. Note that for the Bark set (sub-figure (**a**)), we failed to find any match

were found. In our case, we declare a match to be correct if the distance after homography projection is less than 2 pixels. For comparison, we repeated the same experiment using a ratio test, where for every feature point we find the first and second closest matches, in the other image (using Euclidean distance in $128D$ feature space), and taking the match only if the ratio of distances is less than 0.6. Results are shown in Fig. 3. As can be seen, Oblivious Image Matching deteriorates as the variation between the two images grows, similar to what was observed for the ratio match. The number of matches found, however, compared to ratio test is about a third.

In another experiment we have computed the confusion matrix, comparing all 48 images against each other and found that indeed the diagonal is very dominant. Specifically, we compared each image against each other image except itself (there are 8 data sets with 6 images in each data set, giving a total of 48 images). In this experiment, we used an alphabet of size 16, allowed for multi-matches and set the fuzzy matching threshold to 0.8. After computing Oblivious Image Matching between all possible pairs of images we computed the mean number of feature matches between every pair of data sets and report the results in Fig. 4. As can be seen, the diagonal is very dominant suggesting that Oblivious Image Matching can indeed detect different images of the same object.

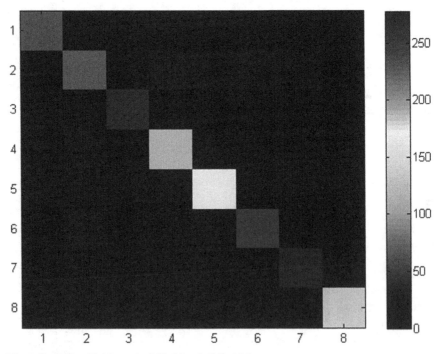

Fig. 4 Confusion Matrix on the Mikolajczyk-Schmid data set

5 Conclusions and Future Work

Many video surveillance problems, such as object detection, recognition and localization, can be reduced to image matching and therefore making video surveillance preserve privacy requires us to develop secure image-matching algorithm. Oblivious Image Matching is a novel, secure, and efficient approach to image matching. By combining the latest in cryptography and computer vision research we have demonstrated an efficient system that shows some promising results. Specifically, we took a recent protocol for secure set intersection and extended it to handle fuzzy matching and applied it both to sets and strings. We then used this novel cryptographic protocol for secure image matching, where images are represented as sets of strings. Oblivious Image Matching was shown to work on real images, but its performance is still not comparable to recent results in object matching and recognition and much work still needs to be done. We plan on conducting larger experiments to validate our approach, as well as combining some geometric constraints in the process to improve results. Finally, we plan to investigate ways to accelerate performance to make the method more suitable to real world scenarios.

References

[AB06] S. Avidan and M. Butman. Blind vision. In *European Conference on Computer Vision*, pages 1–13, 2006.

[AEMM07] S. Avidan, A. Elbaz, T. Malkin, and R. Moriarty. Oblivious image matching. Technical Report cucs-030-07, Columbia University, 2007.

[BNJ03] D. Blei, A. Ng, and M. Jordan. Latent dirchilet allocation. *Journal of Machine Learning Research*, 3:993–1022, 2003.

[CGKS95] B. Chor, O. Goldreich, E. Kushilevitz, and M. Sudan. Private information retrieval. In *IEEE Symposium on Foundations of Computer Science*, pages 41–50, 1995.

[CMS99] C. Cachin, S. Micali, and M. Stadler. Computationally private information retrieval with polylogarithmic communication. *Lecture Notes in Computer Science*, 1592:402–414, 1999.

[FFFP04] L. Fei-Fei, R. Fergus, and P. Perona. Learning generative visual models from few training examples. In *Workshop on Generative-Model Based Vision, IEEE Proc. CVPR*, 2004.

[FNP04] M. Freedman, K. Nissim, and B. Pinkas. Efficient private matching and set intersection. In *Advances in Cryptology – (EUROCRYPT 2004)*, volume 3027, pages 1–19, Springer-Verlag, 2004.

[Gol04] O. Goldreich. *Foundations of Cryptography*. Cambridge University Press, 2004.

[Hof99] T. Hofmann. Probabilistic latent semantic indexing. In *SIGIR*, pages 50–57, 1999.

[Low04] D. G. Lowe. Distinctive image features from scale-invariant keypoints. *International Journal of Computer Vision*, 60(2):91–110, 2004.

[MS04] K. Mikolajczyk and C. Schmid. Scale and affine invariant interest point detectors. *International Journal of Computer Vision*, 60(1):63–86, 2004.

[MS05] K. Mikolajczyk and C. Schmid. A performance evaluation of local descriptors. *IEEE Transactions on Pattern Recognition and Machine Intelligence*, 27(10):1615–1630, 2005.

[NS06] D. Nistér and H. Stewénius. Scalable recognition with a vocabulary tree. In *IEEE Conference on Computer Vision and Pattern Recognition*, pages 2161–2168, 2006.

[SZ03]   J. Sivic and A. Zisserman. Video google: A text retrieval approach to object matching in videos. *International Conference on Computer Vision*, pages 1470–1477,
2003.

[SZ08]   J. Sivic and A. Zisserman. Efficient visual search for objects in videos. *Proceedings
of the IEEE*, 96(4), 2008.

[Yao82]   A. C. Yao. Protocols for secure computations. In *Proc. 23rd IEEE Symposium on
Foundations of Comp. Science*, pages 160–164, Chicago, 1982.

Respectful Cameras: Detecting Visual Markers in Real-Time to Address Privacy Concerns

Jeremy Schiff, Marci Meingast, Deirdre K. Mulligan,
Shankar Sastry and Ken Goldberg

Abstract To address privacy concerns regarding digital video surveillance cameras, we propose a practical, real-time approach that preserves the ability to observe actions while obscuring individual identities. In the Respectful Cameras system, people who wish to remain anonymous wear colored markers such as hats or vests. The system automatically tracks these markers using statistical learning and classification to infer the location and size of each face. It obscures faces with solid ellipsoidal overlays, while minimizing the overlay area to maximize the remaining observable region of the scene. Our approach uses a visual color-tracker based on a 9D color-space using a Probabilistic Adaptive Boosting (AdaBoost) classifier with axis-aligned hyperplanes as weak hypotheses. We then use Sampling Importance Resampling (SIR) Particle Filtering to incorporate interframe temporal information. Because our system explicitly tracks markers, our system is well-suited for applications with dynamic backgrounds or where the camera can move (e.g., under remote control). We present experiments illustrating the performance of our system in both indoor and outdoor settings, with occlusions, multiple crossing targets, lighting changes, and observation by a moving robotic camera. Results suggest that our implementation can track markers and keep false negative rates below 2%.

1 Introduction

Since September 11, 2001, security concerns have led to increasing adoption of surveillance systems, raising concerns about "visual privacy" in public places. New technologies allow for the capture of significantly more detailed information than the human eye can perceive. Surveillance technologies are additionally empowered by digital recording, allowing footage to be stored indefinitely, or processed and combined with additional data sources to identify and track individuals across time and physical spaces. Robotic cameras can be served to capture high-resolution

J. Schiff (✉)
Department of EECS, University of California, Berkeley, CA, USA
e-mail: jschiff@eecs.berkeley.edu

A. Senior (ed.), *Protecting Privacy in Video Surveillance*,
DOI 10.1007/978-1-84882-301-3_5, © Springer-Verlag London Limited 2009

images over a wide field of view. For example, the Panasonic KX-HCM280 pan-tilt-zoom camera costs under $750 and has a built-in web-server and a 21 × optical zoom (500 Mpixels per steradian). The applications of these surveillance technologies extend beyond security, to industrial applications such as traffic monitoring and research applications such as observing public behavior.

McCahill et al. estimate that there are approximately 4 million public surveillance cameras deployed in the UK [35]. The USA has also deployed a number of camera systems in cities such as New York and Chicago for public monitoring [4, 36, 37]. Deployments of such large-scale government-run security systems, in conjunction with numerous smaller-scale private applications, raise fundamental privacy concerns.

In this chapter, we explore an approach we call "Respectful Cameras," that allows monitoring of activity but hides the faces of people who choose to wear recognizable markers such as hats or vests that are made available. We show an example of the Respectful Cameras system's output in Fig. 1. The system allows human actions to be observable so that people can monitor what is going on (i.e., at a construction site or airport terminal) for security or public relations purposes. We envision such a system being made widely available, as these markers would be cheap, unobtrusive, and easily mass-produced. For example, we could provide inexpensive hats of a particular color or pattern at the border of the space where cameras are present, similar to the respectful hats or leg-coverings that are made available at the entrance of churches and synagogues.

Existing face and people tracking methods have difficulty tracking in real-time under moving backgrounds, changing lighting conditions, partial occlusions, and across facial orientations. We investigate a new approach that uses markers worn by

Fig. 1 A sample video frame is on *left*. The system has been trained to track green vests such as the one worn by the man with the outstretched arm. The system output is shown in the frame on the *right*, where an elliptical overlay hides the face of this man. The remainder of the scene including faces of the other two workers wearing orange vests, remain visible. Note how the system successfully covers the face even when the vest is subjected to a shadow and a partial occlusion. Please visit "http://goldberg.berkeley.edu/RespectfulCameras" for more examples including video sequences

individuals to simplify the quality of face or person detection required for obscuring individual identity, providing a method for individuals to opt-out of observation. These markers provide a visual cue for our system by having the features of the marker such as color, size, and shape to be distinguishable from the background. We use the location of the marker to infer the location of the faces of individuals who wish to "opt-out" of observation.

Recent advances in computer processing have made our algorithms utilizing AdaBoost and Particle Filtering feasible for real-time applications. Our approach learns a visual marker's color model with Adaptive Boosting (AdaBoost), uses the model to detect a marker in a single image, and finally, applies Particle Filtering to integrate temporal information.

2 Related Work

Protecting the privacy of individuals has become increasingly important as cameras become more ubiquitous and have greater capabilities, particularly resolution and zoom. Examples of this interest includes The National Science Foundation (NSF) funding of TRUST [1], a research center for security and privacy, and privacy has been the subject of recent symposia such as Unblinking [2].

Changes in surveillance ubiquity and capabilities raise questions about the fair balance of police power (the inherent authority of a government to impose restrictions on private rights for the sake of public welfare, order, and security) to monitor public places versus the citizens' freedom to pass through public spaces without fear of government monitoring. According to Gavison, a loss of privacy occurs through visual surveillance by the extent we are known by others and subject to their attention [22]. He discusses our expectation that our actions are observable only by those we see around us, and thus we can judge how we should act. Nissenbaum describes how the high-resolution and zooming capabilities of cameras applied to visual surveillance also violate the contextual expectations of how people will be perceived in public [38]. This places the burden upon an individual to conduct himself or herself as if every move could be recorded and archived. Finally, it should be noted that it is not just surveillance that threatens privacy, but also the ability to be identified [49].

Researchers such as Hampapur et al. have analyzed the system architecture requirements of surveillance systems and built such a system [25]. Chen et al. built a system for people detection, tracking, and recognition [11] using gait analysis, face detection, and face recognition. As visual privacy is a significant concern of such systems, a number of researchers have explored how to integrate privacy systems into these surveillance systems [10, 12, 18, 48, 56]. Others such as Chinomi et al. have evaluated different methods for obscuring people in video data [13]. Google has started experimenting with automated face blurring in Google Street View [23].

The ability to find the faces or full bodies of people is necessary for automated visual privacy. Applicable methods include face detection [8, 9, 50, 51], face tracking [15, 42], people detection [52], and people tracking [39, 53]. Unfortunately, these methods have difficulty detecting and tracking in real-time for domains with partial occlusions, arbitrary pose, changing backgrounds, and changing lighting conditions [30, 55]. Alternatively, Background Subtraction methods, such as Gaussian Mixture Models [31], can be applied to obscure foreground objects. These methods are generally not designed to disambiguate between different moving objects so that we could obscure only the people of interest and leaving other objects such as moving cars visible. However, work such as that of Senior et al. [47] uses object models as a post-processing step to disambiguate between objects and compensate for occlusions. Many Background Subtraction methods will eventually determine that a stationary person is part of the background, which will cause the stationary person to become unobscured. Also, these systems struggle with domains using robotic cameras, as the system will not have a background-model for the new region, which may contain people to be obscured. In contrast, because our system explicitly tracks markers, it is well adapted for scenes observed by robotic cameras.

Approaches to object detection employ statistical classification methods including AdaBoost [40, 51], Neural Networks [17], and Support Vector Machines (SVMs) [41]. Rather than using the person as the feature, we track a visual marker worn by the individual, and use a form of AdaBoost [20] to track the color of that feature. AdaBoost is a supervised learning approach that creates a strong statistical classifier from labeled data and a set of weak hypotheses, which poorly classify the labeled data. Rather than conventional AdaBoost that provides a binary label, we use Probabilistic AdaBoost [21, 32], which provides the probability of an input's label that we use in our Particle Filter.

When using AdaBoost for detecting objects, either pixel-based or region-based features can be used. Pixel-based approaches such as ours use a set of features for each pixel in the image, while region-based use features defined over a group of pixels. Typical region-based approaches explore applying Haar wavelet features to pixel regions [7, 51]. Avidan describes the use of a pixel-based method [6] where each pixel's initial feature vector contains the RGB values, as well as two histograms of oriented gradients similar to those used in Scale Invariant Feature Transform (SIFT) features [34]. These SIFT features are commonly used for problems such as the correspondence between images or in object detection. Rather than incorporating gradient information, our pixel-based approach uses multiple color spaces as our feature vector.

The research community has also investigated the use of skin color as a mechanism for face detection. One common approach is verifying if each color satisfies a priori constraints [33], another is performing machine learning [16] to model face color. Others use multivariate Gaussians [3, 54] and Gaussians Mixture Models [24] to represent the face colors. Most approaches use a color space other than RGB such as Hue, Saturation, Value (HSV) or YCrCB, but in contrast to our work, few use more than a single color space. It is also common to use pixel color as a pre-processing step to prune out image regions before using a more powerful intensity-based face detector [54]. As these systems evolve and are used in industry, it is important that these systems are trained over a wide variety of races and skin-tones so that the system does not work for some, and not for others.

Sharing our motivations of robust detection, the Augmented Reality community also simplifies object detection with visual markers for tracking and calibrating. Zhang et al. compared many of these methods [57]. Kohtake et al. applied visual markers to simplify object classification to ease the User Interaction problem of taking data stored in one digital device and moving it to another by pointing and selecting physical objects via an "infostick" [29].

Tracking can be used with object detection to enhance robustness. One common method of tracking, Particle Filtering [5, 44], is used to probabilistically estimate the state of a system, in our case, the location of a visual marker, via indirect observations, such as a set of video images. Particle Filtering provides a probabilistic framework for integrating information from the past into the current estimation. Particle Filtering is non-parametric, representing the distributions via a set of many samples, as opposed to parametric approaches that represent distributions with a small set of parameters. For instance, Kalman Filtering [27] represents distributions by a mean and a variance parameter. We choose Particle Filtering because our observation model is non-Gaussian, and thus methods like Kalman Filtering will perform poorly.

Perhaps closest to our approach, both Okuma et al. [39] and Lei et al. [32] also use a probabilistic AdaBoost formulation with Particle Filtering [32]. However, both assume a classifier per tracked-object (region-based), rather than classifier per-pixel. As our markers use pixel-based color, we do not need to classify at multiple scales, and we can explicitly model shape to help with robustness to partial obstructions. Okuma's group applies their approach of dynamic weighting between a Particle Filter and an AdaBoost Object Detector to tracking hockey players. Rather than weighting, our approach directly integrates AdaBoost into the Particle Filter's observation model. Lei et al. use a similar approach to ours, and perform face and car tracking. However, unlike Lei, our formulation can track multiple objects simultaneously.

A preliminary version of chapter appeared as a paper in IROS 2007 [46].

3 System Input

Our system relies on visual markers worn by individuals who wish to have their face obscured. Our input is the sequence of images from a video stream. Let i be the frame number in this sequence. Each image consists of a pixel array where each pixel has a red, green, and blue (RGB) component.

4 Assumptions

We use the location and form-factor of each visual marker as a proxy for a location and form-factor of a corresponding human head. Thus, we assume there is an offset between the marker's location and the estimated face's location. Similarly, we assume the face's size will be proportional to the size of the visual marker. Intuitively, this means that as the marker's size shrinks, the face will shrink proportionally.

We make the following additional assumptions:

- Whenever a person's face is visible, then the visual marker worn by that person is visible.
- In each frame, all visible markers have a minimum number of visible, adjacent pixels.

5 System Output

Our objective is to place solid ellipses to obscure the face of each individual wearing a marker, while minimizing the overlay area to allow observation of actions in the scene.

For each frame in the input stream, the system outputs a set of axis-aligned elliptical regions. These regions should completely cover all faces of people in the input image who are wearing markers. The ith output image has a set of elliptical regions E_i associated with it. Each element in E_i is defined by a center-point, denoted by an x and y position, and major and minor axis r_x and r_y:

$$E_i = \{(x, y, r_x, r_y)\} \tag{1}$$

The ith output video frame is the same as the ith input frame with the corresponding regions E_i obscured via solid ellipses.

Failing to detect a marker when one is present (false negative) is worse than placing an ellipse where there is no face (false positive).

6 Three Phases of System

Our solution consists of three phases: (A) offline learning of a statistical classifier for markers, (B) online marker detection, and (C) online marker tracking.

6.1 Phase A: Offline Training of the Marker Classifier

We train a classifier offline, which we then use in the two online phases. For classification, we use the statistical classifier, AdaBoost, which performs supervised learning on labeled data.

6.1.1 Input and Output

A human "supervisor" provides the AdaBoost algorithm with two sets of samples as input, one for pixels colors corresponding to the marker T_+ and one for pixels colors corresponding to the background T_-. Each element of the set has a red value r, a green value g, a blue value b, and the number of samples with that color m.

Thus, the set of colors corresponding to marker pixels is

$$T_+ = \{(r, g, b, m)\} \tag{2}$$

and the sample set of pixels that correspond to background colors

$$T_- = \{(r, g, b, m)\} \tag{3}$$

As we are using a color-based method, the representative frames must expose the system across all possible illuminations. This includes maximum illumination, minimal illumination, the object under a shadow, and any potential hue effects caused by lighting phenomena such as a sunset. We discuss the AdaBoost formulation in more detail in Section 7.1.

We use a Probabilistic AdaBoost formulation that produces a strong classifier $\eta : \{0, \ldots, 255\}^3 \mapsto [0, 1]$. This classifier provides our output, a prediction of the probability that the RGB color of any pixel corresponds to the marker color.

6.2 Phase B: Online Static Marker Detector

For static detection, each frame is processed independently. This phase can be used on its own to determine marker locations, or can be used as input to a dynamic method such as what we describe in Phase C.

6.2.1 Input and Output

The Marker Detector uses as input, the model generated from AdaBoost as well as a single frame from the video stream.

We can use the marker detector without tracking to infer the locations of faces. This would produce for the ith image, a set of regions E_i as defined in Section 5, to obscure each face. We represent the state of each marker in the ith image as a bounded rectangle. We denote the set of rectangular bounding regions for each marker in image i as R_i. Each rectangular region is represented by a centerpoint, denoted by an x and y position, and its size, denoted by a width Δx and a height Δy:

$$R_i = \{(x, y, \Delta x, \Delta y)\} \tag{4}$$

There is an explicit mapping between the size and location of the bounding regions R_i and the sizes and locations of elliptical overlays E_i. The rectangles in R_i are restricted by the assumptions described in Section 4, but have the flexibility to change its shape as the marker moves around the observed space. When used as a component of a marker tracker, the detector supplies the same set of rectangles for initializing the tracker, but also determines for each pixel the probability $P(I_i(u, v))$ that each pixel (u, v) corresponds to the visual marker in image I_i.

6.3 Phase C: Online Dynamic Marker Tracker

The dynamic marker tracker uses temporal information to improve the Online Detector. We do this by using information from the Static Detector along with a Particle Filter for our temporal model.

6.3.1 Input and Output

The dynamic marker tracker uses both the classifier determined in the training phase and output from the static image recognition phase. We process a single frame per iteration of our Particle Filter. Let the time between the previous frame and the ith frame be $t_i \in \mathbb{R}_+$, and the ith image be I_i. We discuss Particle Filtering in more depth in Section 9.1, but it requires three models as input: a prior distribution, a transition model, and an observation model. We use the Static Marker Detector to initialize a Particle Filter for each newly detected marker. We also use the probabilities $P(I_i(u, v))$, supplied by the Static Marker Detector, to determine the posterior distribution of a marker location for each Particle Filter, given all previously seen images.

The output for the ith frame is also the set of regions E_i as defined in Section 5.

7 Phase A: Offline Training of the Marker Classifier

To train the system, a human "supervisor" left-clicks on pixels in a sample video to add them to the set T_+, and similarly right-clicks to add pixels to set T_-.

In this phase, we use the two sets T_+ and T_- to generate a strong classifier η, which assigns the probability that any pixel's color corresponds to the marker, providing $P(I_i(u, v))$. Learning algorithms are designed to generalize from limited amounts of data. For instance, with the AdaBoost algorithm, we needed a thousand labeled training samples. Also, as our classification algorithm is linear in the number of dimensions of our dataset (9 in our formulation) and number of hyperplanes used as weak hypotheses in the model (20 in our experiments), we can evaluate this classifier in realtime.

7.1 Review of AdaBoost

AdaBoost uses a set of labeled data to learn a classifier. This classifier will predict a label for any new data. AdaBoost constructs a strong classifier from a set of weak hypotheses.

Let X be a feature space, $Y \in \{-1, 1\}$ be an observation space, and $\{h : X \to Y\}$ be a set of weak hypotheses. AdaBoost's objective is to determine a strong classifier $H : X \mapsto Y$ by learning a linear function of weak hypotheses that predicts Y given X. At each iteration from $t = (1 \ldots T)$, AdaBoost incrementally adds a new weak hypothesis h_t to the strong classifier H:

$$f(x) = \sum_{t=1}^{T} \alpha_t h_t(x) \tag{5}$$

and

$$H(x) = \text{sign}(f(x)) \tag{6}$$

Let $\eta(x) = P(Y = 1 | X = x)$, and define AdaBoost's loss function $\phi(x) = e^{-x}$. The objective of AdaBoost is to minimize the expected loss or

$$E(\phi(yH(x))) = \inf_{H} [\eta(x)\phi(H(x)) + (1 - \eta(x))\phi(-H(x))] \tag{7}$$

This is an approximation to the optimal Bayes Risk, minimizing $E[l(H(X), Y)]$ with loss function

$$l(\widehat{Y}, Y) = \begin{cases} 1 & \text{if } \widehat{Y} \neq Y \\ 0 & \text{otherwise} \end{cases} \tag{8}$$

To determine this function, we use a set of training data $\{(x_i, y_i) | x_i \in X, y_i \in Y\}$ sampled from the underlying distribution.

AdaBoost is an iterative algorithm where at each step, it integrates a new weak hypothesis into the current strong classifier, and can use any weak hypothesis with error less than 50%. However, we use the greedy heuristic where at each iteration, we select a weak hypothesis that minimizes the number of incorrectly labeled data points [51]. We use a standard AdaBoost classifier of this form in Phase B, trained on our labeled data.

7.1.1 Recasting AdaBoost to Estimate Probabilities

Typically, as described in [45], AdaBoost predicts the most likely label that an input will have. Friedman et al. describe how to modify the AdaBoost algorithm to produce a probability distribution, rather than a binary classification [21]. The modified strong classifier determines the probability that an input corresponds to a label of 1 (as opposed to -1) and is defined by

$$\eta(x) = P(Y = 1 | X = x) = \frac{e^{2f(x)}}{1 + e^{2f(x)}} \tag{9}$$

We use this probabilistic formulation to determine the probability that each pixel corresponds to a marker, as $\eta(x) = P(I_i(u, v))$, in Phase C.

7.2 Determining Marker Pixels

We begin by applying Gaussian blur with standard deviation σ_I to the image, which enhances robustness to noise by integrating information from nearby pixels. We use these blurred pixels for T_+ and T_-. We then project our 3D RGB color space into the 2D color spaces, HSV [19], and LAB [26] color-spaces. HSV performs well over varying lighting conditions because value changes over varied lighting intensities, while Hue and Saturation do not. LAB is designed to model how humans see color, being perceptually linear, and is particularly well suited for determining specularities. This projection of RGB from T_+ and T_- into the 9D RGBHSVLAB color space is the input to AdaBoost.

For weak hypotheses, we use axis-aligned hyperplanes (also referred to as decision stumps), each of which divides the space along one of the 9D into two sets. These hyperplanes also have a +/− direction, where all 9D tuples that are in the direction and above the hyperplane are labeled as visual marker pixels, and all other tuples are non-marker pixels. The hyperplane separating dimension d at a threshold j is described by:

$$h_{d,j}(X) = \begin{cases} 1 & \text{if } X[d] \geq j \\ -1 & \text{otherwise} \end{cases} \tag{10}$$

Our set of weak hypotheses also includes the complement of these hyperplanes $\overline{h_{d,j}}(X) = -h_{d,j}(X)$. By projecting the initial RGB space into the additional HSV and LAB spaces, we provide more classification flexibility as we have more weak classifiers. For the weak hypothesis, AdaBoost chooses the dimension and threshold at each round that minimizes the remaining error. The algorithm terminates after running for some constant number, n, iterations. There are many ways to set n, for instance, splitting the data into a learning set and a validation set. In this technique, learning is applied to the learning set, and the generalization accuracy is evaluated on the validation set. Thus, we can observe how our model performs not on the data it is exposed to, but at predicting other unobserved data.

Rather than using the learning set and validation set directly, we went through a calibration process where we recorded video, exposing the marker to all areas in the viewing range of the camera and over varied lighting conditions and marker orientations. We went through the process of collecting an initial set of 100 marker pixels and 100 background pixels, and varied n from 5 to 50. If there were still patches of the background or marker that were misclassified, we would add these mistakes to the model, and repeat the learning. For instance, if a portion of the background was misclassified as the marker, we would add some of those pixels to the background set, and repeat the learning. This iterative approach provided an intuitive way for the user to distinguish between the marker and the background.

8 Phase B: Online Static Marker Detector

This section describes our marker detection algorithm, using only the current frame. Once we have the strong classifier from AdaBoost, we apply the following steps: (1) Apply the same Gaussian blur to the RGB image as we did for training, (2) Classify each pixel in the image, (3) Cluster marker pixels, and (4) Select all clusters that satisfy the constraints.

8.1 Clustering of Pixels

To determine the pixels to marker correspondence, we apply the connected-component technique [43]. The connected component algorithm is applied to an image with two types of pixels, foreground and background pixels, or in our case, marker and non-marker. Connected component will recursively group adjacent foreground pixels into the same cluster. We assign a unique group ID to each cluster's pixels. Thus, a connected group of marker pixels would be determined to correspond to the same marker as they have the same group ID. This yields a set of marker pixels for each visual marker in the frame.

To remove false positives, we enforce additional constraints about each identified marker cluster. We verify there are at least ζ_1 pixels in the cluster, and that ratio of width (Δx) to height (Δy) falls within a specified range from ζ_2 to ζ_3:

$$\zeta_2 \leq \frac{\Delta x}{\Delta y} \leq \zeta_3 \tag{11}$$

Requiring at least ζ_1 pixels per cluster prunes out false positives from small areas of color in the background that do not correspond to the marker. We also found that in some backgrounds, there would be long vertical or horizontal strips similar to our marker color, which would be incorrectly labeled as a marker as it was the same color. However, our markers have a bounded ratio between width and height. Using this knowledge helps remove these false positives.

9 Phase C: Online Dynamic Marker Tracker

We use Particle Filtering to incorporate temporal information into our models, improving robustness to partial occlusions. Particle Filtering requires a probability distribution for the likelihood of the state given the current, indirect observations. We provide this Observation Model by extending the theory from our Static Marker Detector from Phase B, using the probability that each pixel corresponds to a marker that is provided by the Probabilistic AdaBoost formulation described in Section 7.1.1.

9.1 Review of SIR Particle Filtering

While there are many types of Particle Filters, we use the Sampling Importance Resampling (SIR) Filter as described in [5, 44]. It is a non-parametric method for performing state estimation of Dynamic Bayes Nets (DBNs) over discrete time. The state at the time of frame i is represented as a random variable Z_i with instantiation z_i and the evidence of the hidden state E_i with instantiation e_i. There are three distributions needed for SIR Particle Filtering: the prior probability distribution of the object's state $P(Z_0)$, the transition model $P(Z_i|Z_{i-1})$, and the observation model $P(E_i|Z_i)$. The prior describes the initial distribution of the object's state. The transition model describes the distribution of the object's state at the next iteration, given the current object state. Lastly, the observation model describes the distribution of observations resulting from a specific object's state. Particle Filtering uses a vector of samples of the state, or "particles," that are distributed proportionally to the likelihood of all previous observations $P(Z_i|E_{0:i})$. At each iteration, each particle is advanced according to the transition model, and then assigned a probability according to its likelihood using the observation model. After all particles have a new likelihood, they are resampled with replacement using the relative probabilities determined via the observation model. This results in a distribution of new particles which have integrated all previous observations and are distributed according to their likelihood. The more samples that are within a specific state, the more likely that state is the actual state of the indirectly observed object.

9.2 Marker Tracking

In this section, we define our transition models and our observation models for our Particle Filter. We also describe how to track multiple markers simultaneously.

9.2.1 Marker Model

The state of a marker is defined with respect to the image plane and is represented by a 6 tuple of a bounding box's center x and y positions, the height and width of the bounding box, orientation, and speed. As can be seen in Fig. 2 this yields:

$$z = (x, y, \Delta x, \Delta y, \theta, s) \tag{12}$$

We model the marker in image coordinates, rather than world coordinates to improve the speed of our algorithms.

9.2.2 Transition Model

The transition model describes the likelihood of the marker being in a new state, given its state at the previous iteration, or $P(Z_i|Z_{i-1} = z_{i-1})$. Our model adds Gaussian noise to the speed, orientation, bounding-box width, and bounding box

Fig. 2 Illustrates the state of a single bounding box (*left*) and the probability mask used for the Particle Filter's observation model (*right*)

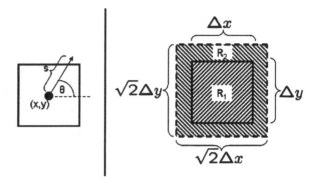

height and determines the new x and y position via Euler integration. Let $W \sim N(0, 1)$ be a sample from a Gaussian with mean zero and standard deviation of one. The mean μ and standard deviation σ for each portion of our model are set a priori. Formally:

$$
\begin{aligned}
x_i &= x_{i-1} + s_i \cdot \cos(\theta_i) \cdot t_i \\
y_i &= y_{i-1} + s_i \cdot \sin(\theta_i) \cdot t_i \\
\Delta x_i &= \Delta x_{i-1} + \sqrt{t_i} \cdot (\sigma_{\Delta x} \cdot W + \mu_{\Delta x}) \\
\Delta y_i &= \Delta y_{i-1} + \sqrt{t_i} \cdot (\sigma_{\Delta y} \cdot W + \mu_{\Delta y}) \\
s_i &= \max(0, \min(s_{\max}, s_{i-1} + \sqrt{t_i} \cdot \sigma_s \cdot W)) \\
\theta_i &= \theta_{i-1} + \sigma_\theta \cdot \sqrt{t_i} \cdot W
\end{aligned}
\tag{13}
$$

At each iteration, we enforce the width and height constraints for each particle described in Section 8.1. The sample from the Gaussian, after being scaled by μ and σ, must be rescaled according to $\sqrt{t_i}$ (as defined in Section 6.3.1) to compensate for changing frame rates.

9.2.3 Observation Model

The observation model describes the distribution of the marker's state given an image, but our formulation gives a probability per pixel, rather than per marker state. We use an objective function as a proxy for the observation model, which has a probability of 1 if the bounding box tightly bounds a rectangular region of pixels with high probability. Let bounding box R_1 be the marker's state and bounding box R_2 have the same midpoint as R_1 but have size $\sqrt{2}\Delta x \times \sqrt{2}\Delta y$. R_1 and R_2 are disjoint. The $\sqrt{2}$ scaling factor makes the areas of R_1 and R_2 be equal. Then:

$$R_1 = \left\{ (u, v) \,\middle|\, |x - u| \le \tfrac{\Delta x}{2}, |y - v| \le \tfrac{\Delta y}{2} \right\} \tag{14}$$

$$R_2 = \left\{ (u, v) \,\middle|\, |x - u| \le \tfrac{\Delta x}{\sqrt{2}}, |y - v| \le \tfrac{\Delta y}{\sqrt{2}}, (u, v) \notin R_1 \right\} \tag{15}$$

$$P_1(Z_i = z_i | I_i) = \frac{1}{\Delta x \Delta y} \left(\sum_{(u,v) \in R_1} P(I_i(u, v)) \right) \tag{16}$$

$$P_2(Z_i = z_i | I_i) = \frac{1}{2\Delta x \Delta y} \left(\frac{\sum_{(u,v) \in R_1} P(I_i(u, v)) +}{\sum_{(u,v) \in R_2} 1 - P(I_i(u, v))} \right) \tag{17}$$

Our final metric used as our observation model is:

$$P(Z | E_t = e_t) = (1 - P_1)P_1 + P_1 P_2 \tag{18}$$

This metric has the essential property that there is an optimal size for the bounding box, as opposed to many other metrics which quickly degenerate into determining the marker region to consist of all the pixels in the image or just a single pixel. For intuition, assume the projection of the visual marker produces a rectangular region. If a particle's bounding region is too large, its objective function will be lowered in region R_1, while if it is too small, then the objective function would be lowered in region R_2. This function yields a probability of 1 for a tight bounding box around a rectangular projection of the marker, yields the probability of 0 for a bounding box with no pixels inside that correspond to the marker, and gracefully interpolates in between (according to the confidence in R_1). We illustrate the two areas in Fig. 2.

9.2.4 Multiple-Object Filtering

Our formulation uses one Particle Filter per tracked marker. To use multiple filters, we must address the problems of: (1) markers appearing, (2) markers disappearing, and (3) multiple filters tracking the same marker. We make no assumptions about where markers can be obstructed in the scene.

For markers appearing, we use the output of the Marker Detection algorithm to determine potential regions of new markers. We use an intersection over minimum (IOM) metric, also known as the Dice Measure [14], defined for two regions R_1 and R_2 is:

$$\text{IOM}(R_1, R_2) = \frac{\text{Area}(R_1 \cap R_2)}{\min(\text{Area}(R_1), \text{Area}(R_2))} \tag{19}$$

If a Marker Detection algorithm has an IOM of more than a specified overlap γ_1 with any of Particle Filter's most likely location, then a Particle Filter is already tracking this marker. If no such filter exists, we create a new marker at this region's location by creating a new Particle Filter with the location and size of the detection region. We choose an orientation uniformly at random from 0 to 2π, and choose speed from 0 to the maximum speed $s_{\max}$ that is chosen a priori.

To address disappearing markers, we require that the probability of the state of at least one particle for a filter exceeds γ_2, otherwise the filter is no longer confident about the marker's location, and is deleted.

Multiple Particle Filters can become entangled and both track the same marker. If the IOM between two Particle Filters' exceeds the same threshold as appearing filters γ_3, we remove the filter that was created most recently. We remove the most recent to maximize the duration a Particle Filter tracks its marker.

10 Experiments

We ran two sets of experiments to evaluate performance. We experimented in our lab where we could control lighting conditions and we could explicitly setup pathological examples. We then monitor performance on video from a construction site as we vary model parameters. All tests involved video from a Panasonic KX-HCM280 robotic camera, transmitting an mJPEG stream of 640×480 images. We ran all experiments on a Pentium(R) CPU 3.4 GHz.

Currently, the system has not been optimized, and we could easily extend our formulation to incorporate parallelism. The rate that we can process frames is about 3 fps, which is approximately $3\times$ slower than the maximum incoming frame rate of 10 fps.

For both the Lab Scenario and Construction Site, we trained the AdaBoost algorithm on 2 one-minute video sequences specific to the environment, using the method described in Section 6.1, exposing the system to many potential backgrounds, location and orientations of the visual markers, and over all lighting conditions that the experimental data experiences. After training AdaBoost, we used the same sequences to calibrate our parameters. In our experiments we used:

$\sigma_{\Delta x}$	$= 25$ pixels	$\sigma_{\Delta y}$	$= 25$ pixels
σ_s	$= 100$ pixels	σ_θ	$= \frac{3}{2}\pi$ radians
$\mu_{\Delta x}$	$= 12.5$ pixels	$\mu_{\Delta y}$	$= 12.5$ pixels
$s_{\max}$	$= 300$ pixels	σ_I	$= 3.7$ pixels
ζ_1	$= 300$ pixels	ζ_2	$= \frac{1}{5}$
ζ_3	$= 5$	γ_1	$= 0.2$
γ_2	$= 0.4$	γ_3	$= 0.2$
# Particles $= 2000$		# Weak Hypotheses $= 20$	

We define an image to be a false negative if any part of any face is visible and to be a false positive if there is an obscuring region in E_i that does not touch any of the faces in image i. These metrics are independent of the number of people in the scene.

To determine the statistics for each experiment, we processed each video with our system and then went through each image, frame by frame, and hand labeled each for false positives and false negatives. We then went through the same sequence twice more to help ensure quality results. This required approximately 30 s per frame, or nearly 60 h of manual labeling for the experiments presented.

10.1 Lab Scenario Experiments

Within the lab, where we can control for lighting changes, we explore scenarios that challenge our system. Our marker is a yellow construction hat, and we assume the face is at the bottom-center of the bounding box and the same size as the hat. We evaluate how the system performs when (1) there are lighting conditions that the system never was trained on, and (2) two individuals (and their respective markers) cross. Lab experiments were run on 51 s of data acquired at 10 frames per second (fps). We summarize our results in Table 1.

Table 1 This table shows the performance of in-lab experiments. To evaluate the system, we place each frame into the category of correctly obscuring all faces without extraneous ellipses, being a false negative but not a false positive, being a false negative but not a false positive, and being both a false negative and false positive. We denote false negatives with FN and false positives with FP

Lab scenario experiments

Experiment	# Frames	Correct	FPs	FNs	FP+FNs
Lighting	255	96.5%	0.0%	3.5%	0.0%
Crossing	453	96.9%	0.0%	3.1%	0.0%

10.1.1 Lighting

In this setup, there is a single person, who walks past a flashlight aimed at the hat during two different lighting conditions. We experiment with all lights being

Fig. 3 Example of a False Negative with the Respectful Cameras System: A sample image frame input on *left image*, with output regions overlayed on *right image*. This sample illustrates where an intense light from a flashlight induced a specularity, causing the classifier to lose track of the hat. As a result, the right image has no solid white ellipses overlaid on the face as it should

on, and half of the lab lights on. In the brighter situation, the flashlight does not cause the system to lose track of the hat. However, in the less bright situation, the hat gets washed out with a specularity and we fail to detect the hat during this lighting problem. An explanation for why the specularity only was visible in the less bright situation is that our camera dynamically modifies the brightness of the image depending on the scene it observes. Thus, in the darker scene, the specularity would have been perceived to be brighter than in the brighter scene. We show one of the failing frames in Fig. 3. In general, the system performs well at interpolating between observed lighting conditions, but fails if the lighting is dramatically brighter or darker than the range of lighting conditions observed during training.

10.1.2 Crossing Markers

In this test, two people cross paths multiple times, at different speeds. Fig. 4 shows how the system merges the two hats into a single-classified hat when they are connected, while still covering both faces. We are able to accomplish this via the biases in our transition model, $\mu_{\Delta x}$ and $\mu_{\Delta y}$, which reduces false-negatives when multiple faces are in a scene. At the following frame in Fig. 5, the system successfully segments what it determined to be a single hat in the previous frame into two hats by creating a new Particle Filter.

10.2 Construction Site Experiments

The construction site data was collected from footage recorded in March, 2007 at the CITRIS construction site at the University of Berkeley, California, under UCB Human Subjects Protocol #2006-7-1.[1] Because we needed to respect the privacy

Fig. 4 Example of Crossing Markers and the Respectful Cameras System: A sample image frame input on *left image*, with output regions overlayed on *right image*. This sample illustrates tracking during a crossing, showing how the Particle Filter grows to accommodate both hats

---

[1] To contact UCB Human Subjects, refer to http://cphs.berkeley.edu/content/contact.htm.

Fig. 5 Example of the Respectful Cameras System: A sample image frame input on *left image*, with output regions overlayed on *right image*. This sample illustrates tracking after a crossing (one frame after Fig. 4), showing how the system successfully creates a second filter to best model the current scene

of the construction workers and restrictions in the protocol, we limited our data acquisition to a 1-week period. The video sequence presented contains a number of difficult challenges, particularly partial obstructions of the marker, significant changes in the background due to the tracking of the moving person with a robotic camera, and lighting differences including sharp changes from shadows. Also, the system observes areas of the scene it was not trained on, as the robotic camera moved 10 times to track the construction worker as he walked throughout the construction site. For the construction site, our marker is a green construction vest and we assume the face is located at the top-center of the vest, as we show in Fig. 1. We first evaluate the performance of the system as we use different color-spaces used for input to AdaBoost. We then evaluate the differences in performance between the Particle Filtered approach from Phase C and the Static Marker Detector from Phase B. All experiments were run on data acquired at 6 fps, simulating that the system can process at this speed, rather than the current capability of 3 fps. This diminished recording speed (the max is 10 fps) was caused by requiring us to view

Table 2 This table shows the performance of experiments at the CITRIS construction site. To evaluate the system, we place each frame into the category of correctly obscuring all faces without extraneous ellipses, being a false negative but not a false positive, being a false negative but not a false positive, and being both a false negative and false positive. We denote false negatives with FN and false positives with FP

Construction site experiments

Experiment	% Correct	FPs	FNs	FP+FNs
Only RGB	19.4%	68.6%	5.1%	6.9%
Only HSV	86.1%	11.5%	1.2%	1.2%
Only LAB	84.3%	10.9%	3.6%	1.2%
All 9 (RGB+HSV+LAB)	93.4%	5.4%	0.6%	0.6%
Static marker detector	82.8%	16.3%	0.0%	0.9%
Dynamic marker tracker	93.4%	5.4%	0.6%	0.6%

Fig. 6 Sample image frame input on *left image*, with output regions overlayed on *right image*. This sample illustrates how without Particle Filtering, even with the 9D color-space, partial occlusions segment the visual marker, resulting in multiple small ellipses

the video stream to move the camera to follow a person during recording, while having the system store a secondary video stream to disk for later experimentation. The data suggests that our system can perform with a 6.0% false positive rate, and 1.2% false negative rate for this real-world application. We summarize our results over a 76-second (331 frame) video sequence from a typical day at the construction site in Table 2.

10.2.1 Color Models

In this test, we investigate how our system performs by using different color spaces, specifically because we are only using simple axis-aligned hyperplanes as our weak hypotheses. We compare the algorithm's performance when just using RGB, just HSV, just LAB, and then the "All 9" dimensional color space of RGB+HSV+LAB. We determined that using all nine is superior in both false positive and false negative

Fig. 7 Sample image frame input on *left image*, with output regions overlayed on *right image*. This sample illustrates how Particle Filtering overcomes partial occlusions, when using the 9D color-space, yielding a single large ellipse

rates. This data suggests that color-spaces that explicitly decouple the brightness from the color (LAB and HSV) perform better than those that do not (RGB). This is probably exacerbated by our choice of weak hypotheses that decouple each dimension.

10.2.2 Particle Filtered Data

In this test, we evaluated performance between a non-Particle Filtered approach, where we just use each frame independently as described in Phase B, and using Particle Filtering as described in Phase C. We can see that the system significantly reduces the number of false-positives from 17.2 to 6.0%, while inducing slightly more false-negatives from 0.9 to 1.2%. There were two extra false-negatives induced by the Particle Filter, one from the shirt being cropped at the bottom of the scene, and one where the previous frame experienced extreme motion blur. We were very strict with our definitions of false-negatives as the face's visible region due to the partially cropped shirt is only 8 pixels wide.

Examples of input and output data can be found in Figs. 8, 9, 10, 11, and 12.

Fig. 8 Input frames from the in-lab crossing experiment

Fig. 9 Output frames showing the Particle Filter with the 9D colorspace performs well under dynamic obstructions

Fig. 10 Input frames from the CITRIS construction site

Fig. 11 Output frames showing using only the RGB colorspace is insufficient

Fig. 12 Output frames using the full 9-dimension colorspace, showing better performance

11 Machine-Learning Discussion

There are a number of other machine-learning techniques other than AdaBoost that can be explored. Other machine-learning based classification approaches include K-Nearest Neighbors, Neural Networks, and SVMs. AdaBoost was a good fit to our problem as our formulation has a fairly low-dimensional space (our problem only has nine dimensions). Also, as we wanted our system to run in real-time, we wanted a lightweight classification approach. We explicitly chose weak hypotheses that were very fast to evaluate, and axis-aligned hyperplanes require only a lookup for the particular dimension, and a comparison with each selected weak hypothesis. This approach is similar to Viola and Jones' [51] motivation of using simple features that are fast to evaluation. A significant advantage of using the greedy selection method for the next weak hypothesis is that the formulation can be thought of as performing a form of feature selection as well. If the H dimension in HSV has poor prediction performance, the weak hypotheses associated with H will not be chosen, making the system more robust. This is possible because our weak hypotheses treat each color dimension independently. Feature selection methods such as wrapping [28] have shown to improve classification performance. The motivation of feature reduction approaches follows the principle Occam's Razor. We are searching for the "simplest" way to predict the classification. This AdaBoost formulation implicitly uses feature selection in the step which chooses the next weak hypothesis according to the greedy heuristic in [51]. Exploration of a very high-dimensional space (like 10,000 dimensions) is computationally very difficult for our approach, as it would require that we explore all weak hypotheses, for each step of the weak hypothesis selection process.

Additionally, we project the RGB space into the HSV and LAB spaces. The original images are provided in RGB, giving us the features in that color-space with no needed computation. As discussed earlier, HSV is more robust to changing lighting conditions, and LAB is better at handling specularities and is designed to be perceptually linear. As shown in our experiments, using this redundant formulation as well as the implicit feature reduction of AdaBoost, effectively utilizes the additional color spaces. If all of the best predictive powers were just in the RGB color space, then the hyperplanes for HSV and LAB would never be selected. We found the chosen weak hypotheses spanned all of the color spaces. Projecting into the other two color spaces gives us $3\times$ the features to explore at each step, improving performance, as we show in our experiments. We also chose to use color space projections rather than other types of projections as we know they were designed to give robust properties such as attempts at being invariant to lighting conditions.

12 Conclusion

We have discussed the Respectful Cameras visual privacy system which tracks visual markers to robustly infer the location of individuals wishing to remain anonymous. We discuss a static-image classifier which determines a marker's location using pixel colors and an AdaBoost statistical classifier. We then extended this to marker tracking, using a Particle Filter which uses a Probabilistic AdaBoost algorithm and a marker model which incorporates velocity and interframe information.

It may be possible to build a Respectful Cameras method directly into the camera (akin to the V-chip) so that faces are encrypted at the hardware level and can be decrypted only if a search warrant is obtained.

While a 1.2% false negative rate for the CITRIS construction is encouraging, we would like it to be even lower to better address privacy applications. One encouraging idea is to run the Respectful Cameras system from multiple cameras, and cross reference the results. Assuming that the false negative rates of multiple cameras is independent, with three cameras, the false-negative rate would be 0.0002%.

For related links, press coverage, videos of our experiments, a discussion of practical and political issues, or to get updates about this project, please visit: http://goldberg.berkeley.edu/RespectfulCameras.

Acknowledgments Thanks to Ambuj Tewari for assisting in formulating the Probabilistic AdaBoost and Jen King for her help with relating this work to policy and law. Thanks to Anand Kulkarni, Ephrat Bitton, and Vincent Duindam for their edits and suggestions. Thanks to Panasonic· Inc. for donating the cameras for our experiments.

This work was partially funded by the a TRUST Grant under NSF CCF-0424422, with additional support from Cisco, HP, IBM, Intel, Microsoft, Symmantec, Telecom Italia, and United Technologies. This work was also partially supported by NSF Award 0535218, and by UC Berkeleys Center for Information Technology Research in the Interest of Society (CITRIS).

References

1. TRUST: Team for research in ubiquitous secure technology. URL http://www.truststc.org/
2. Unblinking: New perspectives on visual privacy in the 21st century. URL http://www.law.berkeley.edu/institutes/bclt/events/unblinking/unblink.html
3. Amine, A., Ghouzali, S., Rziza, M.: Face detection in still color images using skin color information. In: Proceedings of International Symposium on Communications, Control, and Signal Processing (ISCCSP) (2006)
4. Anderson, M.: Picture this: Aldermen caught on camera. Chicago Sun-Times (2006)
5. Arulampalam, S., Maskell, S., Gordon, N., Clapp, T.: A tutorial on particle filters for on-line non-linear/non-Gaussian Bayesian tracking. IEEE Transactions of Signal Processing **50**(2), 174–188 (2002)
6. Avidan, S.: Spatialboost: Adding spatial reasoning to AdaBoost. In: Proceedings of European Conference on Computer Vision, pp. 386–396 (2006)
7. Bahlmann, C., Zhu, Y., Ramesh, V., Pellkofer, M., Koehler, T.: A system for traffic sign detection, tracking, and recognition using color, shape, and motion information. In: IEEE Proceedings of Intelligent Vehicles Symposium, pp. 255–260 (2005)
8. Bourdev, L., Brandt, J.: Robust object detection via soft cascade. Proceedings of IEEE Conference Computer Vision and Pattern Recognition (CVPR) **2**, 236–243 (2005)
9. Bradski, G., Kaehler, A.: Learning OpenCV: Computer Vision with the OpenCV Library, 1st edn. O'Reilly (2008)
10. Brassil, J.: Using mobile communications to assert privacy from video surveillance. Proceedings of the IEEE International Parallel and Distributed Processing Symposium, p. 8 (2005)
11. Chen, D., Bharusha, A., Wactlar, H.: People identification across ambient camera networks. In: International Conference on Multimedia Ambient Intelligence, Media and Sensing (AIMS) (2007)
12. Chen, D., Yang, J., Yan, R., Chang, Y., Tools for Protecting the Privacy of Specific Individuals in Video, EURASIP Journal on Applied Signal Processing, (2007)

13. Chinomi, K., Nitta, N., Ito, Y., Babaguchi, N.: PriSurv: Privacy protected video surveillance system using adaptive visual abstraction. In: S. Satoh, F. Nack, M. Etoh (eds.) MMM, *Lecture Notes in Computer Science*, vol. 4903, pp. 144–154. Springer (2008)
14. Dice, L.R.: Measures of the amount of ecologic association between species. Ecology **26**(3), 297–302 (1945)
15. Dornaika, F., Ahlberg, J.: Fast and reliable active appearance model search for 3-D face tracking. IEEE Transactions of Systems, Man and Cybernetics, Part B **34**(4), 1838–1853 (2004)
16. Fang, J., Qiu, G.: A colour histogram based approach to human face detection. International Conference on Visual Information Engineering (VIE), pp. 133–136 (2003)
17. Feraud, R., Bernier, O.J., Viallet, J.E., Collobert, M.: A fast and accurate face detector based on neural networks. IEEE Transactions of Pattern Analysis and Machine Intelligence (PAMI) **23**(1), 42–53 (2001)
18. Fidaleo, D.A., Nguyen, H.A., Trivedi, M.: The networked sensor tapestry (NeST): A privacy enhanced software architecture for interactive analysis of data in video-sensor networks. In: Proceedings of ACM Workshop on Video Surveillance & Sensor Networks (VSSN), pp. 46–53. ACM Press, New York, USA (2004)
19. Foley, J.D., van Dam, A., Feiner, S.K., Hughes, J.F.: Computer Graphics Principles and Practice. Reading, Mass.: Addison-Wesley, New York (1990)
20. Freund, Y., Schapire, R.E.: A decision-theoretic generalization of on-line learning and an application to boosting. Computer and System Sciences **55**(1), 119–139 (1997)
21. Friedman, J., Hastie, T., Tibshirani, R.: Additive logistic regression: A statistical view of boosting. Annals of Statistics **28**(2), 337–407 (2000)
22. Gavison, R.: Privacy and the limits of the law. 89 Yale L.J., pp. 421–471 (1980)
23. Google Inc.: Privacy FAQ. URL http://www.google.com/privacy_faq.html#toc-street-view-images
24. Greenspan, H., Goldberger, J., Eshet, I.: Mixture model for face-color modeling and segmentation. Pattern Recognition Letters **22**(14), 1525–1536 (2001)
25. Hampapur, A., Borger, S., Brown, L., Carlson, C., Connell, J., Lu, M., Senior, A., Reddy, V., Shu, C., Tian, Y.: S3: The IBM smart surveillance system: From transactional systems to observational systems. Acoustics, Speech and Signal Processing, 2007. ICASSP 2007. IEEE International Conference on **4**, IV-1385-IV-1388 (2007)
26. Jain, A.K.: Fundamentals of digital image processing. Prentice Hall International (1989)
27. Kalman, R.: A new approach to linear filtering and prediction problems. Transactions of the American Society of Mechanical Engineers, Journal of Basic Engineering, pp. 35–46 (1960)
28. Kohavi, R., John, G.H.: Wrappers for feature subset selection. Artificial Intelligence **97**(1–2), 273–324 (1997)
29. Kohtake, N., Rekimoto, J., Anzai, Y.: InfoStick: An interaction device for inter-appliance computing. Lecture Notes in Computer Science **1707**, 246–258 (1999)
30. Kong, S.G., Heo, J., Abidi, B.R., Paik, J., Abidi, M.A.: Recent advances in visual and infrared face recognition: A review. Transactions of Computer Vision and Image Understanding (CVIU) **97**(1), 103–135 (2005)
31. Lee, D.S.: Effective gaussian mixture learning for video background subtraction. IEEE Transactions of Pattern Analysis and Machine Intelligence **27**, 827–832 (2005)
32. Lei, Y., Ding, X., Wang, S.: AdaBoost tracker embedded in adaptive Particle Filtering. In: Proceedings of International Conference on Pattern Recognition (ICPR), vol. 4, pp. 939–943 (2006)
33. Lin, H.J., Yen, S.H., Yeh, J.P., Lin, M.J.: Face detection based on skin color segmentation and SVM classification. Secure System Integration and Reliability Improvement (SSIRI), pp. 230–231 (2008)
34. Lowe, D.G.: Distinctive image features from scale-invariant keypoints. In: International Journal of Computer Vision, vol. 20, pp. 91–110 (2003)
35. McCahill, M., Norris, C.: From cameras to control rooms: The mediation of the image by CCTV operatives. CCTV and Social Control: The Politics and Practice of Video Surveillance-European and Global Perspectives (2004)

36. Moore, M.T.: Cities opening more video surveillance eyes. USA Today (2005)
37. New York Civil Liberties Union (NYCLU): Report documents rapid proliferation of video surveillance cameras, calls for public oversight to prevent abuses (2006). URL http://www.nyclu.org/whoswatching_pr_121306.html
38. Nissenbaum, H.F.: Privacy as contextual integrity. Washington Law Review **79**(1) (2004)
39. Okuna, K., Taleghani, A., de Freitas, N., Little, J., Lowe, D.: A boosted Particle Filter: Multitarget detection and tracking. In: Proceedings of Conference European Conference on Computer Vision (ECCV) (2004)
40. Opelt, A., Fussenegger, M., Pinz, A., Auer, P.: Weak hypotheses and boosting for generic object detection and recognition. In: Proceedings of Conference European Conference on Computer Vision (ECCV), pp. 71–84 (2004)
41. Osuna, E., Freund, R., Girosi, F.: Training support vector machines: An application to face detection. Proceedings of IEEE Conference Computer Vision and Pattern Recognition (CVPR), pp. 130–136 (1997)
42. Perez, P., Hue, C., Vermaak, J., Gangnet, M.: Color-based probabilistic tracking. In: Proceedings of European Conference on Computer Vision (ECCV), pp. 661–675 (2002)
43. Rosenfeld, A.: Connectivity in digital pictures. Journal of the ACM (JACM) **17**(1), 146–160 (1970)
44. Russell, S., Norvig, P.: Artificial Intelligence: A Modern Approach, 2nd edn. Pearson Education (1995)
45. Schapire, R.E., Singer, Y.: Improved boosting algorithms using confidence-rated predictions. Computational Learing Theory, pp. 80–91 (1998)
46. Schiff, J., Meingast, M., Mulligan, D.K., Sastry, S., Goldberg, K.: Respectful cameras: Detecting visual markers in real-time to address privacy concerns. In: International Conference on Intelligent Robots and Systems (IROS), pp. 971–978 (2007)
47. Senior, A., Hampapur, A., Tian, Y., Brown, L., Pankanti, S., Bolle, R.: Appearance models for occlusion handling. Journal of Image and Vision Computing (IVC) **24**(11), 1233–1243 (2006)
48. Senior, A., Pankanti, S., Hampapur, A., Brown, L., Tian, Y.L., Ekin, A., Connell, J., Shu, C.F., Lu, M.: Enabling video privacy through computer vision. IEEE Security & Privacy **3**(3), 50–57 (2005)
49. Shaw, R.: Recognition markets and visual privacy. In: UnBlinking: New Perspectives on Visual Privacy in the 21st Century (2006)
50. Turk, M., Pentland, A.: Face recognition using Eigenfaces. In: Proceedings of IEEE Conference Computer Vision and Pattern Recognition (CVPR), pp. 586–591 (1991)
51. Viola, P., Jones, M.: Rapid object detection using a boosted cascade of simple features. Proceedings of IEEE Conference on Computer Vision and Pattern Recognition (CVPR) **1**, 511 (2001)
52. Wu, B., Nevatia, R.: Detection of multiple, partially occluded humans in a single image by Bayesian combination of edgelet part detectors. IEEE International Conference on Computer Vision (ICCV) **1**, 90–97 (2005)
53. Wu, B., Nevatia, R.: Tracking of multiple, partially occluded humans based on static body part detection. IEEE Conference on Computer Vision and Pattern Recognition (CVPR) **1**, 951–958 (2006)
54. Wu, Y.W., Ai, X.Y.: Face detection in color images using AdaBoost algorithm based on skin color information. In: International Workshop on Knowledge Discovery and Data Mining (WKDD), pp. 339–342 (2008)
55. Yang, M., Kriegman, D., Ahuja, N.: Detecting faces in images: A survey. IEEE Transactions of Pattern Analysis and Machine Intelligence (PAMI) **24**(1), 34–58 (2002)
56. Zhang, W., Ching, S., Cheung, S., Chen, M.: Hiding privacy information in video surveillance system. Proceedings of IEEE International Conference on Image Processing (ICIP) **3**, II-868-71 (2005)
57. Zhang, X., Fronz, S., Navab, N.: Visual marker detection and decoding in AR systems: A comparative study. In: International Symposium on Mixed and Augmented Reality, pp. 97–106 (2002)

Technical Challenges in Location-Aware Video Surveillance Privacy

Jack Brassil

Abstract Though designing, deploying, and operating a video surveillance system in a public place is a relatively simple engineering task, equipping operational systems with privacy enhancing technology presents extraordinarily difficult technical challenges. We explore using mobile communications and location tracking to enable individuals to assert a preference for privacy from video surveillance. Rather than prohibit or defeat surveillance, our system – *Cloak* – seeks to discourage surveillers from distributing video without the authorization of the surveilled. We review the system architecture and operation, and demonstrate how privacy can be enhanced while requiring no change to existing surveillance technology. We use analysis and simulation to explore the solution's feasibility, and show that an individual's video privacy can be protected even in the presence of the many sources of error (e.g., dense crowds, unsynchronized clocks, unreliable communications, location error, location signal loss) we anticipate in a deployed system. Finally, we discuss the key technical, social, and legal barriers to *Cloak's* large-scale deployment, and argue that the pervasive use of camera phones requires the focus of efforts on surveillance privacy technology to shift to limiting dissemination rather than limiting video capture.

1 Introduction

We have become accustomed to the alarm bells sounding with the release of each new report specifying the growth in the number of fixed video surveillance cameras and associated closed circuit television systems operating in public spaces [1, 2]. Many of the public surveillance systems are operated by municipal agencies and are sanctioned to enhance routine operations including automobile and pedestrian traffic monitoring, or permit relatively inexpensive remote policing in an effort to deter

J. Brassil (✉)
HP Laboratories, Princeton, NJ 08540, USA
e-mail: jtb@hpl.hp.com

A. Senior (ed.), *Protecting Privacy in Video Surveillance*,
DOI 10.1007/978-1-84882-301-3_6, © Springer-Verlag London Limited 2009

crime. Operators of such systems frequently adhere to an acceptable use policy – often published – for their CCTV system, addressing matters such as the proper storage and dissemination of captured video content.

A large number of other video surveillance systems are privately owned and operated, though in many cases these systems capture images of people and objects in public spaces (e.g., building mounted perimeter security systems, sidewalk Automatic Teller Machines). The intended purpose of these systems is typically the protection of private property, and restrictions on the use of video captured by such systems tend to be at the discretion of the system's owner. Canada, however, has recently introduced new guidelines to assist private organizations in maintaining surveillance privacy [3].

Concern about the threat to privacy associated with dedicated surveillance systems seems warranted. Cases of misuse or unauthorized video dissemination are reported with regularity. Many systems are far from secure, often relying on low-cost analog video technology and electronic transmission that is easily tapped. Worries about "alternative use" of recorded content remain unabated, and public discourse on privacy issues seems slow to move forward [4].

But the threat to privacy of these conventional fixed position camera systems pales in comparison to the threat posed by the proliferation of camera phones; approximately 370 million camera phones were sold in 2005 [5]. Such phones are not only pervasive in both public and private spaces, but also the combination of their mobility and operator (i.e., owner) control permits them uninhibited access to locations and targets unavailable to conventional surveillance cameras. Though people are often the targets of surveillance, we are equally concerned about photographing objects; an image of a sensitive document bearing confidential information may require greater protection than an image of its owner. Though in this chapter we will routinely refer to a person seeking privacy while moving through a public space, the technology we discuss applies to arbitrary mobile objects (e.g., automobile license tags, credit card transactions).

Though the primary purpose of a camera phone is not to serve as a privately owned and operated surveillance device, it is quite capable of that role. The sophistication of both cameras and video signal processing has grown enormously as computing power has increased exponentially over time. And disseminating content has never been easier or more accessible; internet content hosting sites such as *Flickr* and *YouTube* have grown enormously popular.

To address these concerns, this chapter presents technology that permits a person (or object) to unambiguously assert a preference for video privacy [6]. A key insight which forms the basis of this solution is that it is crucial to distinguish between two activities – being surveilled, and subsequently having the captured video or images distributed. That is, we make the following distinction; while being surveilled may present a potential *threat* of privacy loss, the widescale public disclosure [7] or dissemination of tangible evidence of one's presence at a particular place and time is an *actual* loss of privacy.

We take the presence of ubiquitous "dumb" video surveillance systems to be immutable. We believe that in many cases those concerned for personal privacy would be satisfied with the assurance that their image is simply not distributed without their permission. Our technology does *not* seek to prevent image acquisition, nor present any technical barriers to captured image distribution. Instead the system seeks to permit captured images and video segments to be reviewed and, if necessary, "sanitized" prior to public release, if this is desired by any person or object in the video itself. In effect, we seek to extend to a very large scale the common courtesy of asking a party for permission to take photographs. We believe that in many – but not all – cases this approach will jointly satisfy the needs of both the surveillers and the surveilled.

The remainder of this chapter is organized as follows. Section 2 describes the operation of our proposed "privacy-enhanced surveillance" system, and establishes the technical feasibility of the system for the case of stationary surveillance cameras. Section 3 introduces some basic detection schemes to identify privacy seekers in the presence of crowds in surveillance footage, and presents simulation results that measure how reliably privacy seekers can be identified given the many potential sources of error (e.g., location uncertainty, clock error) that will arise in an actual deployment. We also discuss how our system can be extended to provide privacy from mobile camera phone surveillance. Section 4 examines some closely related technologies to support surveillance privacy, and the next section looks at the ever widening gap between technology and law. In the final section we close with a summary of our investigation.

2 System Architecture and Operation

Our system, called *Cloak*, places the burden of sanitization on video owners seeking public dissemination of content they own. It also places the burden of *asserting* the preference for privacy on the individual interested in retaining privacy. We believe that this division of labor is appropriate, based on the following assumptions:

- While many of those traversing public spaces might choose to cloak on an occasional basis, relatively few will choose to cloak on a frequent or continuous basis. Hence we propose a system where those seeking privacy must "opt-in".
- The vast majority of captured surveillance video has little obvious value and will not be disseminated. Hence, our system is designed to require no change to existing infrastructure, nor require any action unless content is to be disseminated.
- A video segment selected for dissemination that contains an image of a person seeking privacy and requiring sanitization will be an uncommon event; most individuals captured in a video will not be seeking privacy protection.
- Even when sanitization is necessary, it will often not interfere with the specific content valued by the content owner. A privacy seeker in an image simply might not be central to the reason an owner seeks dissemination. In this case both the privacy objective of the surveilled and the dissemination objective of the surveiller can be jointly met.

Beginning with this set of assumptions certainly seems non-intuitive. For instance, why design a system for relatively light use? First, we suspect that while many people are interested in obtaining increased privacy, few will be willing to bear any associated cost or inconvenience, no matter how minimal, for an unfamiliar service that is difficult to value. As we will see, Cloak does not depend on any of these assumptions, but certain aspects of system design would likely change if alternative assumptions were made.

Our proposed privacy-enhanced surveillance system works as follows. A person entering a public space potentially subject to surveillance elects to be in a Privacy Assertion (PA) state by carrying and activating a Privacy-Enabling Device (PED). A PED is a mobile navigation and communications device containing

- a clock,
- a unique identifier,
- one or more location tracking devices, such as a Global Positioning System (GPS) receiver,
- a wireless, mobile data communication link, and
- a non-volatile data storage device.

The bandwidth required for the communication link (e.g., < 1 kbs) is a small fraction of that offered by current wireless, broadband, wide-area data services (e.g., EV-DO). A PED should be equipped with a small amount of storage (e.g., < 32 MB flash memory) to preserve location information during wireless link dropout periods. Tight synchronization between the PED clock and surveillance video recording device clocks is not required. A PED should be inexpensive, as much of this functionality is present in most mobile phones in use today. While certain existing cellular telephone-based location services are not sufficiently precise for this application (e.g., 50 m accuracy in Enhanced 911 Phase II handset-based solutions), they can serve as useful redundant location systems when a primary GPS system loses signal acquisition.

Indeed, dedicated object location tracking devices and associated web-based infrastructure are already in use. One example is the Zoombak A-GPS Locator [8], which provides "continuous" location updates to a central location tracking site at a specified interval between 5 min and 1 h. Integrating both cellular and GPS location service permits the device to continue to acquire location information in environments where signal information is unavailable to one or the other location-tracking technologies.

From a user's perspective entering a PA state is as easy as toggling a "privacy switch" on one's PED. A PED in PA state periodically captures and timestamps its location coordinates (e.g., 1 location per second) and either transmits them immediately or stores them locally (for later transmission). A PED requires no manual intervention when active and communicating in real-time. Note, however, that real-time transmission might not be possible if the communications link connectivity is intermittent or the channel is unreliable. Non-real-time operation might require the PED operator to initiate uploading of locally stored location information when reliable communications become available. Of course, timely delivery reduces the risk that surveillance video or images are disseminated prior to upload.

A location *clearinghouse* receives communications from each active PED. The clearinghouse indexes and stores received information by location. Note that maintaining the complete uncompressed trajectory of a single PED consumes < 500 KB of memory per PA hour; cleverly compressed trajectories would consume considerably less. Though it might seem that recording paths would be storage-intensive, a typical user only requires roughly the same amount of storage as would be consumed by taking a single digital photo each day.

Suppose a surveiller (i.e., video content owner) wishes to disseminate a captured video. The surveiller queries the clearinghouse to determine if *any* PED was active in the field-of-view of its camera during the time interval the video was captured. For now let us limit our attention to fixed surveillance cameras rather than mobile camera phones; we will return to a discussion of how the system can be extended to mobile cameras later. For stationary-mount cameras, finding active PEDs in a camera's field-of-view requires that the surveiller know's the camera's location, and also be able to calculate how each location in the camera's 3D field-of-view corresponds to its position in the acquired 2D image; calculating such projections can be a one-time event. We will discuss the effect of subsequent camera misalignment and other sources of error later in this chapter.

A surveiller queries the clearinghouse via a communication protocol. For example, a sequence of queries can be used to determine if *any* PED traversed the camera's field of view during the time interval of the video segment. An initial query may use only coarse-grain location information (e.g., "Were any PEDs within distance d of location (x, y, z) during time interval $[t_1, t_2]$?"). We will later argue that even under a scenario where the density of PEDs traversing surveilled spaces is high, the probability that a randomly chosen video segment requires sanitization prior to dissemination (i.e., a *hit*) is low.

In the event of a hit both the video segment from the surveiller and the associated PED paths or trajectories from the clearinghouse are forwarded to a video *sanitizer*. The sanitizer strives to modify the video segment to respect the privacy asserted by the photographed PED users. We ideally envision this video processing to be entirely automated, though the required level of sanitization and the sophistication of that process depends on the specifics of the case, and can vary from trivial to implement to extremely complex. We will discuss sanitization technologies again in Section 4. If the sanitizer can modify the video clip to jointly meet the privacy requirements of the photographed PED carrier and the video owner, the resulting clip is returned to the owner for dissemination. Figure 1 presents a sample of how a single image might appear after sanitation.

Before we begin a more detailed look at the range of technical, social and legal issues associated with deploying Cloak, let us take a moment to establish what Cloak is *not*. Cloak does not seek to prevent or deter anyone from taking photographs or creating videos in public spaces. In particular, the system does not interfere with surveillance systems engaging in authorized remote policing. Cloak does no

Fig. 1 The privacy objective
of the surveilled and the
image dissemination
objective of the surveillers
can often be jointly satisfied.
In this image the identity of
the man in the foreground is
protected, though the image's
commercial value might
center on the second
conversing couple
(*background, right*)

"smart" video processing at video creation time; all video information is captured. Cloak places no burden on those not seeking surveillance privacy. Cloak requires no change to existing cameras or surveillance systems, save a requirement to time-stamp videos to facilitate off-line processing. Finally, Cloak does not alter the video ownership rights of a surveiller.

2.1 Discussion

Is building Cloak even technically feasible? To answer this question, let us begin with a very simple example. Suppose we have a single fixed camera primarily trained on a public space. We are given a sufficiently long duration video clip (e.g., 60 s) which shows two people traversing the space, and for simplicity let us say the two arrive and depart the video at different times. Next suppose that one is a PED carrier, and the other is the party of interest to the surveiller (i.e., the reason for dissemination), and we are given the location information reported by the PED.

Even assuming the many potential sources of error, including poor clock synchronization, considerable error in location reported by the PED, camera location error and subsequent misalignment, etc. the likelihood of being unable to determine which of two individuals is the privacy-seeker in the video is slight. It is often the case that a crude estimate of the arrival and departure times to and from the scene are enough to distinguish between two independent travelers moving through a scene. Upon identifying the privacy seeker, manually removing that party via video editing would often not interfere with the video owner's desire to preserve the presence of the other person. Indeed, examples of such editing are often presented on broadcast television, where surveillance videos of criminal activity are post-processed to remove the identities of other present parties (e.g., to protect potential witnesses).

While the above construction assures us that the *Cloak* system can be successfully implemented for very simple use scenarios, the next section focuses on far more complex and interesting scenarios. Some of the questions we seek to answer with our investigation are:

- Can we overcome the many potential sources of location tracking error to correctly identify a PED carrier?
- Can we pinpoint a PED carrier within a large, dense crowd?
- How much time must a PED carrier be present in a video to be reliably identified?

Before turning to these technically challenging questions, let us first take a closer look at several of the principal objections that are commonly raised by those skeptical of deploying the Cloak system.

- *Voluntary Compliance* Cloak's most dubious property is that the system relies on voluntary compliance by video owners to scrub their content prior to dissemination. Technology alone does not appear to be capable of protecting privacy; only societal pressure or law can enforce compliance with the unambiguous desire of the privacy seeker. However, technology *can* be used to assert one's preference for video privacy, and to provide proof of that assertion should one's preference be ignored. A person whose privacy is asserted but ignored and violated can use *Cloak* to demonstrate this fact. Clearly, ignoring a person's privacy preference, particularly one going to the effort and expense of enabling technology to make the assertion, will earn little public good will. Public scorn can be an effective deterrent to violations by institutions owning content (e.g., municipalities) as well as broadcasters (e.g., television, newspaper, web hosting sites). Indeed, it is possible to imagine a sanitized video bearing a visible logo indicating its "privacy protected" state; such an indication could conceivably *earn* good will for the video owner.
- *Trusted Third* Parties Privacy seekers must ultimately place trust in both the location clearinghouse and the sanitizer, even if some basic level of anonymity is afforded using one-time identifiers (e.g., the location clearinghouse need not know the identity of an individual whose location is being recorded). Surveillers receive no information on the surveilled except for their preference for privacy as ultimately indicated by their scrubbed image. Sanitation, of course, brings together images and trajectories, but no additional explicit identifying information is necessarily required.
- *Location Privacy* Individuals have a visceral objection to having their location tracked. The paradox inherent in *Cloak* is that individuals perceive that they must risk sacrificing location privacy to achieve video surveillance privacy.

  But do they? To begin with, if you are carrying a cell phone, how much location privacy do you have? By entering a public space a person implicitly accepts that he or she might lose anonymity at any moment and their presence will become known. But a PED need only be enabled when the possibility of surveillance is real, not at all times. Without it, if one is indeed surveilled, then not only is location revealed, but it is now potentially revealed to a much wider audience in a potent, tangible form (i.e., video).
- *Misuse by Authorities* In principle a law enforcement agency could mine the location clearinghouse to track a subscriber's movements. But the same is true

of other location-sensing systems (e.g., Enhanced 911, Loopt) or automobile toll or credit card transactions, though perhaps to a lesser extent.

Cloak can be enhanced in a variety of ways, and some of these approaches can mitigate these concerns. For the sake of brevity, we will omit an exhaustive discussion of the many possible system embellishments. To consider one example, however, a PED device can potentially specify a preferred Quality of Privacy (QoP). Examples of parameters that can determine service quality include retention time of location data, type of entity (e.g., person, automobile) to cloak, and the degree of desired video "scrubbing." Interestingly, the communication loop can be closed; QoP requirements can conceivably require the surveiller to obtain the explicit consent of the surveilled prior to video dissemination. Such an interaction might require the surveilled to examine and authorize scrubbed content prior to dissemination, or even involve a negotiation of distribution rights.

3 Analysis and Simulation Results

Suppose there are P people (or objects) traversing the field-of-view of a single camera in some time interval $[t_0, t_0 + D]$, and exactly one of those people carries an active PED. The PED reports its location each second, though both its estimate of time and location may be inaccurate; neither are synchronized with the surveillance system. Suppose a sanitizer is independently given the PED carrier's recorded, timestamped path and the recorded, timestamped surveillance video. Given a large value of P, how should the sanitizer correctly pinpoint the PED carrier in the video, and how likely is the sanitizer able to do so?

Let $s(t)$ be the *actual* location of the PED at time t with $s = \{x, y, z\}$. Let $\hat{s}(t)$ be the PED's own estimate of its location. We will assume that the error in a PED's location estimate is bounded at each time instant, i.e.

$$|s(t) - \hat{s}(t)| < \epsilon. \tag{1}$$

For an inexpensive Garmin GPS 18 USB receiver [9], the advertised bound for location error is $\epsilon < 3$ m (Wide Area Augmentation Service enabled) and $\epsilon < 15$ m (Standard Positioning Service), for 95% of measurements. For simplicity let us first consider a *time synchronous* system; we assume that the PED's clock and surveillance system clocks are perfectly time-synchronized. We will revisit this assumption later.

We will also assume that image analysis enables us to discern the distinct people (or objects) in a scene, though in general this is not required for sanitization. Let $v_i(t) : i \in P$ be the chosen "center" of the ith discernible object at time t in the captured video, where $v = \{l, m\}$ is a point in the 2D image coordinate system. The sanitizer determines the path (i.e., trajectories) of each discernible object in the video segment, i.e., $v_i(t) : i \in P, t \in [t_0, t_0 + D]$. The sanitizer also receives the *estimated* trajectory of the PED $\hat{s}(t)$ as recorded while traversing the 3D space in the camera's field of view. Using knowledge of the camera location and perspective, the sanitizer projects that trajectory onto the 2D image coordinate space, i.e.,

$$\tilde{s}(t) = T[\hat{s}(t)].\tag{2}$$

Hence, $\tilde{s}(t)$ represents an approximate trajectory for one of the P objects in the video. Our objective is to determine to which object the approximate trajectory most closely corresponds.

To find that corresponding object (i.e., PED carrier) we compare the given approximate trajectory to each of the P object trajectories discerned from image analysis. To do so we choose to use one of the following two heuristics; either minimize the Mean Square Error (MSE) or (absolute) Linear Error (LE). That is, we find the object i such that

MSE

$$\int_{t}^{t+D} |v_i(t) - \tilde{s}(t)|^2 \mathrm{d}t < \int_{t}^{t+D} |v_j(t) - \tilde{s}(t)|^2 \mathrm{d}t\tag{3}$$

or

LE

$$\int_{t}^{t+D} |v_i(t) - \tilde{s}(t)|\mathrm{d}t < \int_{t}^{t+D} |v_j(t) - \tilde{s}(t)|\mathrm{d}t\tag{4}$$

for $0 < i \le P,\ 0 < j \le P, i \ne j$.

We next turn to simulation to determine the probability of correctly identifying a single active PED among P discernible objects given a noisy representation of its path. Since we have assumed that a PED updates its location periodically, we model its trajectory in discrete rather than continuous time. Further, since our location-sensing device is assumed imperfect, we can approximate location (and the projection of location to the image coordinate system as defined by the transformation T in Equation 2) as discrete-valued variables.

Selecting the most appropriate mobility model for simulating the movement of the P objects in a video greatly depends on where a camera is trained, and the type of objects in that scene. For example, vehicles photographed passing through a highway toll booth have relatively predictable motion, while pedestrians in a shopping mall might appear to move randomly. Further, correlations between the movement of different objects in a scene can vary greatly. Consider a camera trained on a busy public escalator where several people in close proximity have roughly the same trajectory – which person is carrying an active PED, the one just stepping off the escalator or the one immediately behind?

Recall that the P objects traverse the 3D volume in the camera's field-of-view, and each object's actual trajectory has an associated 2D trajectory in the image coordinate system. Since the transformation from a 3D trajectory to a 2D trajectory is deterministic, we can model object mobility in either coordinate system with no loss of generality; we choose to model mobility in the simpler 2D image coordinate system. Note, of course, that a trajectory in image space does not in general have a unique corresponding trajectory through the volume. A preferred approach would be to work with 3D mobility models (or better, to measure actual paths empirically) and transform those into the 2D image space.

Object motion can now be represented by a walk on an infinite 2D grid. To make matters concrete let us say that grid points correspond to a separation of 1 m in the camera field-of-view, and the camera field has approximately a 10,000 m^2 window (corresponding to grid points [0–99, 0–99]). Such a large, open space might correspond to the size of an outdoor public park or square.

Now let us introduce a simple mobility model. Suppose that at time $t_0 = 0$ each of the P objects enters the grid at location $v_i(0) \equiv v(0) = (0, 0)$; this corresponds roughly to the entire group entering the field-of-view simultaneously at the same location, as if entering through a single portal (i.e., hallway or door). Let each subsequent object step be independent from step-to-step, and independent of every other object step. Suppose that each object path follows a *biased random walk* [15, 16] with the following non-zero transition probabilities:

$$p[l + 2|l] = 0.25 \quad p[m + 2|m] = 0.25 \tag{5}$$

$$p[l + 1|l] = 0.25 \quad p[m + 1|m] = 0.25 \tag{6}$$

$$p[l|l] = 0.25 \quad p[m|m] = 0.25 \tag{7}$$

$$p[l - 1|l] = 0.25 \quad p[m - 1|m] = 0.25 \tag{8}$$

That is, in each step each object moves with equal probability either ahead or backward 1 m, or ahead 2 m, or does not move at all, in each dimension l (horizontal) and m (vertical).

Observed from directly above, an object traversing a surface under this model could appear at times to stop, to reverse course, or to vary speeds. The group of P objects would appear to be heading very roughly to the same destination, as if the group was entering a square room at one corner and moving toward the diagonally opposite corner. Though in principle an object could leave and return to the camera's field-of view (possibly multiple times), we will observe objects for a sufficiently long period that taking this event into consideration is unnecessary. Suppose we consider a time interval of duration $D = 200$ s (i.e., our observation interval is $t \in [0, 199]$); on average an object will drift 100 m both horizontally and vertically during that interval, so a typical object will appear to move across the camera's entire field-of-view.

Now let us explore the effect of a PED's error in estimating its location on our ability to correctly identify the PED carrier. We introduce two location error models, each intended to capture all potential sources of location error. Each model is applied independently to each coordinate $\{l, m\}$ in the 2D image coordinate system at each step in the object's path. For the l dimension we have

Biased Uniform error

$$p[|l - \tilde{l}| = d] = 1/W \quad d \in \left[a - \frac{W-1}{2}, a + \frac{W-1}{2} \right] \tag{9}$$

where W is an odd-valued integer greater than 1 m, and a is a non-negative integer, or

"Worst Case" error

$$p\left[|l - \tilde{l}| = -\frac{W-1}{2} \right] = 0.25$$

$$p\left[|l - \tilde{l}| = +\frac{W-1}{2} \right] = 0.25 \tag{10}$$

$$p\left[|l - \tilde{l}| = 0 \right] \qquad = 0.5$$

An identical model is separately written for the m coordinate. Our uniform error distribution has mean a (i.e., $E[|l - \tilde{l}|] = a$), permitting us to examine cases where a PED's observed location has a fixed offset error (typically of a few meters). We chose to consider the "Worst Case" error distribution because we anticipated that MSE detection would perform relatively poorly when the maximum location error is realized in half the location updates, on average. Unless noted, in each of our simulations we considered $P = 1000$ objects traversing the grid, and we present error rates averaged over 10, 000 iterations of 200 s walks.

Let us now determine how well we can correctly identify the single PED carrier as the location error distribution width W increases in the absence of bias. Figure 2 shows that under MSE detection the error distribution width would have to exceed 41 m before we guessed incorrectly in 10,000 scenes. Similarly, the figure shows no errors under LE detection with $W \leq 27$ m, though note that the LE detection error rate climbs much more rapidly than the MSE detection error rate under uniformly distributed location error. Nonetheless both of these results compare very favorably with worst case GPS location error (Equation 1). As we predicted the error rate for the MSE algorithm under the "Worst Case" error distribution climbs much more rapidly with increasing W than under the uniform error distribution.

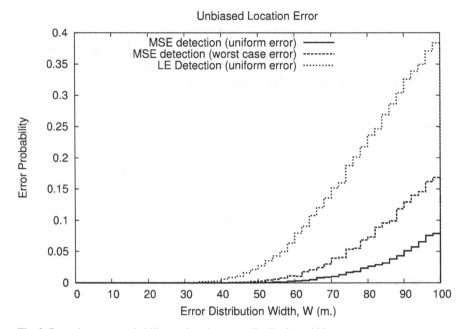

Fig. 2 Detection error probability vs. location error distribution width

Figure 3 presents a set of sample paths for a typical iteration of our simulation. Each black dashed line depicts one of the P object trajectories. For clarity we show only a randomly selected 100 of the 1000 object trajectories. The 200 + points indicated the erroneous sequence of locations reported by the PED carrier during the 200 s observation interval when moving under an unbiased, uniform error model with an error width of $W = 59$ m. Given those locations, the MSE detection scheme had an easy task of correctly identifying the path corresponding to the actual PED carrier (highlighted with □ symbols). The path highlighted with ■ symbols corresponds to the path among the 1000 that is furthest in distance from the reported trajectory. Remarkably, despite this noisy path report, the MSE algorithm is able to identify the PED carrier correctly in 99.75% of the 10 000 iterations.

Next let us consider how error rates are affected by a fixed offset in location reported by the PED carrier. For a uniform distribution with a mean of a meters, we seek the value of the largest distribution width W that results in a detection error rate exceeding 1%. Table 1 shows that error rates can climb sharply as this fixed offset climbs; a fixed offset greatly reduces the location error variability that can be tolerated. In other words, if a PED carrier is always mis-reporting its location by a few meters, it is increasingly likely that the detection algorithm will select another trajectory as associated with the PED, even if the location error variability is shrinking.

Next we consider the effect of the absence of synchronization between a PED's clock and the surveillance system clock(s). Figure 4 shows how the detection error

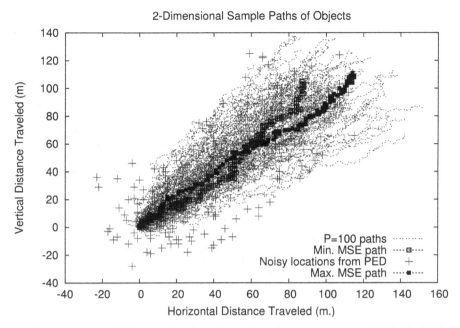

Fig. 3 Sample paths of 100 randomly select object trajectories among a group of 1000. The PED's actual trajectory (□) is selected correctly, despite the seeming randomness and wide range of the PED's reported positions (+). The trajectory of the most distant object (in the mean square sense) is also shown (■)

probability varies as we increase both the unbiased uniform distribution width W and the time difference between the surveillance system clock and the PED clock for a group of 100 objects traversing the grid.

Note how the LE detection scheme degrades relatively slowly as asynchrony grows from 0–4 s, while the MSE scheme error rate climbs catastrophically after about 2 s. For very low timing error ($\leq$ 2 s), detection performance is determined largely by the location error distribution width W. In a practical system, it appears it would be necessary to ensure that clocks remained roughly in synchrony. In either case, these observations lead us to speculate that it might be beneficial to develop a

Table 1 The mean and width of a biased uniform location error distribution that result in an error rate higher than 1% for each detection

	Distribution width (W)	
Mean (a)	LE	MSE
4	$W < 27$	$W < 41$
3	$27 \leq W \leq 35$	$41 \leq W \leq 57$
2	$37 \leq W \leq 41$	$61 \leq W \leq 67$
1	$43 \leq W < 45$	$69 \leq W < 73$
0	$45 \leq W$	$73 \leq W$

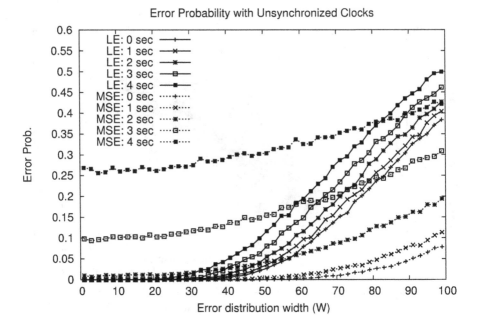

Fig. 4 Detection error rates increase with increasing timing error and location error

multi-pass detection scheme. In such a system, one would perform the first detection pass under the assumption of synchrony, then subsequent passes assuming growing asynchrony, searching for the absolute minimum error across all passes.

What if we increase the number of objects P to choose from in a scene? Figure 5 shows that under the random walk model the detection performance decreases relatively slowly as we increase the object density in the presence of unbiased uniform location error. This too is unsurprising, for if we observe independent walks for a sufficiently long period k we expect to be able to distinguish between many objects (i.e., $P \ll 2^k$).

Dropouts, or the loss of location signal acquisition, is a familiar nuisance to GPS automobile navigation system owners. But dropouts can quickly become a significant source of detection error when dropouts coincide with surveillance of a PED carrier. We model this phenomenon as an on–off process where the probability of staying in the "connected" state (i.e., location signal acquired) and "disconnected" state are Bernoulli processes with probabilities α and β, respectively. Hence the duty cycle, or fraction of time in the connected state, is $D = \frac{\alpha}{\alpha+\beta}$. Let us make the rather severe assumption that during periods of disconnection from the location service the PED continues to report its last known location. Figure 6 shows how the detection error probability can increase dramatically with decreasing duty cycle. In this example, the mean time spent in the connected state is 8 s, and the mean in the disconnected state is $8 \times (\frac{1-D}{D})$ s. There are, however, simple ways to make considerable improvements on this result. For example, one can imagine the PED

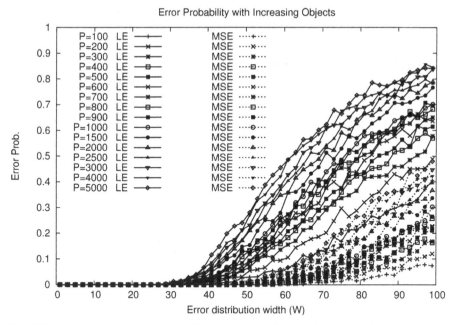

Fig. 5 Detection error rate increases relatively slowly with increased object density

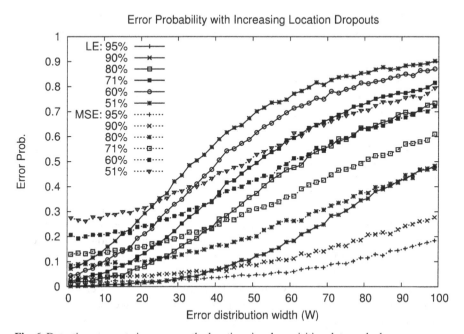

Fig. 6 Detection error rate increases as the location signal acquisition duty cycle decreases

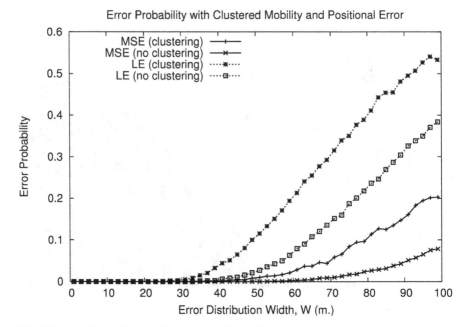

Fig. 7 The combined effect of clustered mobility and location error

delaying location reports until the location is re-acquired, and then sending a set of location updates estimating its previous positions (e.g., using linear interpolation between the last known location in the most recent connection state and the first location in the current connection state).

So far we have limited our attention to models of mobility in which each person's movement is independent of every other person's movement. But in many situations one's motion depends on the motion of others nearby; people traveling together move in tightly knit groups, and a chain of automobiles stops if one in front stops. Hence we developed a "clustering" mobility model in which each person's movement depends in part on the movement of the PED carrier. The PED carrier effectively serves as the "center" of a cluster of size P; those lagging behind the PED carrier increase their "speed" and/or change their direction to catch up, and those ahead slow down. Figure 7 depicts the effects of both clustering and uniform location error as the error distribution width W varies. As expected the detection error rate increases when compared to independent motion. Nonetheless, despite the lower variability of distance between objects detection performance remains high.

Let us turn to the technical challenges faced by the sanitizer. Let us assume a sanitizer is given a video, a sanitization request, and access to the location database. The task faced is to jointly satisfy the privacy objective of the surveilled while preserving the image dissemination objective of the surveiller. Achieving such an outcome can be relatively trivial, or entirely infeasible.

As an example of the former case, a sanitizer might quickly determine that a video simply does not include images of the privacy seeker (i.e., a false alarm), or that the video can be readily "cut" to remove such images. Basic video cuts are easily achieved with commonly available, open-source video processing tools. At the other extreme, the sanitizer might quickly determine that the privacy and dissemination objectives are at complete odds. This would ordinarily be the case for a video taken by a paparazzo of her targeted subject, if the subject was seeking privacy by carrying a PED.

Somewhere between these two extremes lies the challenge of video obfuscation. Here we typically wish the sanitizer to obscure only part of a video. Any number of obfuscation techniques (e.g., blackout, pixellation) are easily available today in widely used software tools. Figure 1 provides a simple demonstration of a pixel blurring operation.

How does a sanitizer know when privacy and dissemination objectives are truly achieved? One approach might be based on an interactive process of scrubbed video review by the privacy seeker and video owner. In general, the more information shared between the parties the higher the likelihood of success. In some cases, one imagines that the sanitizer could serve as a mediator between the parties.

To this point we have considered only fixed surveillance cameras, and we have not addressed the challenging special case of remotely controlled cameras that offer panning, tilting, and zoom functions. But these cameras only begin to address the significant challenges we face in striving to support mobile surveillance cameras in the Cloak system. In the case of fixed surveillance cameras, we expected each camera to know its position, and to know the location of objects in its fixed field-of-view. While the former requirement can be reasonably applied to mobile cameras – at least to the same extent that location knowledge is expected of PEDs – it is difficult to imagine how the latter requirement could be realized. So instead, let us suppose that *every* PED within a radius r of an operating mobile camera at each time t is potentially in the camera's current field-of-view. That is, we will identify every PED carrier that could possibly have been photographed by the mobile camera at each instant during the video clip's duration.

To initiate this process, each surveillance video taken from a mobile camera to be disseminated is accompanied by the camera trajectory, indicating the camera's estimate of its location at 1 s intervals during the filming. Let $\hat{\mathbf{c}}(t)$ be the camera's own estimate of its location in the filming time interval $[t, t + k]$. The sanitizer queries the location clearinghouse to determine if there exists a PED trajectory $\hat{\mathbf{s}}(t)$ satisfying

$$|\hat{\mathbf{s}}(t) - \hat{\mathbf{c}}(t)| < r \tag{11}$$

during the interval $[t, t + k]$.

In general this is a significant computational task. Suppose we define a region sufficiently large to enclose the mobile camera during the filming interval. If N PEDs are known to be present in that region for all or part of the interval, then a brute force algorithm to identify the subset of those PED carriers who came within distance r of the mobile camera is $O(Nk)$.

After completing such a task the location clearinghouse has now identified a set of PED carriers who *might* appear in the video. Of course, in many situations almost none of them will actually appear.

At this point, few courses of action remain open to a sanitizer to respect the privacy requested by the PED carriers. One approach is to initiate a negotiation with each PED carrier to privately review the video to confirm that she is indeed not a photographed party. In the event she is, a manual sanitization would be initiated with her assistance.

Of course, disclosure of the pre-sanitized video to a PED carrier who was not present in the video introduces a risk of subsequent disclosure (or even dissemination of the video itself) to a larger audience – exactly what the process is seeking to avoid. Here, however, we must ultimately rely on the benevolence of the community of PED carriers to respect each other's desire for privacy.

Before moving on let us take a moment to summarize what we have learned in this section. We have presented a collection of simulations to explore the feasibility of constructing *Cloak* using existing mobile communications, location technologies and video processing systems. We are keenly aware that each of these technologies is imperfect, and each can at times perform poorly in the challenging operational settings where we expect Cloak to be deployed.

Our first concern was maintaining a high PED detection rate given current technologies that imprecisely measure a carrier's location. But the results of Fig. 2 suggest that we can use far more imprecise location measurement than is currently widely available with inexpensive GPS receiver technology. We also showed in Fig. 6 that signal dropouts so common in GPS systems can be tolerated with modest reductions in detection rates, though applying simple location estimation techniques would increase performance during these dropout intervals.

Figure 3 highlights our considerable ability to correctly pick out a specific PED carrier even in a crowd of PED carriers moving along a roughly similar course, while Fig. 5 shows that the detection rates remain high even as the size of the crowd grows to a large size. In both cases, of course, we are relying on the target carrier to remain in the surveillance camera's field-of-view for an extended time period, and for the target carrier to move through the scene largely independently of other carriers. To take matters a bit further, Fig. 7 shows that a target PED carrier can also be readily detected when moving together in relatively tight clusters of other carriers.

An additional problem we anticipated that motivated our simulations is lowered detection rates caused by the lack of time synchronization between surveillance camera recording equipment and PED carriers. Figure 4 indicates that even a few seconds off synchronization can degrade performance considerably, so this problem must be solved in an actual system. One approach is to enhance existing surveillance recording systems by providing them with the same clock source used by PED carriers. An alternate approach might involve using a different but relatively accurate time source, such as the *Network Time Protocol*. Both of these approaches suffer from the need to supplement existing surveillance recorders with new, more accurate time sources. In both cases to maintain the highest detection rates it might also be desirable for a sanitizer to use a more sophisticated, multi-pass detection algorithm which presumes imperfect time synchronization between recorder and PED carrier.

It is important to note that we have made a large number of assumptions in developing our simulations, and we have yet to address a number of easy-to-anticipate real-world considerations. As a simple example consider the variety of problems that we have yet to confront with even well-engineered, fixed-mount camera installations: scenes are typically viewed obliquely rather than from above, camera mounts might tilt and sag over time, scene lighting changes over time, objects occasionally block scene elements, etc.

In summary, our simulations give us confidence that a number of potentially significant barriers to *Cloak's* feasibility appear to be surmountable. While this is considerably short of an assurance of a practical system, it does encourage us to take the next step in our investigation – creation of a small-scale experimental prototype for laboratory and field evaluation.

4 Related Technologies

The automated analysis and processing of surveillance video is a central area of study for the computer vision and pattern recognition research community. IBM researchers have developed the *Privacy Camera* [10], an intelligent camera, or more precisely, a camera connected to a computer that performs real-time video analysis. The camera edits out certain pre-determined video content such as a person in a scene. Though both *Cloak* and the *Privacy Camera* effectively sanitize video, it is worth noting the differences between them. Our system does not edit video in real-time, yet it is designed to sanitize any video produced by any camera. Our video editing is driven by object trajectories; the objects themselves can be of arbitrary type and are not known a priori. We do not rely on information about a scene or objects in a scene. Indeed, in our work we have sought to de-emphasize computationally intensive video processing, preferring to rely on positional information rather than information in the video itself. To our disappointment our research has uncovered relatively little work on mobility modeling for people or objects, and this appears to be a fertile area for future research [11, 12].

Intelligent mobile peer-to-peer systems are also an emerging technology that can either amplify or further threaten surveillance privacy. *Smart Camera Networks* such as *Facet* [13] create networks of cooperating mobile phone cameras. Though the intent of this system is to create composite images, they make use of location data of network participants, and may serve as a foundation to help Cloak address non-fixed surveillance systems. But these networks also bring the challenge of addressing the unanticipated problem that surveillance videos can be dynamically stitched together to form composite surveillance video. This raises some very intriguing questions about ownership of derived and/or synthesized surveillance video which is well outside the scope of our study.

Technology useful in video sanitization is also advancing quickly. In particular, emerging *in-painting* [14] techniques promise to permit sanitized videos to appear unsanitized. This is achieved by not only removing objects but also synthesizing perceptually plausible filler for the sanitized pixels.

Location-based services are also taking rapid hold, in part due to technological advances in GPS receivers and the application of wireless internet and cellular telephone technology to the development of "social networks". Personal location "sharing" services such as *Loopt* go to some effort to distance their service offerings from "tracking" services, as used to manage commercial vehicle fleets. Fortunately, as location services have evolved so have efforts by standards bodies to securely process networked location information to protect the privacy of participants; much of the work on protocols, privacy preference specifications, threat analysis and location data formats developed by the IETF *Geopriv* Working Group [17] would be directly applicable in the deployment of a location clearinghouse for Cloak.

Video privacy and surveillance is also a subject of considerable interest in the legal, political science, and social science research communities. Interested readers are strongly encouraged to examine the seminal privacy treatise by Warren and Brandeis [18], which serves as a foundation for current privacy law. This work anticipated the erosion of privacy due to advancing technology, correctly predicting the need for ongoing expansion in privacy law, and the article holds up astonishingly well more than a century after it was written. But despite their insight, the authors could not possibly have anticipated the degree to which technology has outpaced law, particularly in just the last decade. Fortunately, there are a growing number of research groups focusing on the intersection of technology, society, and privacy. The *Surveillance Project* [19] at Queen's University is another resource available to those interested in studying various aspects of video privacy.

Cloak invites immediate analogies with the "National Do Not Call" registry [20] as implemented for telephone solicitation call blocking. The systems are similar in that users must opt-in to assert their privacy preference. Both systems are designed to discourage rather than impede an action by an unknown and frequently unwanted third party. Social and legal frameworks must be established to ensure compliance, which must be monitored and enforced. Of course, a surveilled party may be entirely unaware of surveillance and has no recourse to "hang up" or "not answer" or even review "caller identification".

An important distinction between Cloak and Do Not Call is that the former addresses privacy in public settings, while the latter was motivated in part due to what was viewed as an intrusion into the home. But mobile phones may be registered in Do Not Call. While this practice seems consistent with the mission of the registrar, the Federal Trade Commission, which is chartered to protect consumers (not homeowners), the registry can be arguably viewed as a precedent for a widely accepted [21] government-sponsored system to protect unwanted technological intrusions in both private *and* public places.

5 Technology and Privacy Law

The near absence of privacy rights for individuals in public spaces ensures that any primer on privacy law be brief. Unlike many countries – particularly in Europe – there is no explicit right to privacy guaranteed by the US constitution. Yet a vast incongruity exists between reality and perception; many citizens believe that legal protections to privacy exist that simply do not. Perhaps even more revealing is the lack of a high-level federal government privacy advocate. In Canada, for example, the mission of the Office of the Privacy Commissioner is to "protect and promote the privacy rights of individuals."

Video surveillance is closely tied with the concept of *territorial privacy*; that is, the fact that our assumption of privacy varies with place. Clearly, one expects a greater degree of privacy in one's home than in more public settings. This distinction was upheld by US courts in the case of Katz vs. United States, 389 U.S. 347 (1967), which established that the Fourth Amendment provides privacy protections in places where a person has a reasonable expectation of privacy. At the same time, courts have supported public video surveillance by policing agencies as a legitimate means of protecting citizens. A person has no reasonable expectation of privacy when entering a crowded public space. Yet some people cherish the relative public anonymity that a dense urban setting can at times provide, suggesting that the notion of privacy in public might be desirable if not achievable.

Privacy rights also vary with the type of surveillance media. Audio communications are subject to Title 1 of the Electronic Communications Privacy Act (1996) [16 U.S.C. Section 2510] requiring warrants for audio "wiretapping". Video surveilling is under no such constraint, and consequently existing public surveillance systems are video-only. We must await future court rulings to determine if objects containing sensitive information (e.g., credit card, driver's license, medical report) are granted any photographic protections.

Perhaps the most shameful demonstration of one's inability to assert one's privacy in public is the street battle routinely waged between celebrities and paparazzi. In each encounter a photographer exploits the absence of their subject's public privacy, and the subject at best feebly indicates their preference for no photography. In the absence of a clear and unambiguous ability to assert one's preference and have it respected, the occasional result is a public skirmish. Both parties invariably believe that they are in the right. The subject believes in his or her "right to be left alone," while the photographer insists that any subject in public is "fair game" and anything less is an assault on their livelihood.

The fundamental problem here, of course, is the inability (i.e., lack of protocol) for one to express one's preference and have that preference respected. In the absence of such a protocol, certain lawmakers have begun to contemplate the flawed notion of a physical "privacy zone" associated with individuals in public spaces [22].

Indeed, technology appears to be rapidly blurring what we traditionally think of as a well-defined line between public and private space. For example, use of a public sidewalk access Automatic Teller Machine (ATM) may arguably constitute a private transaction occurring in a public space, as may be a credit card exchange with a street vendor. Recent incidents have raised questions about the intrusiveness of Google's Street View video-mapping service [23]; we are left to consider the possibility that the "line" will be redrawn by technological advances, not by social consensus.

6 Conclusion

We have discussed a novel combination of mobile communications and navigation technology to permit individuals to assert a preference for privacy from video surveillance. We know of no other active research program that shares the ambitious agenda to universally supplement today's surveillance systems with privacy-enhancing technology. Our simulations demonstrate that an individual's privacy can be protected even in the face of the many sources of error we expect to encounter in a deployed system. Though our investigation remains at an early stage – particularly in understanding its applicability to the rapidly growing number of mobile camera phones – our initial work suggests that there are no significant technical barriers to large-scale system deployment. However, we have relied very heavily on simulation, and have made a large number of simplifying assumptions that we would not expect to hold in practical settings. Nonetheless, we are delighted by the promising early results, and the next step in our investigation will be to gather empirical evidence with a small-scale prototype.

Today's surveillance systems are rather primitive, technically unsophisticated tools. But with anticipated advances in technology we expect this to change. We believe that if individuals were aware of the extent that they are surveilled, and had the option to protect their images from distribution, that many would choose to do so.

References

1. New York Civil Liberties Union Report, "Who's Watching? Video Camera Surveillance in New York City and the Need for Public Oversight," http://www.nyclu.org/pdfs/surveillance_cams_report_121206.pdf, 2006.
2. Electronic Privacy Information Center, "Video Surveillance," http://www.epic.org/surveillance.
3. Government of Canada News Centre, "Privacy Commissioners Release New Video Surveillance Guidelines," http://news gc.ca/web/view/en/index.jsp?articleid=383707.
4. D.J. Solove " 'I've Got Nothing to Hide' and Other Misunderstandings of Privacy," *San Diego Law Review*, Vol. 44, p. 745, 2007.
5. "InFoTrends/CAP Ventures Forecasts 2009 Camera Phones at 847 Million Units," http://www.digitalcamerainfo.com/content/InFoTrends-CAP-Ventures-Forecasts-2009-Camera-Phones-Sales-At-847-Million-Units.htm, 2005.
6. J. Brassil, "Using Mobile Communications to Assert Privacy from Video Surveillance," *Proceedings of the First Workshop on Security in Systems and Networks (IPDPS 2005)*, Denver CO, April 2005.
7. D.J. Solove, "A Taxonomy of Privacy," *University of Pennsylvania Law Review*, Vol. 154, No. 3, p. 477, January 2006.
8. Zoombak LLC, http://www.zoombak.com/.

9. Garmin GPS 18 USB Receiver Technical Specifications, http://www8.garmin.com/manuals/ 425_Technical Specification.pdf.
10. Privacy Camera, IBM Research, http://www.research.ibm.com/peoplevision/videoprivacy. html.
11. A. Senior, "Tracking People with Probabilistic Appearance Models," *Workshop on Privacy Enhancing Technologies*, 2003.
12. I. Haritaoglu and M. Flickner, "Detection and Tracking of Shopping Groups in Stores," *Conference On Computer Vision and Pattern Recognition*, 2001.
13. P. Bolliger, M. Köhler, and K. Römer, "Facet: Towards a Smart Camera Network of Mobile Phones," http://www.vs.inf.ethz.ch/pub/papers/ /bolligph-facet2007.pdf, 2007.
14. S-C., Cheung, J. Zhao, and M.V. Venkatesh, "Efficient Object-based Video Inpainting," *IEEE International Conference on Image Processing (ICIP)*, 2006.
15. J. Wozencraft and I. Jacobs, *Principles of Communications Engineering*, Wiley, New York, 1965.
16. A. Papoulis, *Probability, Random Variables, and Stochastic Processes*, McGraw-Hill, New York, 1965.
17. IETF Geopriv Working Group, http://www.ietf.org/. html.charters/geopriv-charter.html/.
18. Samuel Warren and Louis D. Brandeis, "The Right to Privacy," *Harvard Law Review* vol. 193, 1890.
19. The Surveillance Project, Queens University, Canada, http://qsilver.queensu.ca/sociology/ Surveillance/overview.htm.
20. "The National Do Not Call Registry," http://www.donotcall.gov
21. The *Harris Poll*, "National Do-Not-Call Registry: Seven in Ten are Registered and All of Them Will Renew Their Registration," Poll #106, October 31, 2007.
22. E. Ferkenhoff, "Lawmakers Raise Concerns Over Shadowing of Ill. Candidate: Seek Privacy Zone to Bar Videotaping," *Boston Globe*, May 31, 2004.
23. M. Helft, "Google Zooms in Too Close for Some," *New York Times*, May 31, 2007.

Protecting Personal Identification in Video

Datong Chen, Yi Chang, Rong Yan and Jie Yang

Abstract In this chapter, we present some studies on protecting personal identification in video. First, we discuss and evaluate automatic face masking techniques for obscuring human faces in video. Second, a user study is presented to reveal that face-masked video can be attacked using pair-wise constraints. Next, we propose an algorithm to show that this type of pair-wise constraint attack can be implemented using state-of-the-art machine learning approaches. Finally, a new obscuring approach is proposed to avoid the pair-wise constraint attack. The proposed approach protects people's identity by obscuring the texture information of the entire body.

1 Introduction

Protecting personal identity in video has gained much research interest in recent years. After September 11th 2001, more and more video cameras have been deployed in a variety of locations for security and monitoring purposes. Through these cameras, people's appearances and activities are recorded and stored in digital forms, which can be easily shared on the Internet or in DVDs. Apart from the benefits brought by these digital video technologies, sharing these video records among the third parties without any privacy-encoding may seriously threaten people's privacy.

The traditional privacy protection method in video (for example, videos in TV channels) is face masking, in which people's faces are manually blocked or blurred in video frames to protect the subject's identification. Manual face masking is a high-cost process because one-second video consists of 30 frames. In other words, in order to mask one person from a 2-minute video, theoretically one needs to work on 3,600 images. Such a high cost makes this manual method not applicable to large volume videos. To develop more feasible and practical technologies of protecting personal identification in video, we first need to answer a number of questions: can face masking be performed more automatically? Is the face masking approach

D. Chen (✉)
School of Computer Science, Carnegie Mellon University, Pittsburgh, PA 15213, USA
e-mail: datong@cs.cmu.edu

A. Senior (ed.), *Protecting Privacy in Video Surveillance*,
DOI 10.1007/978-1-84882-301-3_7, © Springer-Verlag London Limited 2009

good enough to protect people's identification? And, is there a better way to obscure person in video if face masking is not a good solution?

In previous research, quite a few researchers took account of privacy protection in video from different points of view. Senior et al. [22] presented a model to define video privacy, and implemented some elementary tools to re-render the video in a privacy-preserving manner. Tansuriyavong et al. [24] developed a system that automatically identified a person by face recognition, and displayed a silhouette image of the person with a name list in order to balance privacy-protection and information-conveyance. Brassil [2] implemented a system to allow individuals to protect privacy from video surveillance for applications of mobile communications. Zhang et al. [29] proposed a detailed framework to store privacy information in surveillance video as a watermark. His system can monitor the invalid person in a restricted area but protect the privacy of the non-impaired persons. In addition, several research groups [13, 15, 30] discussed the privacy issues in the computer supported cooperative work domain. Furthermore, Newton et al. [16] proposed an algorithm to preserve privacy by de-identifying facial images. Boyle et al. [1] discussed the effects of blurring and pixelizing on awareness and privacy. In the following sections, we focus on face masking technology, one of the most common approaches to encoding video for protecting personal identity.

2 Automatic Face Masking Techniques

The cost of manually masking faces in video is very high and it is expensive to process large video collections. A video stream captured by a surveillance camera in 24 h consists of 2,592,000 frames of image (at 30 fps) and more than 79 million image frames per month. Besides being a huge amount of data, most surveillance videos are real-time streaming, which requires processing in real time also. One of the best tools to cut down the cost is automatic face masking systems. An automatic face masking module first detects and tracks faces in video frames, and then creates obscuring masks using the detected face locations and scales. In this chapter, we only discuss the details of face detection and tracking process, which must achieve a high recall in order to protect patients' privacy. Large variances on face poses, sizes, and lighting conditions are major challenges in analyzing surveillance video data, which cannot be covered by either profile faces or even intermediate estimations. In order to achieve high recall, we utilize a new forward–backward face localization algorithm by combining face detection and face tracking technologies.

2.1 Face Detection in Images

Many visual features have been used to detect faces, such as color [25] and shape [4], which are effective and efficient in some well-controlled environments. Most recent face detection algorithms employ texture features and appearances and train face detectors statistically using learning techniques, such as Gaussian mixture models [23], Principal Components Analysis (PCA), neural networks [19], and Support Vector Machine (SVM) [17]. Viola and Jones [26] achieved an important milestone in face detection. They applied the boosting technique to combine multiple weak classifiers to achieve fast and robust frontal face detection. In comparison to face detection in images, faces in video tend to have more poses. To detect faces in varying poses, profile faces [20] and intermediate pose appearance estimations [10] have been studied, but the problem remains a great challenge.

2.2 Robust Face Detection in Video

We evaluated the Scheiderman–Kanade [20] face detector, one of the most accurate face detectors at the end of 2007, on video data. The detector extracts wavelet features in multiple subbands from a large number of labeled images and trains neural networks using a boosting technique. In our test, the detector failed in 80% of non-frontal faces because a rich set of head poses in video were not trained in the face profiles. We proposed a compensative algorithm to improve the face detection by locating human heads using shape information of head-and-shoulder in video frames.

2.2.1 Background Subtraction

Background subtraction is used to segment foreground, usually containing people and other moving objects, from background. Here, we assume that all videos are captured with fixed cameras. A background can be dynamically learned by using the kernel density estimation (KDE) [8]. In a KDE algorithm, a set of video frames $\bar{A} = (\bar{A}_{t_1}, \bar{A}_{t_2}, \ldots, \bar{A}_{t_n})$ observed in the past are first stored as the background model. Let $\bar{A}_t(x)$ be a pixel value at a location x in frame $\bar{A}_t$. The probability of this observation is then defined as:

$$\Pr\left(\overline{A_t}(x)\right) = \frac{1}{n} \sum_{i=1}^{n} \alpha K\left(\overline{A_t}(x), \overline{A_{t_i}}(x)\right), \tag{1}$$

where K is a kernel function defined as a Gaussian function:

$$K(x_1, x_2) = \frac{1}{\sqrt{2\pi\sigma^2}} e^{-\frac{\|x_1 - x_2\|^2}{2\sigma^2}}. \tag{2}$$

The constant σ is the bandwidth. Using the color values of a pixel, the probability can be estimated from:

$$\Pr\left(\overline{A_t}(x)\right) = \frac{1}{n} \sum_{i=1}^{n} \alpha \prod_{j \in (R,G,B)} \frac{1}{\sqrt{2\pi\sigma^2}} \exp\left(-\frac{\left(\overline{A_t}(x)^j - \overline{A_{t_i}}(x)^j\right)^2}{2\sigma^2}\right), \tag{3}$$

Fig. 1 Feature extraction of
head-and-shoulder detector

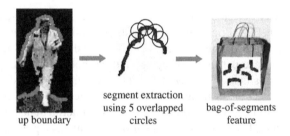

up boundary
    segment extraction
using 5 overlapped
circles
    bag-of-segments
feature

where α is the weight associated with the number appearance samples in the
model A:

$$\alpha = \frac{1}{|\bar{A}|}. \tag{4}$$

Given a background model and a new image, foreground regions can be extracted
by computing the probability of each pixel in the image using Equation (3) with a
cutoff threshold [8].

2.2.2 Head–shoulder Detector

Head-and-shoulder patterns can be detected from other foreground shapes by training a classifier. We use bag-of-segments feature to represent head-and-shoulder
patterns. To extract this feature, we first locate the up boundaries of the foreground
(the foreground pixels that are immediately below at least one background pixel)
from a background-subtracted image. Randomly selecting 10% of boundary pixels,
we extract segments using the 5-overlapped-circle template by localizing each pixel
in center of middle circle. The 5-overlapped-circle shown in the middle of Fig. 1.
The related positions among the 5 circles are fixed. We apply six 5-overlapped-circle
templates in different scales to detect head-and-shoulder pattern in multiple scales.
The template extracts 5 segments at each location as shown in Fig. 1. We represent
each segment using the 2nd, 3rd, and 4th orders of moments after normalizing with
the first order of moment. SVMs with Gaussian kernels are trained as classifier for
recognizing head–shoulder patterns. In our experiments, SVM classifiers trained
with 1,500 examples obtain 92% accuracy in a test set consisting 1,000 examples.

2.3 Face Tracking

Another tool for improving face detection in video is face tracking. Face tracking
follows a human head or facial features through a video image sequence using
temporal correspondences between frames. For privacy protection, one can track
human heads instead of faces, which can be achieved more precisely by tracking
segmented regions [11], color models, color histograms [18, 21, 27], or shapes [4].
A tracking process includes predicting and verifying the face location and size in an

image frame given the information in the consecutive frames. Kalman filters [9] and particle filters can be used to perform the prediction adaptively. To start a tracking, a face or head has to be pre-located in at least one frame.

2.4 Combination of Detection and Tracking

To effectively locate human faces in video, we propose a bi-directional tracking algorithm to combine face detection, tracking, and background subtraction into a unified framework. In this algorithm, we first perform background subtraction to extract foreground and then run face detection on the foreground. Once a face is detected, we track the face simultaneously in both backward and forward directions in video to locate misdetected faces (usually non-frontal faces). Faces are tracked using an approach based on online region confidence learning [5]. This approach associates different local regions of a face with different confidences on the basis of how discriminative they are from their background and the probability of being occluded. To this end, face appearances are dynamically accumulated using a layered representation. Then a detected (or tracked face in previous frame) face area is partitioned into regular and overlapping regions. Tracking confidences of these regions are learned online by exploiting the most powerful features to discriminate the regions from their local background and the occlusion probability in the video. The learned confidences are modeled as bias terms in a mean-shift tracking algorithm. This approach has the advantage of using region confidences against occlusions and a complex background [4].

The performance of this tracking-based face detection algorithm is evaluated on a public CHIL database (chil.server.de). In 8,000 testing frames, the algorithm located 98% of the faces (recall) in the ground truth with at least 50% of the area covered by the detection results. A located face is masked with a white block, which is 2.5 times larger than the detected scale to ensure the obscure of entire face.

3 Risk of Exposure People Identification in Face Masked Video

Common knowledge holds that individuals are difficult to be identified after masking their faces. In fact, this is not always true. Some people can identify their family members or close friends by body shape and typical actions. For people who are unfamiliar with the masked subjects, we did the following study which shows that identifications of face-masked subjects can still be statistically revealed through pair-wise constraint attack. A pair-wise constraint means that people can determine that two face-masked portraits belong to the same person by using clothing, shape, or other cues as alternative information, even though the person's face is still hidden. It cannot directly reveal the identification of the subject but there may be a high risk of identifying people in face-masked images by collecting enough pair-wise constraints. Our study tries to answer two questions. One question is how well people can obtain these types of pair-wise constraints, another is whether these pair-wise constraints can be used to reveal identifications of face-masked individuals?

To answer the first question, we performed the following user study. We only display human silhouette images with masked faces to some human volunteers. All human volunteers involved in this study have no knowledge about the subjects in the images. A screen shot of the interface is shown in Fig. 2. In each experiment, we display one image on the top-left corner as target and display 20 images below as candidates. All images were face-masked and were randomly selected from the pre-extracted foreground image pool, which contains 102 video sequences of 21 different subjects. These video sequences were captured by a surveillance camera in a nursing home environment in 6 days. We ensure that none of the candidates is sampled from the same video sequence that contains the target. We also ensure that only one candidate really matches the target. A volunteer is asked to pick one image from the candidates, which he/she believes that is the same person as the target.

Totally 160 runs are performed by 22 volunteers. In all 160 labeled pair-wise constraints, 140 constraints correctly correspond to the identities of the subjects and 20 of them are errors, which achieved an overall 89% accuracy. The results show that unfamiliar human annotators could label the pair-wise constraints with reasonably high accuracy from face-masked images.

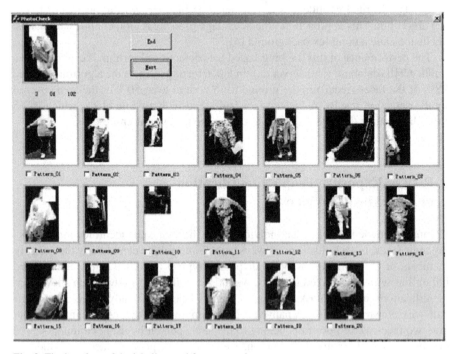

Fig. 2 The interface of the labeling tool for user study

4 Discovering People's Identities Using Pair-Wise Constraints

Furthermore, we show how pair-wise constraints can be used to reveal individual's identification with the help of computer-based classification techniques. Suppose you have a large collection of face-masked images captured from an institute, which involves a relatively small number of people, e.g., a dozen people. One wants to identify every person in these images but only has a few photos with the identifications of the subject from a third party. In a pair-wise constraint attack, he can hire a group of people to collect a large number of pair-wise constraints in the face-masked images and then use the following algorithm to train classifiers for identifying the subjects.

The algorithm uses imperfect pair-wise constraints $\{(x_i, x_j)\}$ on top of labeled photos $\{(y_k, x_k)\}$ to train a better classifier. The idea is to incorporate the additional pair-wise constraints into a margin-based discriminative learning. Typically, the margin-based discriminative learning algorithms focus on the analysis of a margin-related loss function coupled with a regularization factor. Formally, the goal of these algorithms is to minimize the following regularized empirical risk:

$$R_f = \sum_{k=1}^{m} L(y_k, f(x_k)) + \lambda \Omega(\| f \|), \tag{5}$$

where x_k is the feature of the kth training example, y_k denotes the corresponding label, and $f(x)$ is the classifier output. L denotes the empirical loss function, and $\Omega(\| f \|)$ can be regarded as a regularization function to control the computational complexity. In order to incorporate the pairwise constraints into this framework, Yan et al. [27] extended the above optimization objectives by introducing pairwise constraints as another set of empirical loss functions,

$$\sum_{k=1}^{m} L(y_k, f(x_k)) + \mu \sum_{i,j} L'(c_{ij}, f(x_i), f(x_j)) + \lambda \Omega(\| f \|_{\mathrm{H}}), \tag{6}$$

where $L'(c_{ij}, f(x_i), f(x_j))$ is called the pair-wise loss function, and c_{ij} is a pairwise constraint between the ith example and jth example, which is 1 if two examples are in the same class, -1 otherwise. In addition, c_{ij} could be 0 if this constraint is not available.

Intuitively, when $f(x_i)$ and $c_{i,j} f(x_j)$ have different signs, the pairwise loss function should give a high penalty, and vice versa. Meanwhile, the loss functions should be robust to noisy data. Taking all these factors into account, Yan et al. [28] chose the loss function to be a monotonic decreasing function of the difference between the predictions of a pair of pairwise constraints, i.e.,

$$L'(c_{i,j}, f(x_i), f(x_j)) = L(f(x_i) - c_{ij} f(x_j)) + L(c_{ij} f(x_j) - f(x_i)). \tag{7}$$

Equation (7) assumes perfect pairwise constraints. In our work, we extend it to improve discriminative learning with noisy pairwise constraints. We introduce an additional term g_{ij} to model the uncertainty of each constraint achieved from the user study. The modified optimization objective can be written as:

$$\frac{1}{m}\sum_{k=1}^{m} L(y_k, f(x_k)) + \frac{\mu}{|C|}\sum_{i,j} g_{ij} L'(c_{i,j}, f(x_i), f(x_j)) + \lambda\Omega(\|f\|_H), \quad (8)$$

where g_{ij} is the corresponding weight for each constraint pair c_{ij} that represents how likely the constraint is to be correctly labeled from the user study. For example, if n out of m unfamiliar personnel consider these two examples as belonging to the same class, we could compute g_{ij} to be n/m. In practice, we can only obtain the positive c_{ij} sign values using a manual labeling procedure or a tracking algorithm. Therefore, we can omit the sign matrix c_{ij} in future discussion.

We normalize the sum of the pair-wise constraint loss by the number of total constraints $|C|$ to balance the importance of labeled data and pair-wise constraints. In our implementation, we adopt the logistic regression loss function as the empirical loss function due to its simple form and strict convexity, that is, $L(x) = \log(1+e^{-x})$. Therefore, the empirical loss function could be rewritten as follows:

$$\frac{1}{m}\sum_{k=1}^{m} \log(1 + e^{-y_k f(x_k)}) + \frac{\mu}{|C|}\sum_{i,j} g_{ij} \log(1 + e^{f(x_i)-y_j f(x_j)})$$

$$+ \frac{\mu}{|C|}\sum_{i,j} g_{ij} \log(1 + e^{y_j f(x_j)-f(x_i)}) + \lambda\Omega(\| f \|_H). \quad (9)$$

4.1 Kernelization

The kernelized representation of the empirical loss function can be derived based on the Representer Theorem [14]. By projecting the original input space to a high-dimensional feature space, this representation could allow a simple learning algorithm to construct a complex decision boundary. This computationally intensive task is achieved through a positive definite reproducing kernel K and the well-known "kernel trick". We derive the kernelized representation as the following formula,

$$\frac{1}{m} \cdot 1^T \log(1 + e^{-\alpha K_P}) + \frac{\mu}{|C|} g_{ij} \cdot 1^T \log(1 + e^{\alpha K'_P}),$$

$$+ \frac{\mu}{|C|} g_{ij} \cdot 1^T \log(1 + e^{-\alpha K'_P}) + \lambda \alpha K \alpha \quad (10)$$

where K_p is the regressor matrix and K'_p is the pair-wise regressor matrix. Please see [27] for more details of their definitions. To solve the optimization problem, we apply the interior-reflective Newton methods to reach a global optimum. In the rest of this chapter, we call this type of learning algorithm a "weighted pair-wise kernel logistic regression" (WPKLR).

4.2 Experimental Evaluations

We applied the WPKLR algorithm to identify people from real surveillance video. We chose the constraint parameter μ to be 20 and regularization parameter λ to be 0.001 based on the testing performance of classifier trained without using any pair-wise constraints. In addition, we used the Radial Basis Function (RBF) as the kernel with ρ to be 0.08. A total of 48 h of video was captured with 4 cameras in the same nursing home as introduced in Section 3 over 6 consecutive days. We used a people tracker [5] to automatically extract the moving sequences of human subjects, and used video sequences that contained only one person. By sampling the silhouette image every half-second from the tracking sequence, we constructed a dataset of 102 tracking sequences and 778 sampled images from 10 human subjects. Among 102 sequences, 22 sequences are used as the training data and the others as testing, unless stated otherwise.

We extracted the HSV color histogram as image features, which is robust in detecting people identities and could also minimize the effect of blurring face appearance. In the HSV color spaces, each color channel is independently quantized into 32 bins, and each image is represented as a feature vector of 96 dimensions. Note that in this video data, one person could wear different clothes on different days in various lighting environments. This setting makes the learning process more difficult, especially with limited training data provided.

Our first experiment is to examine the effectiveness of pair-wise constraints for labeling identities. We trained classifiers by using the 22 training sequences with noise-free, pair-wise constraints (manually corrected), noisy constraints (real constraints labeled by humans), and weight constraints proposed in this section. Performance is measured by the person recognition accuracy of the trained classifiers as used in Figs. 3 and 4. The learning curve of noisy constraint is completely based on the labeling result from the user study, but uniformly weighted all constraints as 1. Weighted noisy constraint uses different weights for different constraints. In current experiments, we simulated and smoothed the weights based on the results

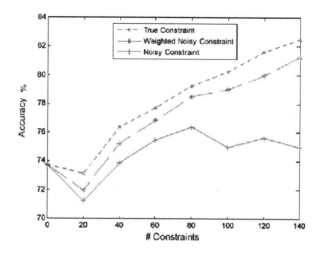

Fig. 3 Accuracies with different numbers of constraints

Fig. 4 Accuracies with
training sets in different sizes

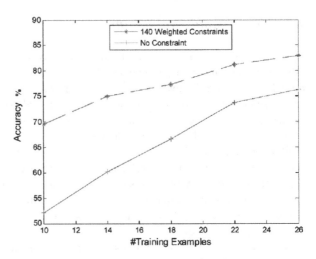

of our user study. The underlying intuition is that the accuracy of a particular constraint can be approximated by the overall accuracy of all constraints with enough unfamiliar personnel for labeling. True constraint assumes that ground truth is available and thus the correct constraints are always weighted as 1, while wrong constraints are ignored. Although the ground truth of constraints is unknown in practice, we intentionally depict its performance to serve as an upper bound of using noisy constraints. Figure 3 demonstrated the performance with the aforementioned three types of constraints. In contrast to the accuracy of 0.7375 without any constraints, the accuracy of weighted noisy constraint grows to 0.8125 with 140 weighted constraints, achieving a performance improvement of 10.17%. Also, the setting of weighted noisy constraint substantially outperforms the noisy constraint, and it can achieve performance near to true constraint. Note that when given only 20 constraints, accuracy is slightly degraded in each setting. A possible reason is that the decision boundary does not change stably with a small number of constraints. However, the performance always goes up after a sufficient number of constraints are incorporated.

Our next experiment explores the effect of varying the number of training examples provided by the ground truth personnel. Figure 4 illustrates the performance with a different number of training examples. In comparison to using only 22 training sequences (shown as "No constraint" in the figure), introducing 140 pair-wise constraints could always substantially improve classification accuracy. Furthermore, pair-wise constraints could make even more noticeable improvement given fewer training examples.

5 Human Body Obscuring

The studies in the previous sections show that identities of people are not completely obscured by only masking the faces, because other people can recognize their familiars by only looking at body appearances. To obscure protected subjects for public access purposes while keeping activity information, Hodgins et al. [12] proposed geometric models, which include stick figures, polygonal models, and NURBS-based models with muscles, flexible skin, or clothing. The advantage of geometric models is the ability to discriminate motion variations. The drawback is that geometric models, such as stick models, are defined on the joints of human bodies, which are difficult to extract automatically from video.

To overcome the shortcoming of the face masking, we propose a pseudo geometric model, namely, edge motion history image (EMHI) to address the problem of body obscuring. EMHI captures the structure of human bodies using edges detected in the body appearances and their motion. Edges can be detected in a video frame, especially around contours of a human body. This detection can be performed automatically, but it is not able to extract edges perfectly and consistently through a video sequence. To integrate noisy edge information in multiple frames and improve the discrimination of the edge based model, we use motion history image techniques.

Let $E_t(x)$ be a binary value to indicate if pixel x is located on an edge at time t. An EMHI $H_t^\tau(x)$ is computed from the EMHI of the previous frame $H_{t-1}^\tau(x)$ and the edge image $E_t(x)$ as:

$$H_t^\tau(x) = \begin{cases} \tau & if\ E_t(x) = 1 \\ \max\left(0,\ H_{t-1}^\tau(x) - 1\right) & otherwise \end{cases} \tag{11}$$

In an EMHI, edges detected by using Canny algorithm are accumulated through the time line to smooth the noisy edge detection results and preserve motion information of human activities. Figure 5 shows an original video frame, its EMHI result, background restoration, and the final obscured image. The proposed EMHI algorithm completely removes the identity information of the woman in pink from the video, while preserving the action information of the woman. The upper left of Fig. 5 is the original image. Figure 5 also illustrates possible ways to protect privacy of specific individuals in video. The lower left of Fig. 5 shows the result of completely removing the woman in pink from the original image. The person is identified and tracked using the technologies proposed in [4, 5]. The upper right of Fig. 5 is the result of applying the EMHI to the entire image. The lower right is the result of applying the EHMI to only the woman (on the left).

The EMHI obscuring process is automatic and does not require silhouettes. The obscured image totally preserves the location of the woman in pink. The body texture is obscured and only body contours are partially preserved, which protects the identity of the woman. The activity of the woman is preserved very well. People can easily tell that someone is walking from this ghost-like image.

6 Conclusions

In this chapter, we have discussed privacy protection in video by face masking. We have shown that faces in video can be detected and masked by computer-based algorithms with reasonable accuracy. However, we prove through a user study that

Fig. 5 An example of people obscured using the EMHI. The original image is shown at the *top-left*.
Its EMHI result is shown on the *top-right*. The *bottom-left* image is the background restoration of
the woman identified from the original video frame. We use the mean background model learned
in the background subtraction introduced in Section 2 to restore the local regions of the woman.
The *bottom-right* image is the final obscured image

face-masked images may still have a chance of exposing people's identifications
through pair-wise attack. The identification accuracy using pair-wise constraints in
the example we provided in this chapter is only a base line result because we only
use color features. In a real attack, the accuracy is expected to be much higher if
shape features are employed. Even in our example, identification accuracy of 83%
can be achieved, which is good enough to identify face-masked subjects in a small
number of candidates. At the end of the chapter, we proposed an EMHI approach
to obscure the entire body. The EMHI approach has better potentials for privacy
protection than face-masking. It is more difficult to be broken by pair-wise attacks
and very easy to be computed even in videos captured by moving cameras. How well
entire body obscure can protect people identification is another interesting research
topic which will be studied in the future. Furthermore, we also need to study whether
the video is still useful after all human bodies are obscured.

References

1. Boyle, M., Edwards, C. and Greenberg, S. The Effects of Filtered Video on Awareness and
   Privacy. In Proc. of CSCW, 2000.
2. Brassil, J. Using Mobile Communications to Assert Privacy from Video Surveillance. In Proc.
   of IPDPS, 2005.

3. Cavallaro, A. Adding Privacy Constraints to Video-based Applications. European Workshop on the Integration of Knowledge, Semantics and Digital Media Technology, 2004.
4. Chen, D., Bharucha, A. and Wactlar, H. People Identification Through Ambient Camera Networks. International Conference on Multimedia and Ambient Intelligence, 2007.
5. Chen, D. and Yang, J. Online Learning Region Confidences for Object Tracking. Proc. Int. Conf. on Computer Vision workshop on Video Surveillance Performance Evaluation of Tracking and Surveillance, 2005.
6. Davis, J.W. and Bobick, A.F. The Representation and Recognition of Human Movement Using Temporal Templates. IEEE Proc. Computer Vision and Pattern Recognition, pp. 928–934, June 1997.
7. Decarlo, D. and Metaxas, D. Deformable Model Based Face Shape and Motion Estimation. Proc. Int'l Conf. Face and Gesture Recognition, 1996.
8. Elgammal, A., Duraiswami, R., Harwood, D. and Davis, L.S. Background and Foreground Modeling using Nonparametric Kernel Density Estimation for Visual Surveillance. Proc. of IEEE, vol. 7, no. 90, pp. 1151–1163, 2002.
9. Gelb, A. Applied Optimal Estimation. ed. MIT Press, 1992.
10. Gong, S., McKenna, S. and Collins, J.J. An Investigation into Face Pose Distributions. Proc. Int'l Conf. Automatic Face and Gesture Recognition, pp. 265–270, 1996.
11. Hager, G. and Toyama, K.X. Vision: A Portable Substrate for Real-Time Vision Applications. Computer Vision and Image Understanding, vol. 69, no. 1, pp. 23–37, 1998.
12. Hodgins, J.K., O'Brien, J.F. and Tumblin, J. Judgments of Human Motion with Different Geometric Models. IEEE: Trans. on Visualization and Computer Graphics, vol. 4, no. 4, December 1998.
13. Hudson, S. and Smith, I. Techniques for Addressing Fundamental Privacy and Disruption Tradeoffs in Awareness Support Systems. In Proc. of ACM Conference on Computer Supported Cooperative Work, 1996.
14. Kimeldorf, G. and Wahba, G. Some Results on Tchebycheffian Spline Functions. J. Math. Anal. Applic., vol. 33, pp. 82–95, 1971.
15. Lee, A. and Girgensohn, A. and Schlueter, K. NYNEX Portholes: Initial User Reactions and Redesign Implications. In Proc. of International Conference on Supporting Group Work, 1997.
16. Newton, E., Sweeney, L. and Malin, B. Preserving Privacy by De-identifying Facial Images. IEEE Transactions on Knowledge and Data Engineering, vol. 17, no. 2, February 2005, pp. 232–243.
17. Osuna, E., Freund, R. and Girosi, F. Training Support Vector Machines: An Application to Face Detection. Proc. Conf. Computer Vision and Pattern Recognition, pp. 130–136, January 1997.
18. Raja, Y., McKenna, S.J. and Gong, S. Tracking and Segmenting People in Varying Lighting Conditions Using Color. Proc. Int'l Conf. Automatic Face and Gesture Recognition, pp. 228–233, 1998.
19. Rowley, H.A., Baluja, S. and Kanade, T. Neural Networks Based Face Detection. IEEE Trans. Pattern Analysis an Machine Intelligence, vol. 20, no. 1, pp. 22–38, January 1998.
20. Schneiderman, H. and Kanade, T. A Statistical Method for 3D Object Detection Applied to Faces and Cars. Proc. Conf. Computer Vision and Pattern Recognition, vol. I, pp. 746–751, 2000.
21. Schwerdt, K. and Crowley, J. Robust Face Tracking Using Colour. Proc. Int'l Conf. Automatic Face and Gesture Recognition, pp. 90–95, 2000.
22. Senior, A., Pankanti, S., Hampapur, A., Brown, L., Tian, Y. and Ekin, A. Blinkering Surveillance: Enabling Video Privacy through Computer Vision. IBM Research Report, RC22886 (W0308-109), 2003.
23. Sung, K.K. and Poggio, T. Example-Based Learning for View-Based Human Face Detection. IEEE Trans. Pattern Analysis and Machine Intelligence, vol. 20, no. 1, pp. 39–51, January 1998.
24. Tansuriyavong, S. and Hanaki, S. Privacy Protection by Concealing Persons in Circumstantial Video Image. In Proc. of PUI, 2001.

25. Terrillon, J.-C., Shirazi, M., Fukamachi, H. and Akamatsu, S. Comparative Performance of Different Skin Chrominance Models and Chrominance Spaces for the Automatic Detection of Human Faces in Color Images. Proc. Int'l Conf. Automatic Face and Gesture Recognition, pp. 54–61, 2000.

26. Viola, P. and Jones, M. Rapid Object Detection Using a Boosted Cascade of Simple Features. Proc. Conf. Computer Vision and Pattern Recognition, vol. I, pp. 511–518, 2001.

27. Wren, C., Azerbayejani, A., Darrell, T. and Pentland, A. Pfinder: A Real-Time Tracking of Human Body. IEEE Trans. Pattern Analysis and Machine Intelligence, vol. 19, no. 7, pp. 780–785, July 1997.

28. Yan, R., Zhang, J., Yang J. and Hauptmann, A. A Discriminative Learning Framework with Pairwise Constraints for Video Object Classification. In Proc. of CVPR, 2004.

29. Zhang, W., Cheung, S. and Chen, M. Hiding Privacy Information in Video Surveillance System. In ICIP, 2005.

30. Zhao, Q. and Stasko, J. The Awareness-Privacy Tradeoff in Video Supported Informal Awareness: A Study of Image-Filtering Based Techniques. GVU Technical Report, GIT-GVU-98-16.

Face De-identification

Ralph Gross, Latanya Sweeney, Jeffrey Cohn, Fernando de la Torre and Simon Baker

Abstract With the emergence of new applications centered around the sharing of image data, questions concerning the protection of the privacy of people visible in the scene arise. In most of these applications, knowledge of the identity of people in the image is not required. This makes the case for image de-identification, the removal of identifying information from images, prior to sharing of the data. Privacy protection methods are well established for field-structured data; however, work on images is still limited. In this chapter, we review previously proposed naïve and formal face de-identification methods. We then describe a novel framework for the de-identification of face images using multi-factor models which unify linear, bilinear, and quadratic data models. We show in experiments on a large expression-variant face database that the new algorithm is able to protect privacy while preserving data utility. The new model extends directly to image sequences, which we demonstrate on examples from a medical face database.

1 Introduction

Recent advances in both camera technology as well as supporting computing hardware have made it significantly easier to deal with large amounts of visual data. This enables a wide range of new usage scenarios involving the acquisition, processing, and sharing of images. However, many of these applications are plagued by privacy problems concerning the people visible in the scene. Examples include the Google Streetview service, surveillance systems to help monitor patients in nursing homes [3], and the collection and distribution of medical face databases (studying, e.g., pain [1]).

In most of these applications knowledge of the identity of people in the image is not required. This makes the case for image de-identification, the removal of identifying information from images, prior to sharing of the data. Privacy protection methods are well established for field-structured data [30]; however, work on

R. Gross (✉)
Data Privacy Lab, School of Computer Science, Carnegie Mellon University, Pittsburgh, PA, USA
e-mail: rgross@cs.cmu.edu

A. Senior (ed.), *Protecting Privacy in Video Surveillance*,
DOI 10.1007/978-1-84882-301-3_8, © Springer-Verlag London Limited 2009

images is still limited. The implicit goal of these methods is to protect privacy and preserve data utility, e.g., the ability to recognize gender or facial expressions from de-identified images. While initial methods discussed in the literature were limited to applying naïve image obfuscation methods such as blurring [23], more recent methods such as the k-Same algorithm provide provable privacy guarantees [14, 25].

In this chapter we review previously proposed naïve and formal face de-identification methods, highlighting their strengths and weaknesses (Section 2). The majority of algorithms operate directly on image data which varies both with identity as well as non-identity related factors such as facial expressions. A natural extension of these methods would use a factorization approach to separate identity and non-identity related factors to improve preservation of data utility. However, existing multi-factor models such as the bilinear models introduced by Tenenbaum and Freeman [33] or tensor models [36] require complete data labels during training which are often not available in practice. To address this problem, we describe a new multi-factor framework which combines linear, bilinear, and quadratic models. We show in experiments on a large expression-variant face database that the new algorithm is able to protect privacy while preserving data utility (Section 3). The new model extends directly to image sequences, which we demonstrate on examples from a medical face database (Section 4).

2 Related Work

The vast majority of previously proposed algorithms for face de-identification fall into one of two groups: ad-hoc distortion/suppression methods [7, 10, 18, 23, 24] and the k-Same [14, 25] family of algorithms implementing the k-anonymity protection model [30]. We describe both categories of algorithms along with their shortcomings in this section.

2.1 Naïve De-identification Methods

Following similar practices in traditional print and broadcasting media, image distortion approaches to face de-identification alter the region of the image occupied by a person using data suppression or simple image filters. These ad-hoc methods have been discussed numerous times in the literature [7, 10, 18, 23, 24], often in the context of computer supported cooperative work (CSCW) and home media spaces where explicit user control is desired to balance between privacy and data utility.

Image-filtering approaches use simple obfuscation methods such as blurring (smoothing the image with, e.g., a Gaussian filter with large variance) or pixelation (image subsampling) [7, 24]. See Fig. 1 for examples. While these algorithms are applicable to all images, they lack a formal privacy model. Therefore, no guarantees can be made that the privacy of people visible in the images is actually protected. As a consequence naïve de-identification methods preserve neither privacy nor data utility as results presented in the next section show.

Work on privacy protection in video surveillance scenarios favors data suppression. Systems typically determine the region of interest in the image through

Fig. 1 Examples of applying
the naïve de-identification
methods blurring and
pixelation to images from the
CMU Multi-PIE database
[15]

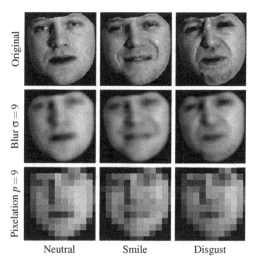

Original   Blur σ = 9   Pixelation p = 9

Neutral   Smile   Disgust

varying combinations of standard computer vision techniques such as background
subtraction [29, 35], object tracking [39], and in some cases face detection [27, 37].
Approaches proposed in the literature then differ in which area of the object to
mask such as the face [8, 21], the silhouette (thereby preserving the body shape)
[20, 31, 38], or the entire bounding box covering the person [12, 38]. The amount
of information transmitted can be further reduced by only indicating the position of
the person in the image by, e.g., a dot and replacing the image area occupied by the
person in the original image with static background in the de-identified image [20].
An alternative approach in the video surveillance space which provides some user
control on the amount of distortion applied in the image was proposed by Dufaux
et al. [11]. Following background subtraction, the regions of interest in the image are
distorted by scrambling the coefficients used to encode the areas in a Motion JPEG
2000 [32] compressed video sequence. The magnitude of change is controlled by
the number of altered coefficients.

2.2 Defeating Naïve De-identification Methods

While naïve de-identification algorithms such as blurring and pixelation have been
shown to successfully thwart human recognition [7, 40], they lack an explicit privacy
model and are therefore vulnerable to comparatively simple attacks. A very effective approach to defeat naïve de-identification algorithms was proposed by Newton
et al. as (manual) *parrot recognition* [25]. Instead of comparing de-identified images
to the original images (as humans implicitly or explicitly do), parrot recognition
applies the same distortion to the gallery images as contained in the probe images
prior to performing recognition. As a result, recognition rates drastically improve,
in effect reducing the privacy protection afforded by the naïve de-identification
algorithms.

We demonstrate this empirically using frontal images from 228 subjects from the
CMU Multi-PIE database [15] displaying *neutral*, *smile*, and *disgust* expressions.

Images are shape normalized using manually established Active Appearance Model labels [9, 22] (see Fig. 1). We then build Principle Component Analysis [19] bases on a small subset of the data (68 subjects representing 30% of the data) and encode the remainder of the data using these basis vectors. With the *neutral* face images as gallery and *smile* and *disgust* images of varying blur and pixelation levels as probes[1] we compute recognition rates using a whitened cosine distance, which has been shown to perform well in face PCA spaces [4]. In Fig. 2 we compare accuracies for relating de-identified to original images with parrot recognition rates. For both blurring and pixelation, parrot recognition rates are significantly higher than the original de-identification rates. For low parameter settings of either of the algorithms, parrot recognition performs even better than using original, unaltered images in both gallery and probe. This is likely due to a reduction in image noise in de-identified images.

In the experiments for Fig. 2, knowledge of the amount of blurring or pixelation present in the probe images was used to de-identify the gallery images with the same amount. This information, however, can be extracted directly from the de-identified probe images for an automatic parrot attack. In the case of pixelation, we simply determine the size of blocks of equal (or approximately equal) pixel intensities in the image. As shown in Fig. 3, the resulting recognition rates are identical to the manual procedure. A similar procedure can be applied in the case of blurring by analyzing the frequency spectrum of the de-identified images.

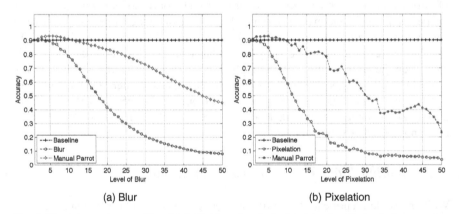

(a) Blur   (b) Pixelation

Fig. 2 Manual parrot recognition for both blurred and pixelated images. Instead of comparing de-identified images in the probe set with original images in the gallery, we apply the same transformation to the gallery images prior to PCA recognition. This was termed *parrot* recognition by Newton et al. [25]. For both de-identification algorithms, recognition rates drastically improve, thereby demonstrating the vulnerability of both privacy protection algorithm to this attack

---

[1] The *gallery* contains images of known subjects. The probe images are compared against the gallery to determine the most likely match [26].

Fig. 3 Automatic parrot recognition for pixelation. We automatically determine the degree of pixelation applied to probe images by determining the size of blocks of equal (or approximately equal) pixel intensities in the image. The same pixelation is then applied to gallery images prior to PCA recognition. The resulting recognition accuracy is identical to the accuracy achieved if ground-truth knowledge of the correct pixelation degree is assumed

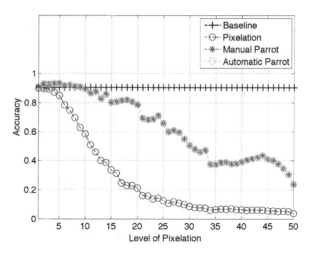

2.3 k-Same

The k-Same family of algorithms [14, 16, 25] implements the k-anonymity protection model [30] for face images. Given a *person-specific*[2] set of images $H = \{I_1, \ldots, I_M\}$, k-Same computes a de-identified set of images $H^d = \{I_1^d, \ldots, I_M^d\}$ in which each I_i^d indiscriminately relates to at least k elements of H. It can then be shown that the best possible success rate for a face recognition algorithm linking an element of H^d to the correct face in H is $\frac{1}{k}$. See [25] for details. k-Same achieves this k-anonymity protection by averaging the k closest faces for each element of H and adding k copies of the resulting average to H^d. See Fig. 4 for an illustration of the algorithm.

While k-Same provides provable privacy guarantees, the resulting de-identified images often contain undesirable artifacts. Since the algorithm directly averages pixel intensity values, even small alignment errors of the underlying faces lead to "ghosting" artifacts. See Fig. 5(a) for examples. To overcome this problem we introduced a model-based extension to k-Same, referred to as k-Same-M in [16]. The algorithm fits an Active Appearance Model (AAM) [9, 22] to input images

Fig. 4 Overview of the k-Same algorithm. Images are de-identified by computing averages over the closest neighbors of a given face in H and adding k copies of the resulting average to H^d

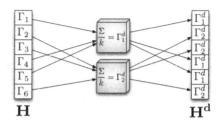

---

[2] In a person-specific set of faces each subject is represented by no more than one image.

Fig. 5 Examples of de-identified face images. Faces shown in (**a**) were de-identified using the appearance-based version of k-Same. Due to misalignments in the face set, ghosting artifacts appear. Faces in (**b**) were de-identified using k-Same-M, the model-based extension of k-Same. In comparison, the images produced by k-Same-M are of much higher quality

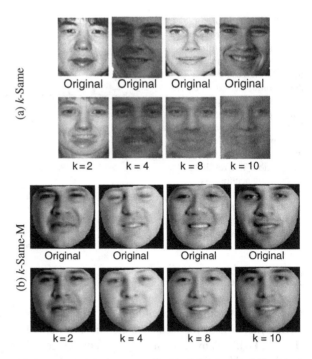

and then applies k-Same on the AAM model parameters. The resulting de-identified images are of much higher quality than images produced by k-Same while the same privacy guarantees can still be made. See Fig. 5(b) for examples.

k-Same selects images for averaging based on raw Euclidean distances in image space or Principal Component Analysis coefficient space [25]. In order to use additional information during image selection such as gender or facial expression labels we introduced k-Same-Select in [14]. The resulting algorithm provides k-anonymity protection while better preserving data utility. See Fig. 6 for examples images from the k-Same and k-Same-Select algorithms.

While k-Same provides adequate privacy protection, it places strong restrictions on the input data. The algorithm assumes that each subject is only represented once in the dataset, a condition that is often not met in practice, especially in video sequences.

2.4 Shortcomings of the k-Same Framework

k-Same assumes that each subject is only represented once in the dataset H, a condition which is often not met in practice. Since k-Same uses the nearest neighbors of a given image during de-identification, the presence of multiple images of the same subject in the input set can lead to lower levels of privacy protection. To demonstrate this we report results of experiments on the Multi-PIE database [15]. Each face in the dataset is represented using the appearance coefficients of an Active Appearance Model [9, 22]. Recognition is performed by computing the nearest neighbors

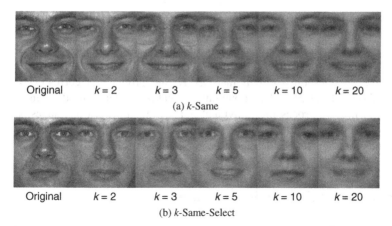

(a) k-Same

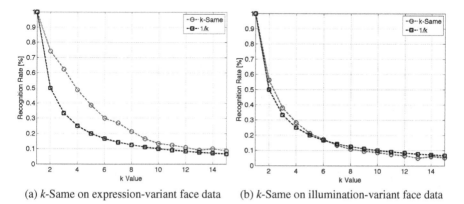

(b) k-Same-Select

Fig. 6 Examples of applying k-Same and k-Same-Select to expression variant faces. Since k-Same-Select factors facial expression labels into the image selection process, facial expressions are preserved better (notice the changing expression in the first row). Both algorithms provide k-anonymity privacy protection

in the appearance coefficient space. In the first experiment, we employ images of 203 subjects in frontal pose and frontal illumination, displaying neutral, surprise, and squint expressions. In the second experiment, we use images of 249 subjects recorded in frontal pose, displaying neutral expressions. Images of five illumination conditions per subject are included in the dataset. In either case, k-Same fails to provide adequate privacy protection. Figure 7 shows face recognition accuracies for varying levels of k. For the expression-variant dataset, accuracies stay well above the $\frac{1}{k}$ rate guaranteed by k-Same for datasets with single examples per class (see Fig. 7(a)). The same observation holds for the illumination-variant dataset for low

(a) k-Same on expression-variant face data   (b) k-Same on illumination-variant face data

Fig. 7 Recognition performance of k-Same on image sets containing multiple faces per subject. (**a**) shows recognition accuracies after applying k-Same to a subset of the CMU Multi-PIE database containing multiple expressions (neutral, surprise, and squint) of each subject. (**b**) shows recognition accuracies after applying k-Same on an illumination-variant subset of Multi-PIE. For both datasets recognition accuracies exceed $\frac{1}{k}$, indicating lower levels of privacy protection

k values (see Fig. 7(b)). We obtain similar results even when class information is factored into the k-Same de-identification process. We can conclude that k-Same does not provide sufficient privacy protection if multiple images per subject are included in the dataset.

k-Same operates on a *closed* face set H and produces a corresponding de-identified set of faces H^d. Many potential application scenarios for de-identification techniques involve processing individual images or sequences of images. k-Same is not directly applicable in these situations. Due to the definition of k-Same, extensions for open-set de-identification are not obvious.

3 Multi-factor Face De-identification

To address the shortcomings of the k-Same framework described in Section 2.4, we proposed a multi-factor framework for face de-identification [13, 17], which unifies linear, bilinear, and quadratic models. In our approach, we factorize input images into identity and non-identity factors using a generative multi-factor model. We then apply a de-identification algorithm to the combined factorized data before using the bases of the multi-factor model to reconstruct de-identified images. See Fig. 8

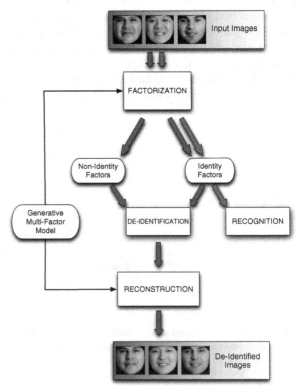

Fig. 8 Overview of the multi-factor framework for face de-identification. Input images are factorized into identity and non-identity components using a generative multi-factor model. The resulting identity parameters could be used for face recognition (*light gray arrows*) or, together with the non-identity parameters for face de-identification (*dark gray arrows*). After de-identification, the bases of the multi-factor model are used to produce de-identified images

for an overview. In the following we first define our unified model (Section 3.1). We then describe two fitting algorithms, the alternating and joint fitting algorithms and compare their performance on synthetic data (Section 3.2). In Section 3.3, we describe how to extend the model to include additional constraints on basis and coefficient vectors. We present results from an evaluation of the algorithm on a face de-identification task in Section 3.4.

3.1 Reconstructive Model

We define the general model M for data dimension k as

$$M_k(\boldsymbol{\mu}, \mathbf{B}^1, \mathbf{B}^2, \mathbf{W}, \mathbf{Q}^1, \mathbf{Q}^2; \mathbf{c}_1, \mathbf{c}_2) =$$

$$(1 \ \mathbf{c}_1^T \ \mathbf{c}_2^T) \underbrace{\begin{pmatrix} \mu_k & \mathbf{B}_k^2 & 0 \\ \mathbf{B}_k^1 & \mathbf{W}_k & \mathbf{Q}_k^1 \\ 0 & \mathbf{Q}_k^2 & 0 \end{pmatrix}}_{\Omega_k} \begin{pmatrix} 1 \\ \mathbf{c}_2 \\ \mathbf{c}_1 \end{pmatrix} \tag{1}$$

with mean $\boldsymbol{\mu}$, linear bases $\mathbf{B}^1, \mathbf{B}^2$, bilinear basis $\mathbf{W}$, quadratic bases $\mathbf{Q}^1, \mathbf{Q}^2$, and coefficients $\mathbf{c}_1$ and $\mathbf{c}_2$. $\mathbf{c}^1 \in \mathbb{R}^{r_1}, \mathbf{c}^2 \in \mathbb{R}^{r_2}, \boldsymbol{\mu} \in \mathbb{R}^d, \mathbf{B}^1 \in \mathbb{R}^{d \times r_1}$ with $\mathbf{B}_k^1 \in \mathbb{R}^{1 \times r_1}$, $\mathbf{B}^2 \in \mathbb{R}^{d \times r_2}, \mathbf{W}_k \in \mathbb{R}^{r_1 \times r_2}, \mathbf{Q}_k^1 \in \mathbb{R}^{r_1 \times r_1}, \mathbf{Q}_k^2 \in \mathbb{R}^{r_2 \times r_2}$. To avoid redundancy, $\mathbf{Q}^1, \mathbf{Q}^2$ could be either symmetric or upper triangular. Here we choose upper triangular.

While Equation (1) defines a quadratic model, it in fact contains lower-dimensional linear, bilinear, and quadratic models as special cases. To illustrate this we set $\mathbf{W} = \mathbf{Q}^1 = \mathbf{Q}^2 = 0$ and obtain

$$M_k^{Lin}(\boldsymbol{\mu}, \mathbf{B}^1, \mathbf{B}^2, 0, 0, 0; \mathbf{c}_1, \mathbf{c}_2) = (1 \ \mathbf{c}_1^T \ \mathbf{c}_2^T) \begin{pmatrix} \mu_k & \mathbf{B}_k^2 & 0 \\ \mathbf{B}_k^1 & 0 & 0 \\ 0 & 0 & 0 \end{pmatrix} \begin{pmatrix} 1 \\ \mathbf{c}_2 \\ \mathbf{c}_1 \end{pmatrix}$$

$$= \mu_k + \mathbf{c}_1^T \mathbf{B}_k^1 + \mathbf{B}_k^2 \mathbf{c}_2$$

the linear model in $\mathbf{c}^1$ and $\mathbf{c}^2$. Similarly, for $\mathbf{Q}^1 = \mathbf{Q}^2 = 0$ we obtain the bilinear model

$$M_k^{Bilin}(\boldsymbol{\mu}, \mathbf{B}^1, \mathbf{B}^2, \mathbf{W}, 0, 0; \mathbf{c}_1, \mathbf{c}_2) = (1 \ \mathbf{c}_1^T \ \mathbf{c}_2^T) \begin{pmatrix} \mu_k & \mathbf{B}_k^2 & 0 \\ \mathbf{B}_k^1 & \mathbf{W}_k & 0 \\ 0 & 0 & 0 \end{pmatrix} \begin{pmatrix} 1 \\ \mathbf{c}_2 \\ \mathbf{c}_1 \end{pmatrix}$$

$$= \mu_k + \mathbf{c}_1^T \mathbf{B}_k^1 + \mathbf{B}_k^2 \mathbf{c}_2 + \mathbf{c}_1^T \mathbf{W}_k \mathbf{c}_2$$

Mixtures of the components yield model combinations, i.e., mixed linear and bilinear, mixed bilinear and quadratic, etc.

The model as defined in Equation (1) is ambiguous, i.e., there exist transformations of $\mathbf{c}^1$, $\mathbf{c}^2$, and $\boldsymbol{\Omega}_k$ that produce identical data vectors. In the linear case the ambiguity is well known:

$$\boldsymbol{\mu}^T + \mathbf{c}_1^T \mathbf{B}^{1^T} = \boldsymbol{\mu}^T + \mathbf{c}_1^T \mathbf{R}\mathbf{R}^{-1}\mathbf{B}^{1^T} \tag{2}$$

for any invertible $\mathbf{R}$. So for $\bar{\mathbf{B}}^{1^T} = \mathbf{R}^{-1}\mathbf{B}^{1^T}$, $\bar{\mathbf{c}}_1^T = \mathbf{c}_1^T \mathbf{R}$ it holds that

$$\boldsymbol{\mu} + \bar{\mathbf{c}}_1^T \bar{\mathbf{B}}^{1^T} = \boldsymbol{\mu} + \mathbf{c}_1^T \mathbf{B}^{1^T} \tag{3}$$

This ambiguity is broken in the case of PCA due to the ordering of the basis vectors according to the corresponding eigenvalues. In the case of the general model defined in Equation (1) arbitrary linear reparameterizations are possible:

$$
\begin{aligned}
M_k(\boldsymbol{\Omega}_k; \mathbf{c}_1, \mathbf{c}_2) &=
(1 \ \mathbf{c}_1^T \ \mathbf{c}_2^T)
\begin{pmatrix}
\mu_k & \mathbf{B}_k^2 & \mathbf{0} \\
\mathbf{B}_k^{1^T} & \mathbf{W}_k & \mathbf{Q}_k^1 \\
\mathbf{0} & \mathbf{Q}_k^2 & \mathbf{0}
\end{pmatrix}
\begin{pmatrix}
1 \\
\mathbf{c}_2 \\
\mathbf{c}_1
\end{pmatrix} \\
&=
(1 \ \mathbf{c}_1^T \ \mathbf{c}_2^T) \,
\boldsymbol{\Phi}_l \boldsymbol{\Phi}_l^{-1} \boldsymbol{\Omega}_k \boldsymbol{\Phi}_r \boldsymbol{\Phi}_r^{-1}
\begin{pmatrix}
1 \\
\mathbf{c}_2 \\
\mathbf{c}_1
\end{pmatrix}
\end{aligned}
\tag{4}
$$

with

$$
\boldsymbol{\Phi}_l =
\begin{pmatrix}
1 & \mathbf{0}_1 & \mathbf{0}_2 \\
0 & \mathbf{R}_{11} & \mathbf{R}_{12} \\
0 & \mathbf{R}_{21} & \mathbf{R}_{22}
\end{pmatrix}, \quad
\boldsymbol{\Phi}_r =
\begin{pmatrix}
1 & \mathbf{0}_2 & \mathbf{0}_1 \\
0 & \mathbf{R}_{22} & \mathbf{R}_{21} \\
0 & \mathbf{R}_{12} & \mathbf{R}_{11}
\end{pmatrix}
$$

and $\mathbf{0}_1 \in \mathbb{R}^{r_1}$, $\mathbf{0}_2 \in \mathbb{R}^{r_2}$, $\mathbf{R}_{11} \in \mathbb{R}^{r_1 \times r_1}$, $\mathbf{R}_{12}, \mathbf{R}_{21} \in \mathbb{R}^{r_1 \times r_2}$, and $\mathbf{R}_{22} \in \mathbb{R}^{r_2 \times r_2}$. The first column of both matrices $\boldsymbol{\Phi}_l$ and $\boldsymbol{\Phi}_r$ must be $(1 \ 0 \ 0)^T$ due to the structure of the coefficient vectors $(1 \ \mathbf{c}_1^T \ \mathbf{c}_2^T)$ and $(1 \ \mathbf{c}_2 \ \mathbf{c}_1)^T$, each with a leading 1. As a consequence of these ambiguities, the model parameters obtained during fitting are not unique. Therefore, special care must be taken to normalize parameters during the synthetic experiments described below.

3.2 Model Fitting

The goal of fitting is to compute the parameters that minimize the model reconstruction error for a given training data set $\mathbf{d} = [\mathbf{d}_1 \dots \mathbf{d}_n]$:

$$\arg\min_{\Gamma, \mathbf{C}_1, \mathbf{C}_2} \sum_{l=1}^{n} \| M(\Gamma; \mathbf{c}_1(l), \mathbf{c}_2(l)) - \mathbf{d}_l \|_2^2 \tag{5}$$

with the bases $\Gamma = (\mu, \mathbf{B}^1, \mathbf{B}^2, \mathbf{W}, \mathbf{Q}^1, \mathbf{Q}^2)$ and coefficients $\mathbf{C}_1 = (c_1(1), \ldots, c_1(n))$, $\mathbf{C}_2 = (c_2(1), \ldots, c_2(n))$.

For the linear model M^{Lin} the corresponding minimization problem is

$$\underset{\mathbf{B}, \mathbf{C}}{\arg\min} \sum_{l=1}^{n} \| M^{Lin}(\mathbf{B}; \mathbf{c}(l)) - \mathbf{d}_l \|_2^2 \tag{6}$$

where we combined the separate bases $\mathbf{B}^1$, $\mathbf{B}^2$ into $\mathbf{B}$ and the coefficients $\mathbf{C}_1, \mathbf{C}_2$ into $\mathbf{C} = (\mathbf{c}(1), \ldots, \mathbf{c}(n))$. Equation (6) can be minimized efficiently by using PCA (see e.g., [5]). This, however, is not the only way. Assuming initial parameter estimates $\mathbf{B}_0$ and $\mathbf{C}_0$, we can minimize the expression in Equation (6) by alternating between computing updates $\Delta \mathbf{B}$ that minimize $\| M^{Lin}(\mathbf{B}_0 + \Delta \mathbf{B}; \mathbf{C}) - \mathbf{D} \|_2^2$ and updates $\Delta \mathbf{C}$ that minimize $\| M^{Lin}(\mathbf{B}_0; \mathbf{C}_o + \Delta \mathbf{C}) - \mathbf{D} \|_2^2$ [34]. Both equations are linear in their unknowns and can therefore be solved directly. In the case of linear models, this alternated least squares algorithm has been shown to always converge to the global minimum [2].

PCA does not generalize to bilinear or quadratic models; however, the alternating algorithm does. (Note that for bilinear models and fully labeled data, the iterative Tenenbaum–Freeman algorithm can be used [33].) We can minimize Equation (5) by solving separately in turn for updates $\Delta \Gamma$, $\Delta \mathbf{C}_1$, and $\Delta \mathbf{C}_2$. See Fig. 9. In each case the corresponding minimization problem is linear in its unknowns and can therefore be solved directly. In order to, e.g., compute the basis update $\Delta \Gamma$ we compute $\arg\min_{\Delta \Gamma} \| \mathbf{E} - \mathbf{T}_{\Delta \Gamma} \Delta \Gamma \|_2^2$, with the current reconstruction error $\mathbf{E} = \mathbf{D} - M(\Gamma; \mathbf{C}_1, \mathbf{C}_2)$ and the constraint matrix $\mathbf{T}_\Gamma$. $\Delta \Gamma$ can be computed in closed form as $\Delta \Gamma = (\mathbf{T}_\Gamma^T \mathbf{T}_\Gamma)^{-1} \mathbf{T}_\Gamma^T \mathbf{E}$. $\Delta \mathbf{C}_1$ and $\Delta \mathbf{C}_2$ are computed in a similar manner.

While the alternating algorithm works well for linear models, it has issues for higher-order models. The linearization into separate component updates ignores the coupling between the bases Γ and coefficients $\mathbf{C}_1, \mathbf{C}_2$. As a consequence, the algorithm is more prone to local minima. To improve performance we propose to *jointly* solve for updates to all parameters at the same time. By dropping second order

The Alternating Fitting Algorithm

Initialization

Randomly initialize $\mu, \mathbf{B}^1, \mathbf{B}^2, \mathbf{W}, \mathbf{Q}^1, \mathbf{Q}^2; \mathbf{C}_1, \mathbf{C}_2$

Iterate

(I1) Compute $\Delta \Gamma$ in
$\arg\min_{\Delta \Gamma} \| M(\Gamma + \Delta \Gamma; \mathbf{C}_1, \mathbf{C}_2) - \mathbf{D} \|_2^2$
Update $\Gamma \leftarrow \Gamma + \Delta \Gamma$
(I2) Compute $\Delta \mathbf{C}_1$ in
$\arg\min_{\Delta \mathbf{C}_1} \| M(\Gamma; \mathbf{C}_1 + \Delta \mathbf{C}_1, \mathbf{C}_2) - \mathbf{D} \|_2^2$
Update $\mathbf{C}_1 \leftarrow \mathbf{C}_1 + \Delta \mathbf{C}_1$
(I3) Compute $\Delta \Gamma \mathbf{C}_2$ in

Fig. 9 The alternating fitting
algorithm

$\arg\min_{\Delta \mathbf{C}_2} \| M(\Gamma; \mathbf{C}_1, \mathbf{C}_2 + \Delta \mathbf{C}_2) - \mathbf{D} \|_2^2$
Update $\mathbf{C}_2 \leftarrow \mathbf{C}_2 + \Delta \mathbf{C}_2$

terms and reorganizing components we can transform the minimization problem $\arg\min_{\Delta\Gamma,\Delta\mathbf{C}_1,\Delta\mathbf{C}_2} \|M(\Gamma + \Delta\Gamma; \mathbf{C}_1 + \Delta\mathbf{C}_1, \mathbf{C}_2 + \Delta\mathbf{C}_2) - \mathbf{D}\|_2^2$ into a similar form as above:

$$\arg\min_{\Delta\Gamma,\Delta\mathbf{C}_1,\Delta\mathbf{C}_2} \| E - \mathbf{T}_{\Gamma,\mathbf{C}_1,\mathbf{C}_2} \begin{pmatrix} \Delta\Gamma \\ \Delta\mathbf{C}_1 \\ \Delta\mathbf{C}_2 \end{pmatrix} \|_2^2 \tag{7}$$

with $\mathbf{E} = \mathbf{D} - M(\Gamma; \mathbf{C}_1, \mathbf{C}_2)$ and the constraint matrix $\mathbf{T}_{\Gamma,\mathbf{C}_1,\mathbf{C}_2}$. Figure 10 summarized the algorithm. See [13] for details.

In order to compare the performance of the alternating and joint fitting algorithms, we use synthetic data with known ground-truth. We randomly generate bases and coefficient matrices (drawn from a zero mean, unit variance normal distribution) and perturb both with varying amounts of noise before initializing the fitting algorithm. For each noise level the bases and coefficients are then normalized to ensure that all models are initialized at the same reconstruction error. We evaluate the fitting algorithms by comparing the ground-truth models with the fitted models.

In all experiments, we report results averaged over five different ground-truth settings with three different initialization settings each for a total of 15 experiments for every model and fitting algorithm. We run every algorithm until convergence (normalized ground-truth error falls below a threshold) or a maximum of 150 iterations, whichever comes first. Figure 11 compares the frequency of convergence for different variations of the joint and alternating fitting algorithms for different initial reconstruction errors. Across all conditions, the joint fitting algorithm performs better than the alternating algorithm. For the combined linear, bilinear, and quadratic model (M+L+B+Q) the joint algorithm converges in 80% of all cases whereas the alternating algorithm only converges in 61% of trials. The difference is even larger for the combined linear and bilinear model (M+L+B) where the joint algorithm converges in 96.2% of all trials compared to 68.6% for the alternating algorithm. The joint fitting algorithm also converges faster, requiring on average 8.7 iterations in comparison to 86.7 iterations for the alternating algorithm (for an initial ground-truth error of 20.0).

The Joint Fitting Algorithm

Initialization

Randomly initialize $\mu, \mathbf{B}^1, \mathbf{B}^2, \mathbf{W}, \mathbf{Q}^1, \mathbf{Q}^2; \mathbf{C}_1, \mathbf{C}_2$

Iterate

(I1) Compute $\Delta = (\Delta\Gamma, \Delta\mathbf{C}_1, \Delta\mathbf{C}_2)$ in
$\arg\min_{\Delta} \|M(\Gamma + \Delta\Gamma; \mathbf{C}_1 + \Delta\mathbf{C}_1, \mathbf{C}_2 + \Delta\mathbf{C}_2) - \mathbf{D}\|_2^2$
Update $\Gamma \leftarrow \Gamma + \Delta\Gamma$

Fig. 10 The joint fitting algorithm

Update $\mathbf{C}_1 \leftarrow \mathbf{C}_1 + \Delta\mathbf{C}_1$
Update $\mathbf{C}_2 \leftarrow \mathbf{C}_2 + \Delta\mathbf{C}_2$

Fig. 11 Comparison of the
convergence frequency for
the alternating and joint
fitting algorithm on synthetic
data. The fitting algorithms
are initialized with
ground-truth data perturbed
by noise of varying
magnitude. Results are shown
for different model
configurations combining the
mean (M), linear (L), bilinear
(B), and quadratic (Q)
components. The joint fitting
algorithm is more robust as
shown by higher frequencies
of convergence across models
and initial perturbations

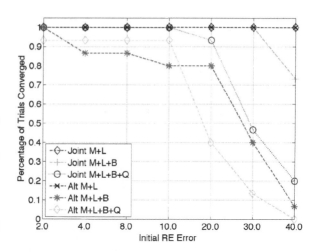

3.3 Multi-factor Models with Constraints

The joint fitting algorithm described in Section 3.2 computes bases and coefficients iteratively by minimizing the model reconstruction error for a given training dataset. See Equation (5). While the resulting model succeeds at reconstructing the data, no other properties (e.g., affinity of class coefficients, basis orthonormality) are enforced. In order to accomplish this we add further constraints to the energy function on the coefficients, the bases or both. We then strive to compute

$$\arg\min_{\Gamma, \mathbf{C}_1, \mathbf{C}_2} \sum_{l=1}^{n} \|M(\Gamma; \mathbf{c}_1(l), \mathbf{c}_2(l)) - \mathbf{d}_l\|_2^2 + \lambda_1 \Theta_1(\mathbf{C}_1, \mathbf{C}_2) + \lambda_2 \Theta_2(\Gamma) \qquad (8)$$

where Θ_1 and Θ_2 refer to sets of constraints. The parameters λ_1 and λ_2 balance the magnitude of the terms.

Let $S^1 = \{s_1^1, \ldots, s_{m_1}^1\}$, $S^2 = \{s_1^2, \ldots, s_{m_2}^2\}$ be sets of coefficient indices of elements in $\mathbf{C}_1$ and $\mathbf{C}_2$, respectively, for which we want to enforce equality. We then strive to compute

$$\arg\min_{\Gamma, \mathbf{C}_1, \mathbf{C}_2} \sum_{l=1}^{n} \|M(\Gamma; \mathbf{c}_1(l), \mathbf{c}_2(l)) - \mathbf{d}_l\|_2^2 +$$

$$+\lambda_{11} \sum_{\substack{s_i^1, s_j^1 \in S^1 \\ s_i^1 \neq s_j^1}} \|\mathbf{c}_1(s_i^1) - \mathbf{c}_1(s_j^1)\|_2^2 + \lambda_{12} \sum_{\substack{s_i^2, s_j^2 \in S^2 \\ s_i^2 \neq s_j^2}} \|\mathbf{c}_2(s_i^2) - \mathbf{c}_2(s_j^2)\|_2^2 \qquad (9)$$

Linearizing the expression in Equation (9) as described in Section 3.2 leads to

$$\arg\min_{\varDelta\varGamma,\varDelta\mathbf{C}_1,\varDelta\mathbf{C}_2} \quad \left\| \mathbf{E}_{RE} - \mathbf{T}_{\varGamma,\mathbf{C}_1,\mathbf{C}_2} \begin{pmatrix} \varDelta\varGamma \\ \varDelta\mathbf{C}_1 \\ \varDelta\mathbf{C}_2 \end{pmatrix} \right\|_2^2 +$$

$$+\lambda_{11}\|\mathbf{E}_{C_1} - \mathbf{T}_{S_1}\varDelta\mathbf{C}_1\|_2^2 + \lambda_{12}\|\mathbf{E}_{C_2} - \mathbf{T}_{S_2}\varDelta\mathbf{C}_2\|_2^2 \tag{10}$$

with the reconstruction error $\mathbf{E}_{RE} = \mathbf{D} - M(\varGamma; \mathbf{C}_1, \mathbf{C}_2)$, the coefficient constraint error for $\mathbf{C}_1$ (defined analogously for $\mathbf{C}_2$)

$$\mathbf{E}_{C_1} = \begin{pmatrix} \mathbf{c}_1(s_{i_1}^1) - \mathbf{c}_1(s_{i_2}^1) \\ \cdots \\ \mathbf{c}_1(s_{i_{m-1}}^1) - \mathbf{c}_1(s_{i_m}^1) \end{pmatrix} \tag{11}$$

and the coefficient constraint matrices $\mathbf{T}_{S_1}, \mathbf{T}_{S_2}$. The problem defined in Equation (10) can be solved as constraint least squares problem with linear equality constraints (see e.g., [6]). To do so we stack the components of Equation (10) and compute

$$\arg\min_{\varDelta\varGamma,\varDelta\mathbf{C}_1,\varDelta\mathbf{C}_2} \quad \left\| \begin{pmatrix} \mathbf{E}_{RE} \\ \lambda_{11} * \mathbf{E}_{C_1} \\ \lambda_{12} * \mathbf{E}_{C_2} \end{pmatrix} - \begin{pmatrix} \mathbf{T}_{\varGamma,\mathbf{C}_1,\mathbf{C}_2} \\ 0 \ \lambda_{11} * \mathbf{T}_{S_1} \quad 0 \\ 0 \quad 0 \quad \lambda_{12} * \mathbf{T}_{S_2} \end{pmatrix} \begin{pmatrix} \varDelta\varGamma \\ \varDelta\mathbf{C}_1 \\ \varDelta\mathbf{C}_2 \end{pmatrix} \right\|_2^2 \tag{12}$$

The solution to Equation (12) can be computed in the same way as the solution to the unconstrained least squares problem. Since the coefficient constraints are added individually and independently for the factors $\mathbf{c}_1$ and $\mathbf{c}_2$, the framework enables semi-supervised learning (see [17]). Constraints on the basis vectors can be enforced in a similar fashion.

3.4 Experiments

In order to evaluate the model proposed in Section 3.3, we use a subset of the CMU Multi-PIE face database [15] containing 100 subjects displaying neutral, smile, and disgust expressions in frontal pose and with frontal illumination. The images were captured within minutes of each other as part of a multi-camera, multi-flash recording. We normalize the face images by manually establishing facial feature point labels, computing an Active Appearance Model [9, 22] over the dataset, and extracting the appearance parameters for all images. We compare privacy protection and data utility of the (ε, k)-map algorithm [13] using two different data representations: the original AAM appearance parameters and the combined $\mathbf{c}_1$ and $\mathbf{c}_2$ parameters extracted from a combined linear and quadratic model. The (ε, k)-map algorithm is a probabilistic extension of the k-Same algorithm described in Section 2.3. For both representations we de-identify the data, reconstruct the (normalized) image, and compute recognition rates using a whitened cosine distance PCA classifier [4] with the de-identified images as probe and the original images as gallery. We evaluate

Fig. 12 Privacy-Data Utility map of the (ε, k)-map algorithm using original and multi-factor representations. We show PCA face recognition and SVM facial expression classification rates for different values of the privacy parameter k. Usage of the multi-factor representation (MF (ε, k)-map) results in higher expression classification accuracies than the original representation while providing similar privacy protection. As comparison we also show results for image blurring

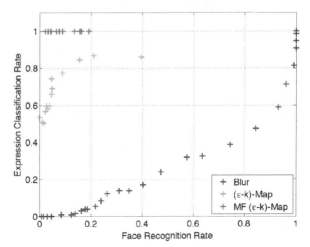

the utility of the de-identified images by computing facial expression classification rates using an SVM classifier (trained on independent original images) [28]. Figure 12 plots the results of both experiments for varying values of k for the original and multi-factor representations. Across all values of k, expression classification on de-identified images based on the multi-factor representation yields better recognition rates while providing the same privacy protection. As comparison, results for simple blurring of the images are included as well. Figure 13 shows examples of smile images de-identified using the proposed framework.

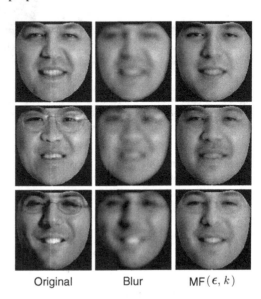

Fig. 13 Examples of smile images de-identified using the multi-factor (ε, k)-map algorithm

Original   Blur   MF(ϵ, k)

4 Conclusion and Future Work

In this chapter, we provided an overview of face de-identification. We described previously proposed naïve as well as formal de-identification algorithms and illustrated their shortcomings. We then introduced a novel de-identification framework using multi-factor models and demonstrated that the algorithm protects privacy (as measured by face recognition performance) while preserving data utility (as measured by facial expression classification performance on de-identified images).

The multi-factor de-identification algorithm described here operates on single images. However, since it is integrated with the Active Appearance Model framework [9, 22], extension of this work to video de-identification is natural. In Fig. 14 we show example frames of applying the algorithm to a video sequence from the UNBC-McMaster Shoulder Pain Expression Archive [1]. This dataset contains image sequences recorded of subjects after shoulder surgery who rotate either their affected or unaffected shoulder, resulting in a range of pain expressions. In Fig. 14 we compare the results from applying the multi-factor and k-Same algorithms. The multi-factor algorithm preserves more of the data utility during de-identification as shown by, e.g., the wrinkles around the eyes of the subject.

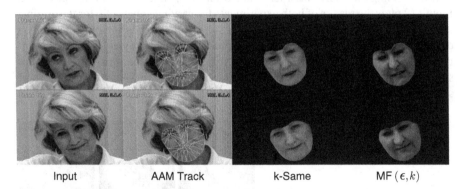

Input   AAM Track   k-Same   MF (ϵ, k)

Fig. 14 Comparison of k-Same and multi-factor de-identification on video sequences. The multi-factor algorithm preserves more of the data utility during de-identification as shown by, e.g., the wrinkles around the eyes of the subject

Acknowledgments This work was supported by the National Institute of Justice, Fast Capture Initiative, under award number 2005-IJ-CX-K046.

References

1. A. Ashraf, S. Lucey, J.F. Cohn, T. Chen, Z. Ambadar, K. Prkachin, P. Solomon, and B.-J. Theobald. The painful face – pain expression recognition using active appearance models. In *ICMI*, 2007.
2. P. Baldi and K. Hornik. Neural networks and principal component analysis: Learning from examples without local minimia. *Neural Networks*, 2(1):53–58, 1989.

3. A. Barucha, C. Atkeson, S. Stevens, D. Chen, H. Wactlar, B. Pollock, and M.A. Dew. Care-media: Automated video and sensor analysis for geriatric care. In *Annual Meeting of the American Association for Geriatric Psychiatry*, 2006.

4. R. Beveridge, D. Bolme, B.A. Draper, and M. Teixeira. The CSU face identification evaluation system. *Machine Vision and Applications*, 16:128–138, 2005.

5. C.M. Bishop. *Neural Networks for Pattern Recognition*. Oxford University Press, 1995.

6. A. Björck. *Numerical Methods for Least Squares Problems*. SIAM: Society or Industrial and Applied Mathematics, 1996.

7. M. Boyle, C. Edwards, and S. Greenberg. The effects of filtered video on awareness and privacy. In *ACM Conference on Computer Supported Cooperative Work*, pages 1–10, Philadelphia, PA, December 2000.

8. Y. Chang, R. Yan, D. Chen, and J. Yang. People identification with limited labels in privacy-protected video. In *International Conference on Multimedia and Expo (ICME)*, 2006.

9. T. Cootes, G. Edwards, and C.J. Taylor. Active appearance models. *IEEE Transaction on Pattern Analysis and Machine Intelligence*, 23(6), 2001.

10. J. Crowley, J. Coutaz, and F. Berard. Things that see. *Communications of the ACM*, 43(3):54–64, 2000.

11. F. Dufaux, M. Ouaret, Y. Abdeljaoued, A. Navarro, F. Vergnenegre, and T. Ebrahimi. Privacy enabling technology for video surveillance. In *Proceedings of the SPIE 6250*, 2006.

12. D.A. Fidaleo, H.-A. Nguyen, and M. Trivedi. The networked sensor tapestry (NeST): A privacy enhanced software architecture for interactive analysis of data in video-sensor networks. In *Proceedings of the ACM 2nd International Workshop on Video Surveillance and Sensor Networks*, 2004.

13. R. Gross. *Face De-Identification using Multi-Factor Active Appearance Models*. PhD thesis, Carnegie Mellon University, 2008.

14. R. Gross, E. Airoldi, B. Malin, and L. Sweeney. Integrating utility into face de-identification. In *Workshop on Privacy Enhancing Technologies (PET)*, June 2005.

15. R. Gross, I. Matthews, J. Cohn, T. Kanade, and S. Baker. Multi-PIE. In *8th International Conference on Automatic Face and Gesture Recognition*, 2008.

16. R. Gross, L. Sweeney, F. de la Torre, and S. Baker. Model-based face de-identification. In *IEEE Workshop on Privacy Research in Vision*, 2006.

17. R. Gross, L. Sweeney, T. de la Torre, and S. Baker. Semi-supervised learning of multi-factor models for face de-identification. In *IEEE International Conference on Computer Vision and Pattern Recognition (CVPR)*, 2008.

18. S. Hudson and I. Smith. Techniques for addressing fundamental privacy and disruption trade-offs in awareness support systems. In *ACM Conference on Computer Supported Cooperative Work*, pages 1–10, Boston, MA, November 1996.

19. I.T. Jolliffe. *Principal Component Analysis*. Springer, second edition, 2002.

20. T. Koshimizu, T. Toriyama, and N. Babaguchi. Factors on the sense of privacy in video surveillance. In *Proceedings of the 3rd ACM Workshop on Continuous Archival and Retrival of Personal Experiences*, pages 35–44, 2006.

21. I. Martinez-Ponte, X. Desurmont, J. Meessen, and J.-F. Delaigle. Robust human face hiding ensuring privacy. In *Workshop on the Integration of Knowledge, Semantics and Digital Media Technology (WIAMIS)*, 2005.

22. I. Matthews and S. Baker. Active appearance models revisited. *International Journal of Computer Vision*, 60(2):135–164, 2004.

23. C. Neustaedter and S. Greenberg. Balancing privacy and awareness in home media spaces. In *Workshop on Ubicomp Communities: Privacy as Boundary Negotiation*, 2003.

24. C. Neustaedter, S. Greenberg, and M. Boyle. Blur filtration fails to preserve privacy for home-based video conferencing. *ACM Transactions on Computer Human Interactions (TOCHI)*, 2005.

25. E. Newton, L. Sweeney, and B. Malin. Preserving privacy by de-identifying facial images. *IEEE Transactions on Knowledge and Data Engineering*, 17(2):232–243, 2005.

26. P.J. Phillips, H. Moon, S. Rizvi, and P.J Rauss. The FERET evaluation methodology for face-recognition algorithms. *IEEE Transaction on Pattern Analysis and Machine Intelligence*, 22(10):1090–1104, 2000.
27. H. Schneiderman and T. Kanade. Object detection using the statistics of parts. *International Journal of Computer Vision*, 56(3):151–177, 2002.
28. B. Schoelkopf and A. Smola. *Learning with Kernels: Support Vector Machines, Regularization, Optimization, and Beyond*. MIT Press, 2001.
29. C. Stauffer and W.E.L. Grimson. Adaptive background mixture models for real-time tracking. In *IEEE International Conference on Computer Vision and Pattern Recognition (CVPR)*, 1998.
30. L. Sweeney. k-anonymity: A model for protecting privacy. *International Journal on Uncertainty, Fuzziness, and Knowledge-Based Systems*, 10(5):557–570, 2002.
31. S. Tansuriyavong and S-I. Hanaki. Privacy protection by concealing persons in circumstantial video image. In *Proceedings of the 2001 Workshop on Perceptive User Interfaces*, 2001.
32. D. Taubman and M. Marcellin. *JPEG 2000: Image Compression Fundamentals, Standards and Practice*. Kluwer Academic Publishers, 2002.
33. J.B. Tenenbaum and W. Freeman. Separating style and content with bilinear models. *Neural Computation*, 12(6):1247–1283, 2000.
34. F. de la Torre and M. Black. A framework for robust subspace learning. *International Journal of Computer Vision*, 54(1–3):117–142, 2003.
35. K. Toyama, J. Krumm, B. Brumitt, and B. Meyers. Wallflower: Principles and practice of background maintenance. In *IEEE International Conference on Computer Vision*, pages 255–261, 1999.
36. M. Vasilescu and D. Terzopoulous. Multilinear subspace analysis of image ensembles. In *Computer Vision and Pattern Recognition*, 2003.
37. P. Viola and M. Jones. Rapid object detection using a boosted cascade of simple features. In *IEEE International Conference on Computer Vision and Pattern Recognition (CVPR)*, 2001.
38. J. Wickramasuriya, M. Alhazzazi, M. Datt, S. Mehrotra, and N. Venkatasubramanian. Privacy-protecting video surveillance. In *SPIE International Symposium on Electronic Imaging (Real-Time Imaging IX)*, 2005.
39. C. Wren, A. Azarbayejani, T. Darrell, and A. Pentland. Pfinder: Real-time tracking of the human body. *IEEE Transactions on Pattern Analysis and Machine Learning*, 19(7): 780–785, 1997.
40. Q. Zhao and J. Stasko. Evaluating image filtering based techniques in media space applications. In *ACM Conference on Computer Supported Cooperative Work*, pages 11–18, Seattle, WA, November 1998.

Psychological Study for Designing Privacy Protected Video Surveillance System: PriSurv

Noboru Babaguchi, Takashi Koshimizu, Ichiro Umata and Tomoji Toriyama

Abstract As video surveillance systems are widely deployed, concerns continue to grow about invasion of privacy. We have built a privacy protected video surveillance system called PriSurv. Although PriSurv protects subject privacy using image processing, criteria of controlling the subject's visual information that is privacy-sensitive should be clarified. Visual information must be disclosed by considering the trade-off between privacy and security. The level of privacy-sensitive visual information that could be disclosed to a viewer is simply called disclosable privacy in this chapter. Disclosable privacy, which deeply involves the personal sense, is affected by many factors. A sense of privacy is individual, but in some cases it might have common factors. In this chapter, we analyze what factors determine and affect disclosable privacy by applying statistical analysis to questionnaire-based experimental results. These results indicate that disclosable privacy is concerned with how much a subject has feeling of closeness to a viewer and expects the viewer's responsibility. They also show that disclosable privacy differs greatly by individuals. Reflecting the obtained findings in PriSurv's design, we adapt PriSurv to reflect a personal sense of privacy.

1 Introduction

To prevent crime and insure public security, video surveillance cameras are being deployed not only in private spaces but also in public spaces. As video surveillance cameras become ubiquitous, concerns continue to grow over possible invasions of privacy [13, 18]. To address the privacy problem, we propose a privacy protected video surveillance system called PriSurv [1, 7]. We assume that PriSurv will be used in a small community composed of general and authorized members. Such communities might include apartment buildings, offices, schools, school zones, residential areas, and so on. In the community, the members can watch each other;

N. Babaguchi (✉)

Department of Communication Engineering, Osaka University, Suita, Osaka 565-0871, Japan
e-mail: babaguchi@comm.eng.osaka-u.ac.jp

A. Senior (ed.), *Protecting Privacy in Video Surveillance*,
DOI 10.1007/978-1-84882-301-3_9, © Springer-Verlag London Limited 2009

members are both subjects of the surveillance videos and viewers at the monitor. PriSurv adaptively protects member's privacy by controlling visual information using image processing. In PriSurv, a subject's appearance in the surveillance video can be changed, depending on the identity of the viewer.

To control visual information based on a personal sense of privacy, the criterion must be clarified for deciding how much visual information is disclosed. Visual information must be disclosed by considering the trade-off between privacy and security. The level of privacy-sensitive visual information that could be disclosed to a viewer is simply called disclosable privacy in this chapter. Disclosable privacy, which deeply involves the personal sense, is affected by many factors. A sense of privacy is individual, but in some cases it might have common factors. Therefore, a psychological approach is required to scrutinize privacy sense.

In this chapter, we clarify the criterion for controlling visual information in accordance with a subject's disclosable privacy by analyzing what influences disclosable privacy. Based on the experimental results, we modify the design principles of PriSurv. We conclude that PriSurv must be adaptable to the personal differences of disclosable privacy as well as to the relation between the viewer and subject, because PriSurv is used by the members themselves of a small community to watch over those of their community.

The rest of this chapter is organized as follows. Section 2 surveys related video surveillance and privacy protection work. In Section 3, we overview PriSurv and describe visual abstraction. In Section 4, we conduct psychological analysis of disclosable privacy through questionnaire-based experiments. In Section 5, we consider our obtained findings about PriSurv's design. Finally, Section 6 concludes this work.

2 Related Work

Video surveillance technologies have attracted great attention and become controversial after the September 11 terrorist attacks on the USA [2]. In particular, the face recognition algorithms implemented in some video surveillance systems increased privacy concerns [5]. Several research projects attempted to prevent face recognition to preserve privacy [8, 16]. Newton et al. [16], Cavallaro et al. [4], and Kitahara et al. [10] proposed methods for protecting subject privacy by such image processing as blurring and mosaicing. Boyle et al. [3] analyzed how a blur and a pixelized video filter impacted both awareness and privacy in a media space. Chang et al. [6] discussed how face masked images for privacy protection can be used to identify people. Wickramasuriya et al. [20] implemented a privacy-preserving surveillance system using RFID tags and image processing. Their study deals with privacy problems associated with simple access control in a room. Senior et al. [18] suggested a method of reconstructing an image using information extracted from the captured image and other sensors to remove privacy information. Zhang et al. [21] proposed a method for embedding privacy information using digital watermarking technology. The embedded information can only be obtained by authorized viewers. Sekiguchi et al. [17] considered more appropriate privacy protection and proposed a system to protect subject privacy in accordance with the requests of viewers and subjects in which more emphasis is placed on the viewer's request than the subject's request for practical use of the surveillance system.

Unfortunately, a personal sense of privacy was barely considered in the existing systems, because viewers are limited to such authorized viewers as police officers and security personnel. Extending the kinds of viewers, we consider flexible privacy protection based on the relation between viewers and subjects. Our goal is to elaborate PriSurv's design through a psychological study [15] that analyzes disclosable privacy to adapt it to a personal sense of privacy.

3 PriSurv

We assume that PriSurv will be used by small communities to watch themselves in their small communities in an area comprised of such persons who are relied on as close friends and family.

Figure 1 shows a schematic image of PriSurv that consists of the following four modules:

Sensor: Consists of surveillance cameras and sensors to obtain personal IDs.

Analyzer: Generates stratified images, each of which corresponds to each subject with an assigned his/her ID from the Sensor.

Abstractor: Controls visual information using privacy protected image processing called *visual abstraction* [7, 12].

Access Controller: Determines which kind of visual abstraction is applied based on the relation between the subject and the viewer.

These modules control the visual information for all subjects based on their disclosable privacy. Registered viewers can watch the original or visually abstracted

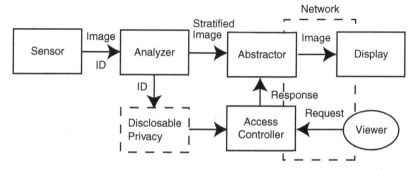

Fig. 1 Schematic image of PriSurv

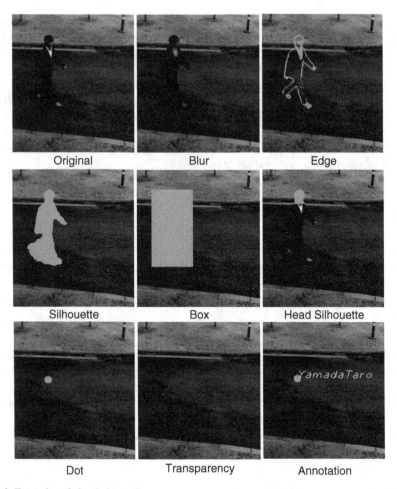

Fig. 2 Examples of visual abstraction

video through networks. Specifically, the subject's appearance in the video can be changed depending on who the viewer is.

Figure 2 shows several examples of processed images using visual abstraction. Here, the name of each abstraction operator is augmented to each image. In particular, *Original* means no abstraction is performed; *Transparency* means a subject is removed from the image/video; *Annotation* means that only the subject's attributes are displayed while hiding her/his appearance. To generate visually abstracted images, background subtraction and stratification are taken into consideration. Background subtraction enables us to separate background and foreground. All foreground subjects are divided into stratified images, each of which corresponds to a subject. The stratified image is processed by such abstraction operators as silhouette, edge, and dot (Fig. 2) to hide the subject's visual information. For details of visual abstraction, see [7].

4 Psychological Analysis of Disclosable Privacy

Through questionnaire-based experiments, we clarify the criterion for controlling visual information in accordance with a subject's disclosable privacy. The results of our previous experiment that involved 32 women ranging from ages 20 to 39 showed that disclosable privacy is affected by the closeness between subjects and viewers [11]. In addition, our preliminary survey with 52 subjects ranging from 20 to 59 showed that people in their 50 s are less sensitive to privacy than those in their 20–40 s. Because PriSurv's aim is to flexibly protect the privacy of subjects who are sensitive to privacy issues, we conducted an experiment involving 187 subjects in their 20–40 s. The age and gender composition is shown in Table 1. Although disclosable privacy was assumed to be affected not only by a one-to-one relation between a subject and a viewer but also by a many-to-one relation between multiple subjects and a viewer, we focused on the one-to-one relation in this experiment. We tested our hypotheses about disclosable privacy using factor analysis to survey at large [14] and cluster analysis to learn the differences among groups.

Table 1 Age and gender composition of subjects

Age	Men	Women
20 s	32	30
30 s	32	33
40 s	30	30
Total	94	93

4.1 Hypotheses and Questionnaires

We denoted our four hypotheses as H1, H2, H3, and H4 as follows:

H1: A subject's disclosable privacy is positively correlated with subject's closeness to a viewer.

H2: A viewer's responsibility expected by a subject is positively correlated with subject's closeness to the viewer.

H3: A subject's disclosable privacy is positively correlated with a viewer's responsibility expected by the subject .

H4: A subject's disclosable privacy is individual.

We conducted an experiment using a questionnaire that consisted of instructions, six questions, and five abstracted images. The following instructions were provided:

The subjects live in a condominium 10 min on foot from the train station. Video surveillance cameras, controlled by the condominium's neighborhood watch group, are located along the street from the station at intervals of 30 m. Members of the neighborhood watch group monitor the videos on a rotating basis. If monitors find that someone in the video is endangered, they can sound an alarm attached to the video surveillance cameras to inform people of an emergency.

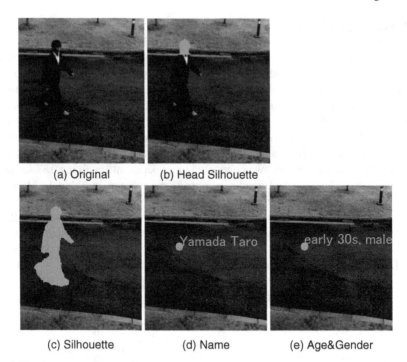

(a) Original   (b) Head Silhouette

(c) Silhouette   (d) Name   (e) Age&Gender

Fig. 3 Five images used in questionnaires

Figure 3 shows the five abstracted images used in the questionnaire. Figures 3 (a–e) are called *Original*, *Head Silhouette*, *Silhouette*, *Name*, and *Age&Gender*, respectively. *Name* and *Age&Gender* are attached annotations. Among the images here, (a) is most disclosing, and (e) is least disclosing.

Let us describe how the questionnaire was given. First, it asked the subjects to imagine four persons encountered in daily life from the most close acquaintance to the least close acquaintance. The four persons are designated as A, B, C, and D from close to not-close. In addition, the police officer and the security guard are designated as P and W, respectively. Next, the subjects were asked the following questions Q1, ..., Q6 if the viewer is either A, B, C, D, P, or W. Q2, Q4, Q5, and Q6 were rated on a seven-point scale: 7 is the greatest, and 1 is the least extent.

Q1: Choose one image to show the viewer from (a) to (e) in Fig. 3 when A, B, C, D, P, or W is watching.

Q2: How much do you feel your privacy is protected when A, B, C, D, P, or W is watching with the images selected at Q1?

Q3: Do you think that a viewer could identify you with the images selected at Q1?

Q4: How much do you feel a viewer has a responsibility to watch you when A, B, C, D, P, or W is watching?

Q5: How much do you feel a responsibility to watch A, B, C, or D when you are watching them?

Q6: How much do you feel a viewer would protect you in an emergency when A, B, C, D, P, or W is watching?

4.2 Analysis of Experimental Results and Discussion

First, we calculated the distribution and the average of the answers for each A, B, C, D, P, or W viewer. Figure 4 shows the distribution of the selected images for each viewer asked at Q1. Figure 4 indicates that subjects selected more *Original* to close persons A and B, and fewer *Original* and more *Silhouette* to not-close persons C and D. To understand the selection of images related to privacy protection, Fig. 5 shows the distribution of selected images Q1 with the average of privacy protection asked at Q2. Figure 5 shows that subjects select images with much visual information to the most close person A, even though they do not feel that their privacy is protected. On the other hand, Fig. 5 shows that subjects select images with little visual information to the most not-close person D because they feel that their privacy is protected. These figures support hypothesis H1: a subject's disclosable privacy is positively correlated with subject's closeness to a viewer.

Next, the average Q4, Q5, and Q6 scores were calculated to investigate the relation between closeness to a viewer and responsibility to watch. Figure 6 shows the average scores of Q4, Q5, and Q6 for each viewer. We found a significant correlation by Pearson's product-moment correlation coefficient. The significance was always 0.999. Table 2 shows the Pearson's product-moment correlation coefficient and significance probability. Pearson's product-moment correlation coefficient reflects

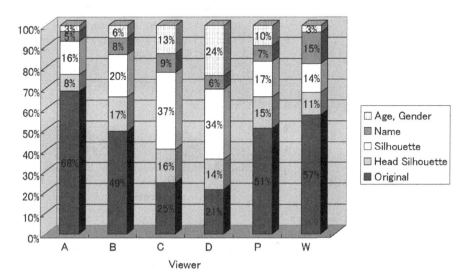

Fig. 4 Selected images for each viewer: A, B, C, D, P, or W

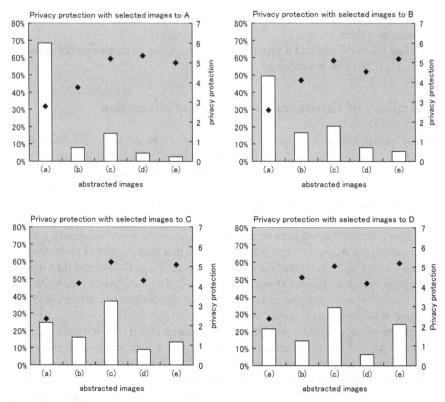

Fig. 5 Selected images and privacy protection

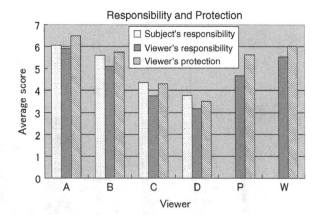

Fig. 6 Average scores of Q4, Q5, and Q6

the degree of linear relationship between two variables ranging from -1 to $+1$. In this case, the variables mean the answers to the questions. The significance level is defined as the probability of deciding to reject the null hypothesis when it is actually true. This decision is often made using significance probability: if the significance probability is less than the significance level, then the null hypothesis is rejected.

Table 2 Pearson's product-moment correlation coefficient

		A	B	C	D
Q4 and Q5	Pearson's product-moment correlation coefficient	0.845	0.787	0.617	0.688
	significance probability	0.000	0.000	0.000	0.000
Q4 and Q6	Pearson's product-moment correlation coefficient	0.345	0.345	0.374	0.524
	significance probability	0.000	0.000	0.000	0.000
Q5 and Q6	Pearson's product-moment correlation coefficient	0.420	0.465	0.520	0.532
	significance probability	0.000	0.000	0.000	0.000

As the significance probability gets smaller, the result becomes more significant. Table 2 shows the correlation between the pair of Q4, Q5, and Q6 for each viewer.

Further, this result shows that the viewer's responsibility expected by subjects (Q4), subject's responsibility to watch (Q5), and protection expected by subjects (Q6) are all positively correlated with closeness to the viewer. This result supports hypothesis H2: a viewer's responsibility expected by a subject is positively correlated with subject's closeness to the viewer.

We then performed factor analysis of Q2, Q4, Q5, and Q6 results. Factors were extracted using the principal factor method, and varimax rotation with Kaiser Normalization [9] was adopted. Seven factors were extracted by considering the decay of the eigenvalues.

Figure 7 shows factor loading after varimax rotation. Factor loading indicates how much the factor affected the questions. Note that when the factor loading values

Questions	Factor 1 Not-close Responsibility Factor	Factor 2 Close Responsibility Factor	Factor 3 Protection Prospect Factor	Factor 4 Duty Responsibility Factor	Factor 5 Not-close Privacy Factor	Factor 6 Close Privacy Factor	Factor 7 Duty Privacy Factor
Q5(D)	**0.837**	-0.015	0.031	0.212	0.037	0.035	0.003
Q4(D)	**0.780**	0.027	0.073	0.115	-0.074	-0.030	-0.059
Q5(C)	**0.765**	0.218	0.144	0.075	0.030	0.014	0.015
Q4(C)	**0.713**	0.320	0.076	0.047	-0.102	-0.057	0.023
Q5(A)	-0.018	**0.891**	0.163	-0.001	0.032	0.023	-0.090
Q4(A)	-0.001	**0.879**	0.121	0.112	0.006	0.001	-0.054
Q4(B)	0.292	**0.830**	0.085	0.054	-0.068	-0.050	0.023
Q5(B)	0.341	**0.755**	0.170	0.052	0.009	-0.043	-0.006
Q6(C)	0.434	0.087	**0.754**	0.066	0.084	0.059	-0.029
Q6(B)	0.116	0.309	**0.663**	0.030	0.093	-0.081	0.111
Q6(A)	-0.182	0.295	**0.623**	0.096	0.134	0.022	0.021
Q6(D)	0.525	0.055	**0.544**	0.212	0.127	0.068	-0.072
Q6(P)	0.232	-0.061	**0.500**	0.484	-0.017	0.023	-0.033
Q5(W)	0.125	0.188	-0.063	**0.788**	0.093	0.035	-0.035
Q5(P)	0.366	0.026	0.058	**0.695**	0.091	0.092	-0.087
Q6(W)	-0.001	0.012	0.366	**0.671**	0.021	-0.061	-0.029
Q2(D)	-0.035	0.014	0.139	0.097	**0.885**	0.010	0.167
Q2(C)	-0.013	-0.027	0.117	0.074	**0.867**	0.236	0.126
Q2(B)	0.027	-0.009	0.052	0.039	0.252	**0.912**	0.124
Q2(A)	-0.028	-0.036	-0.041	0.027	-0.004	**0.805**	0.315
Q2(W)	-0.026	-0.079	0.036	-0.065	0.085	0.310	**0.858**
Q2(P)	-0.017	-0.030	0.012	-0.076	0.213	0.128	**0.833**

Fig. 7 Factor loading after varimax rotation

Table 3 Factor contribution, contribution ratio after rotation, and Cronbach's coefficient α

	Factor contribution	Contribution ratio (%)	Cumulative ratio (%)	α
Not-close responsibility factor	3.32	15.1	15.1	0.847
Close responsibility factor	3.22	14.6	29.7	0.920
Protection prospect factor	2.23	10.1	39.9	0.806
Duty responsibility factor	1.96	8.9	48.8	0.793
Not-close privacy factor	1.74	7.9	56.7	0.900
Close privacy factor	1.69	7.7	64.4	0.872
Duty privacy factor	1.63	7.4	71.8	0.879

on some questions are higher than other questions, the factor strongly affected the questions. Table 3 shows the factor contribution, i.e., the contribution ratio after rotation and Cronbach's coefficient α calculated from the interpretation questions. Factor contribution is a square sum of factor loading that indicates how much the factor covers the whole questionnaire. We can see the degrees of the effect of each factor on the whole questionnaire from Table 3.

The following seven factors cover 70% of the variability in the questionnaire because the sum of the factor contribution is 71.8%. Factors with loading greater than 0.48 were subjects for analysis and are named based on our interpretation as follows:

Factor 1: *Not-close Responsibility Factor* is characterized by high loading on the subject's responsibility to watch a not-close person and the not-close person's responsibility expected by subjects.

Factor 2: *Close Responsibility Factor* is characterized by high loading on the subject's responsibility to watch a close person and the close person's responsibility expected by subjects.

Factor 3: *Protection Prospect Factor* is characterized by high loading on the protection expected by subjects.

Factor 4: *Duty Responsibility Factor* is characterized by high loading on the police officer and the security guard's responsibility and the protection expected by subjects.

Factor 5: *Not-close Privacy Factor* is characterized by high loading on the privacy protection if the not-close person is watching.

Factor 6: *Close Privacy Factor* is characterized by high loading on privacy protection if the close person is watching.

Factor 7: *Duty Privacy Factor* is characterized by high loading on privacy protection if the police officer or the security guard is watching.

The factor analysis results indicate that the viewer related to the factors is classified into three groups: close persons A and B; not-close persons C and D; persons on duty P and W. This classification is observed especially on factors related to responsibility and privacy protection.

Table 4 Cluster details

Cluster	Number	Average age	Ratio of men	Ratio of women
C1	58	31.6	0.47	0.53
C2	84	34.9	0.49	0.51
C3	23	32.7	0.43	0.57
C4	22	36.5	0.50	0.50
total	187	33.8	0.50	0.50

After factor analysis, we conducted a hierarchical cluster analysis on the Q1 score to investigate individuality for selecting images. The Ward method [19] was applied to link groups. Considering their size, we adopted four clusters to specify the individuality of the selected images. The number of people belonging to each cluster is indicated in Table 4. Clusters are designated as C1, C2, C3, and C4. Clusters C1, C2, C3, and C4 have 58, 84, 23, and 22 people, respectively. The average age of each cluster is indicated, but no significant age difference was found by t-test. Gender is almost evenly distributed in all clusters.

To investigate the tendency of selecting images, the percentage of selected images for each viewer for each cluster is shown in Fig. 8. Figure 8 shows the following tendencies:

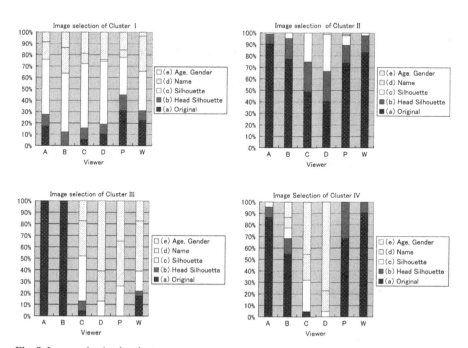

Fig. 8 Image selection by clusters

C1: C1 selects images with little visual information such as *Silhouette* except for persons on duty P and W.

C2: C2 selects images with a lot of visual information such as *Original* and *Head Silhouette* to all viewers.

C3: C3 selects images with a lot of visual information such as *Original* only to close persons A and B.

C4: C4 selects images with a lot of information to *close* persons A and B and persons on duty P and W, while with little information to *not-close* persons C and D.

Each cluster has a clear feature for selecting images. This shows that disclosable privacy differs greatly among individuals. The result supports hypothesis H4: a subject's disclosable privacy is individual.

Next, we investigate other features of the clusters to determine the different reasons for selecting images, especially related to the seven factors extracted by factor analysis. First, the relation between the clusters and the seven factors was considered. We introduce a subscale score in terms of the average score of the questions used to analyze the factors. The subscale score is calculated for each factor for each subject. For instance, a subscale score of *Not-close Responsibility Factor* is calculated by the sum of the scores of Q4 and Q5 when C and D are viewers divided by four, the number of questions. Then we compare the average subscale scores by applying analysis of variance (ANOVA), a technique for comparing the means of two or more groups based on variance.

Table 5 shows the ANOVA results for each factor and each cluster. The average subscale score, the F value, and significance probability are shown in Table 5. The bold values are significantly different compared to the other clusters. The F value measures the distance between individual distributions used by ANOVA .

The ANOVA results show significant differences on the significant level of 0.05 or 0.01 among clusters of the five factors: *Not-close Responsibility Factor*, *Close Responsibility Factor*, *Not-close Privacy Factor*, *Close Privacy Factor*, and *Duty Privacy Factor*.

In addition, multiple comparisons are conducted by a Bonferroni *t*-test for these factors. Table 6 shows the difference of the average subscale scores, standard error, and significance probability between the pairs of the clusters with significant differences. For example, the difference of the average subscale score of *Not-close Responsibility Factor* between C2 and C3 is 0.7966, and the significance probability is 0.045.

We can derive the following features for clusters C1 to C4:

C1: The average subscale score of the *Close Responsibility Factor* is significantly lower than the other clusters, and the average subscale score of the *Close Privacy Factor* is significantly higher than the other clusters.

C2: The average subscale score of the *Not-close Responsibility Factor* is significantly higher than C3, and the average subscale score of the *Not-close Privacy Factor* is significantly lower than the other clusters.

Table 5 ANOVA results

	Average subscale score					F value	Significance probability
	C1	C2	C3	C4	Total		
Not-close responsibility factor	3.6509	**4.0357**	**3.2391**	3.5682	3.7634	3.000	**0.032**
Close responsibility factor	**5.2069**	5.8512	5.8152	6.0568	5.1337	4.006	**0.009**
Protection prospect factor	5.0414	5.2881	4.9652	4.9636	5.1337	1.169	0.323
Duty responsibility factor	5.3966	5.6131	4.9891	5.5795	5.4652	2.106	0.101
Not-close privacy factor	4.8966	**3.6369**	4.8478	4.6818	4.2995	8.774	**0.000**
Close privacy factor	**4.7500**	2.9107	2.8913	3.4091	3.5374	14.197	**0.000**
Duty privacy factor	3.9483	**2.8036**	**4.8913**	3.2727	3.4706	11.832	**0.000**

Table 6 Bonferroni *t*-test results

Factor	Cluster		Average difference	Standard error	Significance probability
Not-close responsibility factor	C2	C3	0.7966	0.2948	0.045
Close responsibility factor	C1	C2	−0.6443	0.2145	0.018
		C4	−0.8499	0.3146	0.045
Not-close		C1	−1.2597	0.2738	0.000
privacy	C2	C3	−1.2109	0.3774	0.009
factor		C4	−1.0449	0.38404	0.043
Close		C2	1.8393	0.2962	0.000
privacy	C1	C3	1.8587	0.4276	0.000
factor		C4	1.3409	0.4345	0.014
Duty	C2	C1	−1.1447	0.2835	0.000
privacy		C3	−2.0877	0.4092	0.000
factor	C3	C4	1.6186	0.4953	0.008

C3: The average subscale score of the *Not-close Responsibility Factor* is significantly lower than C1, and the average subscale score of the *Duty Privacy Factor* is significantly high. The average subscale score of the *Duty Responsibility Factor* is the lowest of the four clusters.

C4: The average subscale score of the *Close Responsibility Factor* is significantly higher than C1, and the average subscale score of the *Close Privacy Factor* is significantly lower than C1. The average subscale score of the *Not-close Responsibility Factor* tends to be low, and the average score of the *Not-close Privacy Factor* is significantly higher than C2.

We interpreted these features with the image selection in Fig. 8 as follows:

C1: C1 selects images with little visual information to the close persons, because C1 does not expect their responsibility. So C1 feels that privacy is protected.

C2: C2 selects images with a lot of visual information to the not-close persons, because C2 expects their responsibility. So C2 feels that privacy is not protected.

C3: C3 selects images with little information about not-close persons and persons on duty, because C3 does not expect their responsibility. So C3 feels that privacy is protected.

C4: C4 selects images with a lot of visual information to the close persons, because C4 expects their responsibility. So C4 feels that privacy is not protected.

These results support hypothesis H3: a subject's disclosable privacy is positively correlated with a viewer's responsibility expected by the subject.

Through all of these analyses, all the hypotheses mentioned in Section 4.1 are supported.

5 Reflected Findings in PriSurv Design

We collected the obtained findings that must be reflected in the PriSurv design as follows:

- Visual information must be controlled based on closeness and responsibility because disclosable privacy is positively correlated with closeness to a viewer and the viewer's responsibility expected by subjects.
- The system must be capable of configuring the personal preferences of image selection because disclosable privacy is individual.
- It is appropriate to control visual information based on viewer's responsibility expected by subjects because in some groups responsibility shows more stable features.

Based on these findings, we refined the schematic image of PriSurv from Figs. 1, 2, 3, 4, 5, 6, 7, 8, and 9. Figure 9 shows the refined schematic image of PriSurv. Subjects can register a "Privacy Policy" that reflects their personal disclosable privacy to adapt to the differences of responsibility and image preferences. Privacy Policy, which describes the kinds of abstracted images depending on the viewer's responsibility expected by subjects, is saved in the Profile Base. To keep the Privacy Policy simple, a responsibility table describes the expected viewer's responsibility one by one. An example of the Privacy Policy is shown in Fig. 10 and is described with XML. Note that the descriptions contain abstraction operators based on viewer responsibility levels expected by subjects. The responsibility table has pairs of viewer responsibility levels and viewer IDs. When subjects are captured by

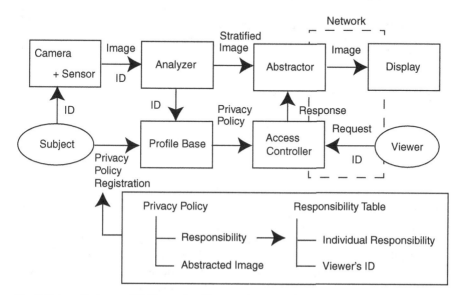

Fig. 9 Schematic image of PriSurv refined by experiment results

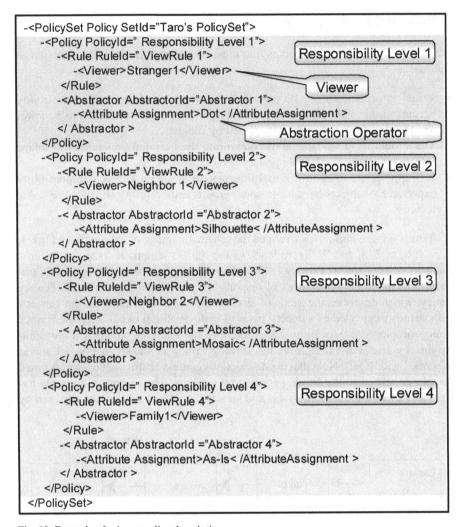

Fig. 10 Example of privacy policy description

video surveillance cameras, the Access Controller reads their Privacy Policy from the Profile Base and adaptively protects their privacy.

6 Conclusion

In this chapter, we investigated the criterion for controlling visual information in accordance with disclosable privacy. Our four hypotheses about sense of privacy were confirmed through questionnaire-based experiments and statistical analysis. Analysis of the experimental results revealed that closeness to a viewer, viewer's responsibility expected by a subject, and abstracted images affected the subject's disclosable privacy. The obtained findings were used to modify PriSurv's design to harmonize it with a personal sense of privacy.

In our experiment, we focused on a one-to-one relation between a subject and a viewer as disclosable privacy; practically it must be considered based on the relation between subjects captured on the surveillance video and a viewer. On the other hand, still images with visual abstraction as shown in Fig. 3 were used in our experiment. Ideally abstracted videos should be considered because people's reactions to videos and still images might be different. Abstracted videos might convey more information than their corresponding still images. Additional analysis from this viewpoint is of our interest. Future work will further investigate the pros and cons of monitoring the abstracted images and the relation between image analysis error and privacy protection.

Acknowledgments This work was supported in part by the Strategic Information and Communications R&D Promotion Programme (SCOPE).

References

1. Babaguchi, N.: Video Surveillance Considering Privacy. In: IPSJ Magazine, Vol. 48, No. 1, pp. 30–36. (2007)
2. Bowyer, K.W.: Face Recognition Technology: Security Versus Privacy. In: IEEE Technology and Society Magazine, vol. 23, No. 1, pp. 9–19. (2004)
3. Boyle, M., Edwards, C., and Greenberg, S.: The Effects of Filtered Video on Awareness and Privacy. In: Proc. of CSCW'00, pp. 1–10, ACM Press. (2000)
4. Cavallaro, A., Steiger, O., and Ebrahimi, T.: Semantic Video Analysis for Adaptive Content Delivery and Automatic Description. In: IEEE Trans. Circuits and Systems for Video Technology, Vol. 15, No. 10, pp. 1200–1209. (2005)
5. Cass, S. and Riezenman, M.J.: Improving Security, Preserving Privacy. In: IEEE Spectrum, Vol. 39, No. 1, pp. 44–49. (2002)
6. Chang, Y., Yang, J., Chen, D., and Yan, R.: People Identification with Limited Labels in Privacy-Protected Video. In: Proc. of ICME2006. (2000)
7. Chinomi, K., Nitta, N., Ito, Y., and Babaguchi, N.: PriSurv: Privacy Protected Video Surveillance System Using Adaptive Visual Abstraction. In: Proc. 14th International Multimedia Modeling Conference, pp. 144–154. (2008)
8. Gross, R., Airoldi, E.M., Malin, B., and Sweeney, L.: Integrating Utility into Face De-identification. In: Proc. 5th Workshop on Privacy Enhancing Technologies, pp. 227–242. (2005)
9. Kaiser, H.K.: The Varimax Criterion for Analytic Rotation in Factor Analysis. In: Psychometrika, Vol. 23, 187–200. (1958)
10. Kitahara, I., Kogure, K., and Hagita, N.: Stealth Vision for Protecting Privacy. In: Proc. 17th International Conference on Pattern Recognition, Vol. 4, pp. 404–407. (2004)
11. Koshimizu, T., Toriyama, T., and Babaguchi, N.: Factors on the Sense of Privacy in Video Surveillance. In: Proc. 3rd ACM Workshop on Capture, Archival and Retrieval of Personal Experiences, pp. 35–43. (2006)
12. Koshimizu, T., Toriyama, T., Nishio, S., Babaguchi, N., and Hagita, N.: Visual Abstraction for Privacy Preserving Video Surveillance. In: Technical report of IEICE. PRMU, Vol. 2006, No. 25, pp. 247–252. (2006)
13. Langheinrich, M.: A Privacy Awareness System for Ubiquitous Computing Environments. In: Proc. 4th International Conference on Ubiquitous Computing, pp. 237–245. (2002)

14. Murakami, Y. and Murakami, C.: The Standardization of a Big Five Personality Inventory for Separate Generations. In: The Japanese Journal of Personality, Vol. 1, No. 8, pp. 32–42. (1999)
15. Murakami, Y. and Murakami, C.: Clinical Psychology Assessment Handbook, pp. 104–124, Kitaohji-Shobo. (2004)
16. Newton, E.M., Sweeney, L., and Malin, B.: Preserving Privacy by De-identifying Face Images. In: IEEE Trans. Knowledge and Data Engineering, Vol. 17, No. 2, pp. 232–243. (2005)
17. Sekiguchi, T. and Kato, H.: Proposal and Evaluation of Video-based Privacy Assuring System Based on the Relationship between Observers and Subjects (Development and Operation of Information Systems). In: Transactions of Information Processing Society of Japan, Vol. 47, No. 8, pp. 2660–2668. (2006)
18. Senior, A., Pankanti, S., Hampapur, A., Brown, L., Ying-Li Tian, Ekin, A., Connell, J., Chiao Fe Shu, and Lu, M.: Enabling Video Privacy Through Computer Vision. In: IEEE Security & Privacy Magazine, Vol. 3, No. 3, pp. 50–57. (2005)
19. Ward, J.H. and Hook, M. E.: Application of a Hierarchical Grouping Procedure to a Problem of Grouping Profiles. In: Educational and Psychological Measurement, Vol. 23, No. 1, pp. 69–82. (1963)
20. Wickramasuriya, J., Alhazzazi, M., Datt, M., Mehrotra, S., and Venkatasubramanian, N.: Privacy-protecting Video Surveillance. In: Proc. SPIE International Symposium on Electronic Imaging, Vol. 5671, pp. 64–75. (2005)
21. Zhang, W., Cheung, S.S., and Chen, M.: Hiding Privacy Information in Video Surveillance System. In: IEEE International Conference on Image Processing, pp. 868–871. (2005)

Selective Archiving: A Model for Privacy Sensitive Capture and Access Technologies

Gillian R. Hayes and Khai N. Truong

Abstract At times, people need or want a record of their previous experiences. Sometimes those records are media other than text-based descriptions or notes. At the same time, a world of constant capture invokes Orwellian fears of surveillance and monitoring in a modern digital Panopticon. Thus, the selective archiving model, in which data are constantly buffered but require explicit input to be archived, represents a compromise through which people can dynamically negotiate their own policies around control, privacy, information access, and comfort. Through multiple formative studies and two deployment studies of selective archiving technologies in very different spaces for very different reasons, we are able to tease out some significant themes about recording in everyday life. In this chapter, we discuss those issues as observed in this work and outline some areas of future research in selective archiving.

1 Introduction

Even under the most informal of circumstances, people may want a record of what occurred. They can use these records to augment their memories, to share experiences with others who were not present, to provide fodder for discussion, or simply to provide an archive for which future uses have not been clearly defined. Thus, many researchers have explored ways in which people can capture, either automatically or manually, the details of experiences. Abowd and Mynatt define the broad problem of capture and access as capturing information so that it can be successfully accessed later [1]. Truong identifies several areas for future exploration of capture and access including capture of information in inherently unstructured or informal settings [17]. In this chapter, we discuss these *natural environment* capture and access problems, which include privacy-sensitive capture of information in

G. R. Hayes (✉)
Department of Informatics, Donald Bren School of Information and Computer Science, University of California, Irvine, CA, USA
e-mail: gillianrh@ics.uci.edu

A. Senior (ed.), *Protecting Privacy in Video Surveillance*,
DOI 10.1007/978-1-84882-301-3_10, © Springer-Verlag London Limited 2009

unstructured, unexpected, and often informal situations so that it can be successfully accessed at a later date.

Capture of information can be extremely difficult when recording that data was not planned beforehand or when the setting is so informal and unstructured that it does not naturally afford recording. At the same time, archiving of information – particularly automatic or semi-automatic archiving – can severely impact individual agency and the ability to manage needs. In this work, we describe a privacy-sensitive solution to capturing data in these everyday situations. The underlying solution presented in this chapter is known as *selective archiving*, in which services are always on and available for recording but require some explicit action to archive data. If no such action is taken, recorded data is deleted automatically after a specified time.

This research focuses on the development and study of socially appropriate ways to archive data about important life experiences during unexpected and unstructured situations. This work involves three significant phases: formative studies to understand the data capture needs of particular populations of users in these situations; design and development of a technical architecture for capture and access in these settings coupled with design and development of applications for two specific domain problems; and evaluation of this solution as it pertains to these domain problems and the overall goal of sensitivity towards privacy, information access, and control-related concerns.

2 Related Work

Several research projects have explored buffering capture streams for quick, near-term review similar to the selective archiving model. Minneman et al. explored the use of near-term access of information captured during structured activity, meetings, with the Where-Were-We application, a service that captures video of the meeting activity [15]. This service allows users to access data from the captured streams during the meeting or much later. Prior to this work, however, Hindus and Schmandt created a near-term audio reminder service, known as Xcapture that provided a "digital tape loop" of audio for a single office and later telephone conversations through a regular PC interface [13]. Dietz et al. later provided a similar capability using the phone device itself as the interface for interacting with the captured audio [2]. The application allows the user to catch up to the live conversation by speeding up the playback using audio processing techniques. With others, we explored the potential usability, usefulness, and acceptability issues involved with the user always being able to review audio from her recent past on a mobile phone [9, 14, 16]. The Personal Audio Loop application (PAL) continuously records audio from the phone's microphone and stores the audio for a user-defined amount of time, allowing a user to replay recent audio snippets.

Video content also can be buffered, as demonstrated by the Where-Were-We application. The SenseCam application from Microsoft Research takes a photograph every few seconds to create a digital record of experiences [4]. The StartleCam application buffers video to capture interesting images of a user's surrounding after the system has detected a change in the user's emotional state [12]. To compensate for latency caused by the sensor as well as the processing of the data points, Startle-Cam buffers a very short amount of video content to allow the application to grab images from seconds ago, when the trigger point occurred.

We were motivated by all of these applications in the development of selective archiving and the Experience Buffers. Whereas each of these applications buffers a particular media, e.g., *video*, we created a model that better takes advantage of the affordances, both socially and technically, of selective archiving by providing an extensible architecture that can include or exclude any of these media types depending on the application and the particular sensitivities of the domain.

3 Selective Archiving as a Model for Recording

Selective archiving is a mechanism for recording that does not require users to pre-determine when they might want to record yet also does not result in the generation of large quantities of unusable or irrelevant or potentially harmful data. In this section, we describe the concept and motivation of selective archiving. We then briefly overview the prototype implementations used to probe and test the concepts of selective archiving. Finally, we describe the implementations of two applications (CareLog and BufferWare) that take advantage of selective archiving to provide needed records in unstructured and potentially sensitive settings.

3.1 Experience Buffers Architecture

The Experience Buffers Architecture (EBA) includes a collection of capture services embedded in an environment that do not archive information in and of themselves [11]. Rather, experience buffers save information for a certain period of time set by the users of the system. During the time period that the information is saved in the buffer, applications can use short range RF to wirelessly request some subset of the buffer's data. After this time has passed, the information disappears. In this way, users of mobile applications can take advantage of environmental capture services if and only if they are present in that environment at the time that the information is captured. They can retrospectively choose to archive a piece of information thereby leveraging the computer's ability to capture information not pre-determined to be of importance and the human's ability to notice that a salient moment has occurred. Currently implemented buffer services include collections of still photographs, video streams, audio streams, and inking. Future data that might be buffered would include sensor network data. Because the architecture is built in such a way that any signal coming in can be recorded to disk, indexed, and removed later as it "times out," any type of sensor data can be buffered that can be recorded in discrete chunks (e.g., one-second intervals).

3.2 CareLog: Selective Archiving in Special Education Classrooms

For children with severe behavior disorders, the implementation of an intervention to minimize problem behaviors can have dramatic effects on quality of life. Unfortunately, these children cannot explain what is causing the behavior (e.g., why they are hitting themselves and others). To get this information, behavior specialists carefully document the context surrounding the behavior and conduct Functional Behavioral Assessment (FBA). FBA in a clinical setting lacks ecological validity and can lead caregivers to the wrong conclusions and ineffective interventions. On the other hand, FBA undertaken in natural settings is very disruptive.

CareLog is a system for the recording of diagnostic behavioral data that allows for teacher control of data archiving and access while simultaneously offloading the burden of beginning those recordings at the appropriate time to capture the right information [7, 8]. CareLog supports the traditional FBA process augmented with additional rich media. Teachers use a simple remote interface that looks like the locking key fob of an automobile to actuate archiving of data to document both what occurred in the past and what is to occur in the future. When any button on that small mobile device is pressed, CareLog saves the media based on pre-configured classroom staff preferences. The teacher can review the incident in greater detail by clicking the "View" button, which produces an Incident Review

Fig. 1 The access interface allows teachers to view all four video streams and one audio feed simultaneously and provide the meta-data required for FBA

window in view mode (see Fig. 1). The reviewing interface includes automatically synchronized video feeds and pre-populated but editable lists of appropriate tags. CareLog also provides some automatic graphing capabilities to support quick evaluations. Users of CareLog can label incidents with extra tags, including antecedents, consequences, and other notes. The analysis interface provides the graphing capabilities traditionally needed in a functional analysis as well as the ability to "drill down" from the high level graphs into individual incidents and their media (see Fig. 2).

CareLog was deployed over 5 months at a special school for behavior disabilities [8]. Four teachers used both traditional and technology enhanced methods for conducting FBAs as part of this quasi-controlled study. The study design was a mix of within and between subjects designs in that each teacher experienced both experimental FBA conditions (within), but each student was only a subject of one FBA (between). The conditions were counterbalanced, with two teachers using the technology-enhanced FBA process first and two using the traditional method first. Teachers were randomly assigned to groups, and thus the students were randomly assigned to treatment conditions. Prior to conducting any

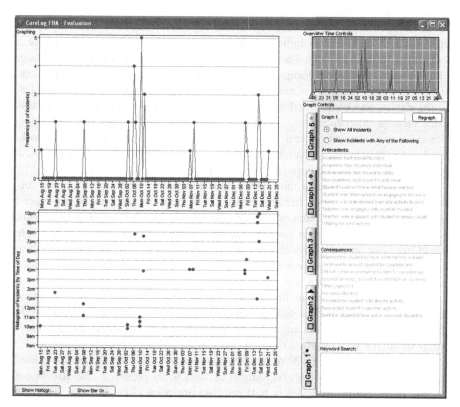

Fig. 2 The graphing and analysis interface. The *upper right* window shows an overview of the available data in graphical format as well as a zooming interface that controls the larger graphs to the *left*

FBAs, all teachers completed one day of in-service training on FBA and use of CareLog.

In each of the four classrooms involved in the study, the CareLog installation included four small webcams installed in ceiling area near the four corners of the classroom with a pen microphone in the ceiling near the center of the room. All other equipment was stacked on top of a bookcase along one wall of each room. Data was synchronized with a laptop to allow teachers and behavior experts to review data in the library, at home, or in any other location that might be more comfortable and quiet than the classroom.

As compared with traditional methods, teachers using CareLog were less error prone and reported reduced workload during the FBA. Furthermore, people used the tools to collaborate spontaneously and reported benefits to distributing work and problem solving across a wider range of individuals.

3.3 BufferWare: Selective Archiving in Semi-Public Spaces

In open and casual spaces, people might not be able to predict when events of interest will occur and often are not prepared for manual recording. To allow people to document such experiences, we designed and deployed a selective-archiving application (called BufferWare) in an informal space for almost 2 years. We chose a social area next to an open stairwell on the third floor of an academic building, which houses media-and-design, computer science, and engineering researchers. Most of the time, the space is unoccupied, but during the afternoon, all three tables, all the chairs, and some standing space are often filled. Typical activities in this space include small meetings, eating, and individual reading and work sessions. The space may also infrequently be used for group discussions unrelated to work, telephone conversations, eavesdropping on conversations on other floors, or as a spot for individuals and groups looking out the windows.

The area itself contained three tables next to three large erasable writing surfaces. We chose this space because it was open, informal, and public not closed off like meeting rooms, which other researchers have already studied. In particular, we embedded a touch-screen into the café table nearest the window, so that people would not have to walk through a recorded space to get to a non-recorded area. A single camera, attached to a PC via video and security cables, provided video recording of the table area. Finally, a microphone glued to the tabletop recorded sound within a space matching the camera viewing angle. The touch screen interface provided two buttons, one for saving and one for purging the data cache. Users could choose how much to save using a double slider. Users could access saved content online through a Web interface (see Fig. 3).

We first deployed BufferWare from September 2005 to June 2006. We posted signs and sent emails to alert building occupants to its presence. We also began logging requests to save or delete buffered data or review clips. In April 2006, we began using motion detectors to log motion in the space. Survey and interview input from the first deployment were used to identify initial usability problems, which we

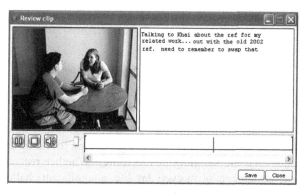

Fig. 3 The BufferWare system: (**a**) The recorded view of a café table nearest to the window augmented with touch screen to provide two buttons, one for saving and one for purging the data cache. (**b**) Users can choose how much to save using a double slider and can send the data to registered users

fixed. We then deployed the second version of BufferWare during September and October 2006. After the second deployment, we moved the BufferWare hardware, which included the camera, microphone, and touch screen interface. We continued to gather motion detector data for the next 30 days to record activity in the space after the equipment had been removed. Throughout this 2-year period, we distributed and collected two surveys (19 respondents for the first and 13 for the second from 100 distributed each time) and conducted 27 interviews regarding the use and understanding of the BufferWare deployment.

During this deployment study, we found that people use three types of knowledge to interpret and understand a new recording technology: physical, social, and experiential [10]. Physical knowledge refers to the portions of the design that are visible and physical and inform people about what a technology is and how to use it. Social knowledge is that embedded in a community, for example, the conventions, laws, and uses of the space. Social knowledge also includes the elements of trust and understanding – or suspicion and confusion – gathered from other social actors in the environment. Experiential knowledge includes the range of information from past experiences with new or similar technologies.

4 Impact of Selective Archiving Model for Recording

Selectively archived segments of data can provide an efficient way to recover and to analyze high quality data that traditionally available. The projects presented in this chapter provide insight about how we can support record-keeping in informal and unstructured settings in a balanced and sensitive way. Furthermore, when examined together, these projects provide a view into the larger generalized problem of unstructured capture and access and the acceptability of capture technologies. These considerations evolved into a set of seven tensions surrounding recording technologies that are presented in this chapter. In this section, we describe those tensions and point to how they should be used by designers of future recording technologies.

4.1 Ownership of Data

Knowing who owns and controls the data allows people to use other methods of negotiation outside of the technology itself (e.g., talking to the owner about what is saved and requesting the stopping of recording). Whether recording in pervasive computing environments or in everyday life, a significant challenge for those impacted by the recording, therefore, is determining who owns the data and by what means one negotiates with them. Issues surrounding who owns the data captured were plentiful throughout the CareLog and BufferWare projects. Furthermore, ownership of the recording equipment itself can signal ownership of the data in some cases.

Typically, in schools, when teachers record behavioral data, they are asked to do so by someone else. They often then turn those records over to the asking party for analysis. In the CareLog deployment, teachers were doing their own analysis. They frequently commented about the value of FBA that they had previously not seen, because they were merely the data collectors.

When discussing the videos that were saved with CareLog, teachers commented that they were very comfortable, because they were in control of the capture. They also knew where the data resided (on a non-networked set of computers in their classrooms). Even though they did not financially own these machines, they believed that they belonged to them temporarily and treated the data as their own. They were the only ones who would access the data for analysis purposes, and they could delete any video segment they had archived at any time. In essence, they could keep control of the data from the beginning to the end of its lifecycle. There was no question that the data belonged to the teacher in charge of the classroom. The non-teacher staff also appeared to recognize that the teacher owned the data collected with CareLog, and that could sometimes be a tension. Staff members would sometimes ask the teacher in the middle of an incident if she had clicked the button to invoke capture. At other times, both teachers and staff made comments that the teacher could request a clip upon walking back in the room after a short break and therefore observe activities that happened while away. In terms of problem solving about student behavior, this functionality is crucial to teachers being able to diagnose events when they are not present. In terms of staff perception, however, a very powerful tool was given to the teachers who are already managers of the entire classroom experience.

The potential concerns were typically resolved in several ways. Teachers often discussed the goals of the project and what was recorded with their staff. We regularly assured everyone involved – teachers and staff – that the records would only be used for the diagnosis and for my research and would not be shared with the principal or other administrative body. Teachers were also more comfortable bringing staff into the recording process when using CareLog than when using the pen and paper method. Thus, staff members were also sometimes given control of archiving, likely empowering them within the classroom and the FBA process and making them more comfortable with the video recording.

In the BufferWare deployment, ownership of the data was much less clear. In fact, we had established no real policy about it. Loosely put, our plan was to keep the data available as long as possible for the registered users, ending access and destroying it when we could no longer maintain access to it, emailing them when we were going to destroy it, and allowing them to keep the data themselves as allowed by Institute policy. Most of this information was never made public in the way of a formal retention and use policy. Instead, people were forced to rely on word of mouth, some simple signs, and policies posted on-line, as is prone to occur in the "real world."

Records were always saved to a particular account (or accounts). Thus, data were intended to be owned by the particular account holders, to be saved, reviewed, or deleted at will. However, little was published (and thus little was known) about where the actual server with the data resided. In fact, the data resided physically on two servers, both of which were in close proximity to the BufferWare space, but few people had this information. Thus, people often questioned where the data might be stored, who physically, legally, and logically owned it, and therefore, what might be done with it.

Perceptions about ownership of data can be complex and nuanced and are central to the acceptability of capture technologies. As researchers and designers in this area, it is crucial to understand three features of systems that might affect these perceptions:

- Physical indicators of data ownership, such as placement and physical access to the servers on which the data resides;
- Ability to capture, to delete, and to access the data (anyone who can do all three is often perceived to be an owner of the data);
- Access to social processes by which to negotiate with the data owner (and the power relationships such as in schools or a place of business that could prevent such processes).

4.2 Choice

Another important aspect of selective archiving – and capture technologies in general – is the presentation of a choice to opt in or out of a capture system. It is easy to argue that choice should be maximized in these cases, and indeed, the technologies and studies for CareLog and BufferWare were designed to maximize choice for involved stakeholders. Despite this intention, however, perception about choice was mixed, and when considered alongside other capture systems such as surveillance cameras and wide range CCTV initiatives, issues of how much choice to support become more complex.

In the CareLog deployment, once a teacher had decided to enroll in the study, the entire classroom was enrolled unless someone objected. In one case, a teacher's aid strongly objected. He expressed that he had a "phobia" of recording and would get nervous and freeze when snapshots and videos were taken at social gatherings. He was moved to another position in the school that did not involve the study, and in fact, everyone involved was happier in the end with the traded jobs for reasons that has nothing to do with the study. The effort was not small, however, and involved approval from the principal and changing of daily activities. Thus, one can easily imagine that other people may have been concerned but not enough to go through that work and thus chose to remain in the recorded classrooms.

Once the choice was made to remain working in an enrolled classroom, people present had very little choice about being captured or not. The cameras for CareLog covered the entire room, and when a researcher was present another handheld camera was used to follow the student of interest. One staff member physically avoided the handheld camera as much as possible, always choosing to work one-on-one with students other than the one being recorded. This staff member, however, could not avoid the overhead cameras that were part of CareLog and expressed comfort with them despite the discomfort with the handheld camera. After further probing of this issue, this staff member described multiple potential reasons for increased comfort, including lesser visibility of that recording and a different view from overhead rather than from face on, but in the end, she was unable to supply a concrete reason for the differences in her perceptions. People may actually experience higher levels of comfort with those technologies that they have little choice about avoiding, a point that needs more inquiry and to which we return later in this section.

In the BufferWare deployment, the choice to be in the study or not and the choice to be recorded or not were both made readily available at each and every interaction with the system and the space. Some people still expressed negative sentiments about not having a choice about the installation of the system more generally, but all those who objected also commented that they could easily choose to go elsewhere or not use the space. People commented that simply avoiding the space was nearly always the easiest choice over gathering more information, trusting the system, pressing delete, or unplugging or covering the recording equipment.

In this situation in which it is easy to choose to avoid capture, people freely described the ways in which they would avoid it. When asked in the same interviews, however, about surveillance cameras, very different reactions were voiced. Even if those people who commented that surveillance cameras were there for safety and therefore in a different class are discounted, there are still examples of people for whom BufferWare is a concern and surveillance cameras less so. When probed further, the reasoning often came down to the lack of choice. Essentially, because people have to accept some amount of recording to drive on the highways, use the bank or grocery store, and enter their office buildings, they do. Interestingly, the one staff member in the CareLog study with a self-described "phobia" of cameras discussed the elaborate ends to which he goes when using such spaces, including mapping out the optimal path in a store before entering so that he could enter with his head down and move quickly through the space, remaining on camera the minimal amount of time possible. Even this individual found ways to tolerate recording when necessary. Thus, any risk and reward models must account for not only the potential risks and rewards of technology use or avoidance but also of the entire setting (e.g., being employed in a space under surveillance, buying groceries).

4.3 Visibility and Awareness of Recording, Archival, and Deletion

The effects of the visibility of recording cannot be underestimated in understanding how recording technologies are perceived. In terms of selective archiving in particular, visibility not only of recording but also of archival and deletion may also affect acceptability and adoption of these technologies.

CareLog was designed to have minimal environmental impact so that the students would not be distracted or concerned about the installation. At the same time, this design also meant that teachers and other staff had minimal visibility of the actual recording equipment, which was mounted discretely to the ceiling. The teacher held substantial visibility into the archival and deletion processes by controlling both the remote that actuated archival and the access software through which deletion is possible. Minimal feedback was supplied to the teacher and staff members about when an event is saved. A small window indicates that an event was saved. Teachers did use this feedback occasionally to check that they had successfully archived some data, but often they were too busy with the incident to check. No feedback about the camera angle was provided during capture, because the entire room was blanketed with fixed cameras. Such feedback might have been helpful, however, because occasionally a camera would fail or stop working, and often the staff would not notice until they went to view the data later.

The staff members other than teachers had little knowledge, unless they asked the teachers directly, of what was archived or deleted. For the protection of the equipment and due to space constraints, all of the teachers had asked to have the monitor on which the feedback window was displayed, placed behind their desks. Thus, this information was relatively inaccessible to most staff members. All of the staff members were briefed extensively about the automatic deletion capabilities inherent to selective archiving, but they had little visibility into whether or not a teacher saved data.

In the BufferWare deployment, visibility and awareness were highly varied across the stakeholders involved. The camera used was a high-end pan-tilt-zoom webcam mounted nearby that looked quite obviously like a camera (as opposed to security cameras that are often more concealed). People who used the space quickly and easily identified it. People who had not used the space during the deployment, however, could not easily see it, due to its placement between two structural elements of the stairwell that blocked most views of it from outside the space.

Feedback about what was being captured within the camera's angle was also shared only with people in the space. This feedback was presented through a small video window on the embedded touch-screen that could be used to control the system. Again, to access this feedback, a person would have to be in the space. Thus, visibility for concerned parties who chose not to be in the space was minimal, a point that caused some unease for some of these people. Furthermore, there was nearly no visibility in the space or otherwise, provided about the microphone's range and status. One person suggested after the first deployment to create a visualization of the captured sound waves that could be mounted vertically nearby. In this way, people outside the space could easily glance to see if they might have been recorded. Likewise, people inside the space intending to record, who often complained about the quality of audio – which had been intentionally reduced to avoid accidental recording of people outside the space – could ensure that what they wanted to capture was indeed saved.

The open visibility of the camera in the BufferWare space was generally considered to be a positive design choice. People expressed that they would not have liked to find out later that there was a camera in place and that seeing it and the LCD display helped them make decisions about the capture. At the same time, however, some people noted that they believed they would have been less concerned about the recording if the camera were less apparent. People expressed conflict between wanting to be aware of the capture and wanting the camera itself to be less visible, thereby reducing self-consciousness and so on. One person even commented that by sitting with his back to the camera, he believed he tended to be more comfortable than his lunch partner who often sat facing him, and therefore facing the camera and had commented about constant reminding of the recording.

The tension between wanting to be aware of capture generally and the potential issues that arise when that awareness comes from constant visibility and reminding should be explored further. Even people who are comfortable with recording generally can become self-conscious or uncomfortable at the specific time of capture. Thus, implementers and users of these everyday recording technologies must consider how to combine awareness, visibility, and notification in ways that are clear but avoid being too blunt and intrusive.

4.4 Trust

Issues of trust and the closeness of the relationships of various stakeholders, including the system creators, maintainers, and researchers can be fundamental to the acceptance of new capture technologies. Selective archiving was designed with features such as automatic deletion of content, but true acceptance requires trust that the policy is being followed and features were implemented as described. Furthermore, trust must exist between those people using and affected by the system. That is to say, those who might be recorded must trust those who are actuating the recording.

In the CareLog deployment, there were multiple opportunities to establish a trusting relationship amongst all concerned parties. Often, the staff members in the classroom already had a strong working relationship. There were only severe conflicts amongst staff members in one room, and in that room, each of those individuals independently developed a trusting relationship with the researchers, often confiding in us about the problems with other staff. We were typically on site four of five school days each week and available by phone, email, and in person to answer questions. Through use of the system, people also reported being confident that the video was in fact being deleted when no one pressed an archive button. In fact, if anything, they expressed concerns about accidentally not recording what they wanted to save.

In one classroom, we also requested additional permissions from the staff and parents to share the videos that had been saved during the study for research purposes. Each person was provided with multiple options for specifying what to be shared or not (e.g., still pictures taken with CareLog vs. full audio and video with CareLog vs. the same with the handheld cameras). All staff members returned the permissions. One of them noted as he handed it to one of us, "I trust you, and there wouldn't be a point to letting you take all this video and then not let you use it." The teacher in the room held the form for the longest time (a few days) considering which elements she would allow to be shared and which she would not. Ultimately, she returned it with permission to share any of the information. When returning it to us, she said that she had decided to "trust [us] not to make [her] look like an idiot."

In the BufferWare deployment, there were many fewer opportunities to develop a trusting relationship. Furthermore, the fact that it was unclear to some people whose project it actually was meant that they were forced to trust the technology more generally, as opposed to the individuals involved. Those people who both knew who the researchers were and already had an established relationship with us commented that these friendships and trusting relationships were essential to accepting the system.

Furthermore, the protections and trust relationship with our university also supported these notions. People commented that if the system were available elsewhere (e.g., a coffee shop or grocery store), they would be much more concerned, because they do not hold the same level of trust with those entities. On the other hand, people who did not associate BufferWare with particular trusted individuals or a trusted institution hesitated greatly about use. In many cases, they expressed distrust of where saved clips were going and for what they might be used. In other cases, they even distrusted that the data were being deleted at all.

An important adoption criterion for any new system, but particularly those that involve recording, is trust of the developers, owners, and maintainers of the system. Simply building in controls such as security of access or automatic deletion is not enough to put people at ease. They must also trust that these controls were implemented as described and are being monitored for potential abuse. Thus, when considering the designs of future capture applications, we must consider not only the affordances of the technology towards such issues as privacy and control of data but also towards building trust relationships and working within the social fabric and cultural constructs of the present context.

4.5 Features of Rich Media

Audio and video both provide an enormous amount of information. Often audio is considered to be even more personal and identifiable than video, but in the CareLog and BufferWare deployments, both were provided synchronously. The reactions to provision of these high bandwidth media were varied across the two cases, and inform our understanding of the features of these media.

In the CareLog case, risk of capturing children on video without guardian consent, in particular is of great concern. In American schools, FERPA guidelines govern school records, and policies often indicate that video recording must only be used with explicit permission [3]. Even without the audio channel, videos of students (and for that matter, photographs) are closely regulated. Early on, we explored the potential use of sophisticated techniques for blurring or blocking uninvolved students or those for whom permission has not been recorded. When these suggestions were described to focus group participants discussing use of video for the care of children with special needs, the answer was unanimously that they would not use them [6]. Participants repeatedly voiced that the assessments would be inaccurate if they did not include the entire situational context.

In that work, five options were provided to 28 participants (professional and familial caregivers of children with autism) on which to reflect about the utility, comfort-level, and other features in terms of their everyday work and lives: manual annotation with no video, fully automated recording, fully automated recording with a location-based filter (see Fig. 4), fully automated capture with a child-based filter (see Fig. 5), and selective archiving of captured video. In the cases involving video, samples were demonstrated, from which the still images in Figs. 4 and 5 were taken. Caregivers noted that with children with special needs, particularly social disorders, observations of the larger context of and the other actors in the environment are a necessity. Thus, a piece of video blurred to protect the privacy and anonymity of the other people nearby would be useless to those practicing in this domain.

Fig. 4 In this video clip, interactions around a toy box are of interest to the caregivers. In the frame on the *left*, the child of interest (*center*) can be seen playing with the toy box. For the child to the right's protection, he was only to be recorded when close to the toy box. Thus, in the frame on the *right*, the interaction between the children is blurred. This video clip mimics a camera-fixed environment recording only interactions in a defined space

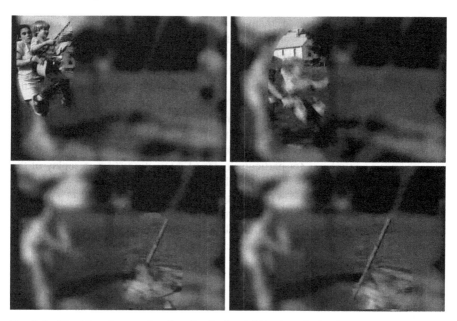

Fig. 5 In this video, the caregiver is only clearly visible when she is close to the child. Otherwise, she is blurred, and the areas around her are clear. These images mimic a fixed camera in an environment configured only to show the child of interest

It is worth noting that assessments conducted in person without video currently tend to rely on the teacher or perhaps one external observer to document the setting. Given that humans can only attend to so much detail at a time and that the behaviors often occur unexpectedly, it is unlikely that these reports would include all of the relevant information either. Similarly, CareLog only captures four camera angles all from the ceiling looking down and one sound stream. Thus, it is unlikely that this account includes the entire relevant context either. Data that may be important, such as temperature or humidity, is lost with this media.

Despite the limitations of audio and video at recreating the entire situational context, use of these rich streams of data did result in observations by the teachers above and beyond what would have been possible in the traditional model. For example, teachers commented on the ability to go back and observe the other students in the room at the time that one student was acting inappropriately, and thus receiving most of the staff attention. They were also able to observe small activities occurring just prior to an intense behavioral incident. These activities may not have been noticed at the first time or may have been forgotten in the impending chaos of the incident. The flexibility of the media meant that a new depth of analysis and understanding could be reached and sometimes more data than that was needed for the task at hand was collected and used for further classroom management activities.

BufferWare also included audio and video, although only one camera angle was used. Whereas the additional information available in this rich media was seen positively in the CareLog case, many people viewed it as overkill and too much of an invasion in the BufferWare case. Often, for example, they simply wanted an easily skimmable audio record of the conversation. Lack of appropriate access interfaces for such skimming meant that people did learn to take advantage of the video channel by holding up signs or gesturing at a particularly important portion of the conversation.

Other people commented that they simply wanted a record of what was on the whiteboard, and the ubiquitous availability of camera phones and digital cameras made explicit capture of the final artifact simpler than use of BufferWare. Better designed access interfaces for particular types of interactions (e.g., a replay of the content of the whiteboard as it was added) would greatly improve the system as it stands. Important to note, however, is that few people actually expressed a need for the full capabilities of audio and video simultaneously in an interaction. Thus, the flexibility built in with full access to this level of media is likely unnecessary in an informal space such as that used in the BufferWare project.

4.6 Face

Concerns about capture technologies can center on the ways in which captured data can be removed from one context and represented in another. The ability for people to manage their own image to others is compromised when one "face" can be removed and reinserted elsewhere. Issues of "face" as defined by Goffman [5] came up repeatedly in analysis of reactions to BufferWare.

Although much more accepted than BufferWare, the CareLog deployment experiment also touched on issues of face and face negotiation by interested stakeholders. During the CareLog deployment, teachers kept control of both capture and access of data saved through the CareLog interface. On the other hand, the researchers controlled the capture of data recorded using the handheld camera. Furthermore, teachers and staff never viewed those videos. In certain ways, they could more easily remember to present themselves in certain ways when a researcher was physically present with the camera. This very presence served as a visible reminder that recording was taking place. As frequently seen in field research, however, the participants tended to get used to our presence and carried on with their work as they likely would without us there.

Occasionally after a particularly intense experience, staff members would comment to us about what was being recorded. For example, an argument ensued between a teacher and a staff member that ended with the staff member being reassigned to a different room. Each of the people involved later apologized to me for having had to witness the argument. Each individual also then mentioned something about the way in which he or she might be portrayed in my video and whether that could or would be used by the school. We assured them that only researchers would view these videos, and that they should not be concerned with anyone else from the school viewing them. We could not assure them honestly that they might not appear negatively on the video, and so we concentrated on assuring them of who might have access. Thus, the faces they wish to present to other school staff, including their principal, would be preserved even if this presentation across the research staff could not be guaranteed. Although they appeared relieved after this situation, another intense afternoon occurred with the same teacher and a student later in the study, and we held a similar conversation. Again, the teacher appeared reassured, but in the end-of-study questionnaire, this same teacher expressed concerns about self-presentation using the handheld video camera, noting that the same worries did not exist for the CareLog recording.

In the BufferWare study, a large number of the expressed concerns about recording had to do with presentation of self and the negotiation of face. People were concerned about personal habits like scratching or nail biting in which they might partake while sitting alone in the space but which they would not want to be recorded and shared with other people. In this case, although it may be embarrassing to be caught doing one of these small habits, it is generally considered of minimal concern when the viewing is transient. When it is recorded and can be shared outside of the context, however, concerns compound.

Another face negotiation issue that came up repeatedly in the BufferWare deployment involved the notions that space around its installation were for work, again bringing to mind boundary negotiation between home and work. People commented that they would not want to be recorded having fun or "goofing off" in this workspace. They did participate in these activities at times, but they reported not wanting to be caught nor recorded participating in them. They also noted that personal phone calls, often taken in the hallway to keep personal and work realms separate, should not be recorded in this work space, albeit a relatively informal space. Finally, people commented that they might engage in peripheral activities often associated with work, such as gossiping, but that these activities should not be recorded and do not meet the formal definition of what should be occurring in the cultural ideal of this particular workspace. Rich media can be a powerful tool to support presentation of self in a desirable way. On the other hand, it can also be a powerful mechanism by which to share information that demonstrates a negative presentation of an individual. Many concerns about simple still photographs center on the way a person looks, with whom they might be and what that might imply, and so on. Audio and video taken out of context can be even more damaging. Thus, face negotiation and concepts of face are important notions for consideration when building capture applications. When the space is relatively informal, such as in BufferWare, and the capture can occur anytime, as in both cases, the potential risk for self-presentation can be quite large.

4.7 Decision Point

Selective archiving includes the inherent assumption that people are best equipped to make decisions about what they want to be recorded after an event has occurred. Deletion occurs automatically for data not marked to be saved, and manual deletion of saved data can occur at any time. However, people must choose to save data in close temporal proximity to the actual event. These choices about the decision point had impact on both the use and the acceptance of these technologies.

If an analyst can predict a problem behavior's occurrence, it is very likely that she/he already knows the function of that behavior and that she/he can implement a behavior intervention plan that will result in its reduction. Thus, FBA inherently requires the documentation of events that cannot be predicted. In this case, then, it is not surprising that the model of choosing to archive something after it occurs would be considered a positive way to make the decision. We had some concerns, however, that the window for decision-making would be too small. That is to say, teachers might remember hours or even days later that they had not saved something they wished that they had. In the end, the risk of false negatives was quite low, however, because they missed so many incidents with the pen and paper method. They rarely if ever considered if they had missed an incident in the CareLog condition. Furthermore, the risk of false positives was much higher. Recording extra information both caused more work for them to watch the videos and put them at risk of recording information that was damaging to a staff member or student without any benefit. In those cases, the manual deletion after they had already archived some piece of video addressed their needs.

In the BufferWare case, provision of after the fact decision-making was reported to be less important, and in fact, uncomfortable in some cases. People commented that notes were good enough for most informal meetings. Activities they would like recorded, such as practice presentations, could be set up ahead of time. Finally, those moments that they really needed to record unexpectedly, those "ah-hah" moments, were fewer and farther between than opportunities in which they expected to need to record. BufferWare's design explicitly lowered the hurdle to beginning recording, but still people reported not needing that type of capture very frequently. Thus, it may simply be that even if made comfortable with recording, there is no optimal decision point for capture technologies for which situations of need are rare.

5 Conclusions

Technologies built to support one domain problem are often appropriated for other uses outside of the research setting. Thus, once the concepts of selective archiving were conceived, it became important to examine how the solution might be interpreted within other everyday situations. Therefore, in addition to exploring the concepts of selective archiving for behavioral assessment, using CareLog, we designed a flexible system that could be used for a variety of purposes and deployed it in a multi-purpose shared space. Together, these two technologies – and their associated deployment studies – provide edge cases from which we can draw a broader understanding of selective archiving as a sensitive model for recording in everyday situations.

Selectively archived segments of data can provide an efficient way to recover and to analyze high quality data than traditionally available. Furthermore, selective archiving provides an interesting model for gathering the rich data needed for diagnostic applications, memory augmentation, and more in a privacy-sensitive way.

In this work, we explicitly engaged the tension points for recording, examining them from both an automated surveillance standpoint as well as from one that invokes selective archiving. By examining the perceptions, adoption, and uses of these technologies together, we highlight features of design – technological and socio-political – that must be considered when deploying capture technologies into everyday, unstructured settings. Who owns the data, not just who owns the capture technologies themselves, is an essential component to making an informed decision about capture technologies. Elements of choice about being in a recording or not also factor in, with people often avoiding those capture technologies they can and tolerating those they have less choice about avoiding.

Of course, without some level of visibility or awareness of these technologies, other considerations would not easily come into play. Like notions of awareness, trust often interacts with and is affected by other concepts. Considerations of such issues as who owns the data and whether or not that can be believed often center on trust. Furthermore, visibility of both capture and of system status and workings can increase both awareness and trust levels. The media to be captured itself often comes with particular affordances that must be considered both by designers and users. An appropriate richness of media should be supplied, no more and no less. Discovering what that level is both at the beginning of a situation and over time is a significant challenge in the creation and use of these capture technologies. Finally, use of recording and decision-making about that recording must fit into the social norms regarding demonstration and negotiation of face.

The CareLog and BufferWare projects provide much insight about how we can support record keeping in informal and unstructured settings in privacy-sensitive, controlled ways. Furthermore, when examined together, these projects provide a view into the larger generalized problem of unstructured capture and access and the acceptability of capture technologies. There is a wide spectrum of domain problems requiring capture and technologies to support those problems, however. These technologies should be explored both in direct consideration of particular domain problems and bearing in mind the themes uncovered in this work. Many of the features that enabled or prevented adoption of selective archiving in both the CareLog and BufferWare projects came from the design of the research, the organizational context, or other areas, with the technology itself holding only one piece of the puzzle. Thus, both selective archiving and other capture technologies should be considered as part of a larger set of socio-technical constructs. These constructs continue to evolve providing a dynamic system into which the placement of selective archiving technologies will likely provide more areas of future research as we continue to examine the uptake and appropriation of them over extended periods of time.

References

1. Abowd G.D. and Mynatt E.D. (2000) Charting Past, Present and Future Research in Ubiquitous Computing. ACM Transactions on Computer-Human Interaction, Volume 7(1): 29–58, March 2000.

2. Dietz P.H. and Yerazunis W.S. (2001) Real-Time Audio Buffering for Telephone Applications. In the Proceedings of UIST 2001: 193–194.
3. FERPA (1974) The Family Educational Rights and Privacy Act (FERPA) (20 U.S.C. § 1232g; 34 CFR Part 99).
4. Gemmell J., Bell G., Lueder R., Drucker S. and Wong C. (2002) MyLifeBits: Fulfilling the Memex Vision. In the Proceedings of ACM Multimedia 2002: 235–238.
5. Goffman E. (1955) On Face-Work: An Analysis of Ritual Elements in Social Interaction. Psychiatry, Volume 81: 213–231.
6. Hayes G.R. and Abowd G.D. (2006) Tensions in Designing Capture Technologies for an Evidence-based Care Community. In the Proceedings CHI 2006: 937–946.
7. Hayes G.R., Gardere L., Abowd G.D. and Truong K.N. (2008) CareLog: A Selective Archiving Tool for Behavior Management in Schools. In the Proceedings CHI 2008: 685–694.
8. Hayes G.R., Kientz J.A., Truong K.N., White D.R., Abowd G.D. and Pering T. (2004) Designing Capture Applications to Support the Education of Children with Autism. In the Proceedings of UBICOMP 2004: 161–178
9. Hayes G.R., Patel S.N., Truong K.N., Iachello G., Kientz J.A., Farmer R. and Abowd G.D. (2004) The Personal Audio Loop: Designing a Ubiquitous Audio-based Memory aid. In the Proceedings of MobileHCI 2004: 168–179.
10. Hayes G.R., Poole E.S., Iachello G., Patel S.N., Grimes A., Abowd G.D. and Truong, K.N. (2007) Physical, Social, and Experiential Knowledge of Privacy and Security in a Pervasive Computing Environment. In IEEE Pervasive Computing, Volume 6(4): 56–63.
11. Hayes G.R., Truong K.N., Abowd G.D. and Pering T. (2005) Experience Buffers: A Socially Appropriate, Selective Archiving Tool for Evidence-Based Care. In the Extended Abstracts of CHI'05: 1435–1438.
12. Healey J. and Picard R.W. (1998) StartleCam: A Cybernetic Wearable Camera. In the Proceedings of ISWC 1998: 42–49
13. Hindus D. and Schmandt C. (1992) Ubiquitous Audio: Capturing Spontaneous Collaboration. In the Proceedings of the CSCW 1992: 210–217.
14. Iachello G., Truong K.N., Abowd G.D., Stevens M.M. and Hayes G.R. (2006) Prototyping and Sampling Experience to Evaluate Ubiquitous Computing Privacy in the Real World. In the Proceedings of CHI 2006: 1009–1018.
15. Minneman S.L. and Harrison S.R. (1993) Where Were We: Making and Using Near-Synchronous, Pre-Narrative Video. In the Proceedings ACM Multimedia 1993: 207–214.
16. Patel S.N., Truong K.N., Hayes G.R., Iachello G., Kientz J.A. and Abowd G.D. (2007) The Personal Audio Loop: A Ubiquitous Audio-Based Memory Aid. In: Joanna Lumsden (Ed.) Handbook of User Interface Design and Evaluation for Mobile Technology.
17. Truong K.N. (2005) INCA: An Infrastructure for Capture & Access – Supporting the Generation, Preservation and Use of Memories from Everyday Life. Georgia Institute of Technology, Ph.D. Dissertation.

BlindSpot: Creating Capture-Resistant Spaces

Shwetak N. Patel, Jay W. Summet and Khai N. Truong

Abstract The increasing presence of digital cameras and camera phones brings with it legitimate concerns of unwanted recording situations for many organizations and individuals. Although the confiscation of these devices from their owners can curb the capture of sensitive information, it is neither a practical nor desirable solution. In this chapter, we present the design of a system, called BlindSpot, which prevents the recording of still and moving images without requiring any cooperation on the part of the capturing device or its operator. Our solution involves a simple tracking system for locating any number of retro-reflective CCD or CMOS camera lenses around a protected area. The system then directs a pulsing light at the lens, distorting any imagery the camera records. Although the directed light interferes with the camera's operation, it can be designed to minimally impact the view of other humans in the environment. In addition to protecting one's personal or private space from unwanted recording, the BlindSpot system can be used to turn spaces, such as industry labs, movie theatres, and private properties, into capture-resistant environments.

1 Introduction

As digital cameras and camera phones have become cheaper and more common, it has also become easier for owners of these devices to record still and moving images anywhere. The pervasiveness of such recording devices creates a legitimate concern among those who wish to retain some level of privacy or secrecy. Companies concerned that camera phones may compromise the security of their intellectual property often ban such devices from their facilities. Although this approach and other legal and social forces may curb inappropriate capture behaviors [1, 3, 9], such practices are not always practical or reliable. Thus, there has been previous

S.N. Patel (✉)

Computer Science and Engineering and Electrical Engineering, University of Washington, Seattle, WA 98195, USA

e-mail: shwetak@cs.washington.edu

A. Senior (ed.), *Protecting Privacy in Video Surveillance*,
DOI 10.1007/978-1-84882-301-3_11, © Springer-Verlag London Limited 2009

work that addressed this challenge by disabling recording features in the cameras through cooperative software [5, 7, 10]. Alternatively, we explored a solution that does not require instrumentation or control of the recording device. We developed a system for safeguarding the environment itself against unwanted recording, called BlindSpot. The system allows people to prevent unwanted recording of their own personal space. Our system actively seeks cameras in the environment and emits a strong localized light beam at each device to neutralize it from capturing while minimally disturbing the natural viewing experience by the human eye.

In this chapter, we summarize some previous work in this area. We then outline the technical underpinnings of our approach, describe a prototype implementation of the BlindSpot system and discuss the advantages and limitations of this approach for safeguarding against digital capture. Finally, we discuss the potential application of the BlindSpot system in industry labs, movie theatres, and private properties to turn those spaces into capture-resistant environments.

2 Related Work

Most technical solutions previously proposed to prevent or react to undesired camera capture require some sort of instrumentation on the capture device. Solutions, such as Safe Haven, leverage the short-range wireless capability available on camera phones (such as Bluetooth or WiFi) to allow the environment to notify the device that the space does not allow photography or other forms of recording [5, 7, 10]. A drawback to this solution is that it requires the camera phone owner to install and use special software on her/his device and respect the privacy constraints of the environment and nearby individuals. For example, Hewlett-Packard's proposed paparazzi-proof camera [8] automatically modifies images when it receives commands from a remote device. This camera includes a facial recognition feature that selectively blurs parts of an image that include faces of particular people. Similarly, Cloak addresses privacy concerns with surveillance cameras by having users carry a "privacy enabling device" (PED) [2]. This device informs the environment that any footage of the carrier of this device must be sanitized later.

Alternatively, a small wearable solution called "Eagle Eye" uses a light sensor to detect a camera's light flash [4]. In response, this device instantaneously flashes back and obscures a portion of the photographic image. However, the device only works against still, flash photography.

We take a significantly different approach from these previous solutions in the design of Blindspot, which enables the definition and creation of capture-resistant environments. First, we actively impede recording at the point of capture, as with Eagle Eye, rather than requiring users to trust cameras to sanitize images after the recording has occurred. Second, unlike many previous solutions, our approach does not rely on any cooperation or instrumentation on the part of the capture devices or the people operating them. Our solution addresses both video capture and still imagery. We focus on being able to protect fixed regions within an environment, such as a wall. Specifically, our solution will minimally impact what an observer in the environment sees while still preventing a camera from being able to record. That is, surfaces in an environment obviously can be covered to prevent capture, but then visitors to the space cannot see anything at all. Additionally, there are numerous commercially available retro-reflective sprays and shields that can also be placed over a surface to reflect light and flashes in a manner that prevents recording. However, these solutions create glare that impacts visibility from the human eye as well as the camera's CCD or CMOS sensor whereas our system does not affect people in the environment.

3 Design Goals for a Capture-Resistant Environment

Our primary goal in addressing this problem was to design a system that prevents certain portions of that space from being recorded with a standard CCD or CMOS camera, thereby producing a so-called capture-resistant environment. This motivation, and review of past related work, highlights the four major design goals for building a capture-resistant environment. First, the environment would not require cooperation or control of the recording devices before, during, or after capture. Second, it should be able to prevent both still images and video recordings. Third, the view of the environment by the naked human eye must be minimally impacted. Finally, we wanted our approach to allow authorized cameras to record. Using a combination of computer vision and projection, our design, described in the next section, actively searches for cameras and systematically blocks them from recording clear pictures, rather than relying on the cameras to remove or alter content after the fact (see Fig. 1).

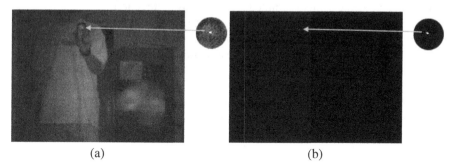

(a)   (b)

Fig. 1 On the *left* is an unprocessed IR view captured by our camera detector with plenty of ambient light in the room. A person holds a camera phone pointed at a region in the environment we want to protect from capture. On the *right* is the processed view. The camera is detected by locating a bright white circular speckle

4 The BlindSpot System

In this section, we present our BlindSpot system, which consists of three components. The first component – the camera detector – actively tracks CCD or CMOS lenses in the environment. When the system detects a camera lens, the second system component – the camera neutralizer – sends a localized beam of light at each camera's lens to obstruct its view of the scene. This technique also works on video cameras. The third part of the system – the capture manager – regulates camera capture within the environment. This component locates and allows permitted devices to record. For each component, we describe the theory of operation and our proof of concept implementation. We then critically evaluate the limitations of our proof of concept prototype, distinguishing the theoretical limits from the current engineering limitations of the specific implementation. We also discuss future extensions of our system.

4.1 Detecting Cameras in the Environment

CCD and CMOS cameras have an optical property that produce well-defined light reflections. Our system tracks these reflections to locate cameras in the local environment.

4.1.1 Theory of Operation

BlindSpot's camera detector leverages the retro-reflective property of the CCD or CMOS sensor lens found on all consumer-level digital cameras. Retro-reflection causes light to reflect directly back to its source, independent of its incident angle. CCD and CMOS sensors are mounted at the focal plane of the camera's optical lens, making them very effective retro-reflectors. By tracking these retro-reflections, we can detect and locate cameras pointed towards a given direction.

There are many objects in the environment that also exhibit the retro-reflective property. Commercial applications of retro-reflection include traffic signs and reflective clothes commonly worn by road construction workers. In addition, the retro-reflective property of the retina at the back of the eye often causes a subject's eyes to glow red in flash photography. This effect has allowed researchers to use a similar approach to ours to track eye movement in gaze tracking systems [6]. As we show later in this chapter, these objects are typically imperfect retro-reflectors and can reasonably be distinguished from CMOS or CCD cameras.

4.1.2 Implementation

In our initial prototype, we used a Sony Digital HandyCam video camera placed in *NightShot* mode to detect cameras in the environment. We arranged IR transmitters and covered the detector's lens with a narrow band pass IR filter (see Fig. 2). This instrumentation projected an IR light beam outwards from the camera and detected any retro-reflective surfaces within the field of view. We intentionally placed the IR illuminator around the perimeter of the detector's lens to ensure a bright retro-reflection from cameras within the field of view of the detector and pointed directly at it or tilted away at slight angles (which we computed to be up to roughly $\pm20°$ for our apparatus). Retro-reflections appeared as a bright white circular speckle through

(a)   (b)

Fig. 2 The *left* picture shows our initial camera detector unit. We outfitted a Sony HandyCam, placed in *NightShot* mode, with a collection of IR transmitters and covered the lens with a narrow band pass IR filter. The *right* picture shows our camera detector coupled with a projector to neutralize cameras in the environment

the IR filtered camera. We initially thought that by flickering the IR light at 5 Hz, we would be able to detect reflective surfaces more easily. Although this approach worked, we later relied on computer vision techniques to detect the reflections and did not need to flicker the IR light.

We detect reflections by simply locating white regions in the camera view above a certain color threshold (in gray). The system disregards all other shades of gray, assuming these reflections come from some surface other than a lens. Because we employ thresholding technique, there is no limit to the number of devices that the camera detector can detect within its cross-section. In the next section, we discuss how to handle false positives and false negatives.

The system effectively tracks cameras and their trajectories at about 15 Hz. A more powerful computer could track at 30 Hz; however, 15 Hz is sufficient because a user must hold the average camera still for at least this period of time to avoid motion blur during capture. The detector camera has about a 45° field of view. We have found that reflections from cameras of varying shapes and sizes can be detected from up to 10 m away. At 5 m away, the cross-section of the detector camera is roughly a 4 m width × 3 m height area (see Fig. 3).

Fig. 3 At 5 m away, the cross-section of the detector camera is roughly a 4 m width × 3 m height area

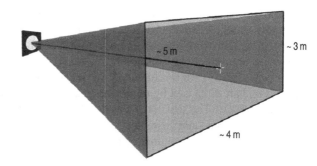

Fig. 4 Current
implementation of the
BlindSpot system

Because the original implementation used a single camera, the system required manual calibration between the camera detector and the neutralizer (described in the next section) to a planar surface. To address this problem, we implemented the current prototype to use two webcams as a stereoscopic vision system for tracking in 3D space (see Fig. 4). This approach supports the flexible placement of the neutralizer and the camera detectors independent of each other.

4.2 Neutralizing Cameras

Once the system detects camera lenses in the environment, the camera neutralizer component emits localized light beams onto detected camera lenses. The strong beam of light forces the camera to take an obscured image.

4.2.1 Theory of Operation

The camera neutralizer leverages the inherent imperfect sensing capabilities of CCD and CMOS cameras that result in two specific effects, blooming and lens flare. Blooming occurs when a portion of the camera's sensor is overloaded, resulting in leakage to neighboring regions. For example, a candle in an otherwise dark setting may cause blobs or comet tails around the flame. Although some cameras are capable of compensating for this effect, they typically only handle moderate amounts of light. Lens flare is caused by unwanted light bouncing around the glass and metal inside the camera. The size of the lens flare depends on the brightness of the entering light. Well-designed and coated optics can minimize, but not completely eliminate, lens flare. By shining a collimated beam of light at the camera lens, blooming and lens flare significantly block any CCD or CMOS camera from capturing the intended image. Some cameras employ bright light compensation algorithms. However, there is typically a delay before the sensor stabilizes. Thus, a flashing light prevents the camera from stabilizing to the light source.

4.2.2 Implementation

To emit a strong localized light beam at cameras, we pair a projector of 1,500 lumens with our camera detector. This unit projects an image of (one or more) spots of varying light at the reflections. Pixels in the projected image change between white, red, blue, and green. This approach prevents cameras from adjusting to the light source and forces the cameras to take a picture flooded with light. In addition, inter-leaving various projection rates neutralizes a larger variety of cameras. The camera neutralizer continuously emits this light beam until the camera lens is no longer detected. Therefore, this approach works against both still image cameras and video cameras.

Our tests show that the projector can still generate an effective localized light beam when we focus it to 5 m away. Although light from a projector can travel much further, its luminance decreases with distance. We estimate that 5 m is roughly the length of a reasonable size for a room. At 5 m away, we can project localized light beams to cover a pyramidal region with a base of 6 m width × 4.5 m height. To ensure that we can neutralize cameras from all angles, we can measure the angle at which users can approach the surface, and accordingly, we can determine how many projectors we must use to cover that range. We can add additional projectors away from the surface to neutralize cameras from further away if needed (see Fig. 5).

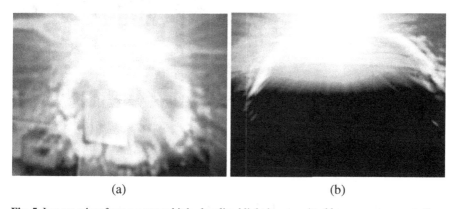

(a)   (b)

Fig. 5 Images taken from a camera hit by localized light beam emitted by our camera neutralizer. The picture on the *left* shows a localized light beam generated using a single color. The picture on the *right* shows a localized light beam generated using color patterns that do not allow the cameras to adjust to the light source (notice the scan line)

4.3 Regulating Camera Capture

Although our system prevents existing cameras from being able to record a fixed surface in our environment, we recognize that there may be circumstances in which it would be appropriate for certain cameras to be permitted to capture. To allow certain cameras to take pictures in the environment, the system simply does not send localized light beams at those devices. However, this feature requires that the environment knows which cameras have been permitted by the owner of the space to take pictures.

One solution we implemented is placing a physical token on the lens side of the camera. The tag is retro-reflective and depicts a 2D glyph. When the camera detector finds this tag within close proximity (1–5 m) of a camera lens and the system validates its authenticity, the camera neutralizer is not activated for that particular camera. The 2D glyph encodes a unique identifier that the system recognizes as valid tags. The owner of the physical space gives out a tag when she wants to permit a specific camera to capture within that space. The owner either removes the tag after the camera has captured information or she removes the 2D glyph from the list of tags the capture-resistant environment permits. A problem with this solution exists when a camera lens is in the detector's field of view but the 2D glyph has been occluded. The glyph must be placed very close to the camera lens to address this problem. If spaced over some distance, our tracker may become confused between the permitted camera lens and another nearby lens (see Fig. 6).

Fig. 6 *Left* shows retro-reflective glyph temporarily attached near a camera phone's lens. *Right* shows sample 5 cm × 5 cm glyph pattern

(a)   (b)

5 Assessing the Design Challenges and Limitations

In this section, we summarize how we addressed our original design goals and the challenges and limitations faced in the design of BlindSpot. We also describe how our approach addresses the potential attacks or workarounds people may use to circumvent the capture-resistant environment. Finally, we also discuss the known theoretical limitations and the engineering deficiency in our prototype.

5.1 Challenges

There are two types of challenges our system faces. First, we must handle the errors involved in detecting cameras. Second, we must address potential attacks or workarounds people may use to circumvent the capture-resistant environment.

5.1.1 Errors in Detecting Cameras

There are two types of errors that can occur in our system. A false positive occurs when the camera detection system mistakenly detects a camera in the environment where one is not actually present. A false negative occurs when the camera detector fails to identify a camera pointing at the capture-resistant space.

Handling False Positives

False positives can result from the detection system interpreting reflections off of metallic or mirrored surfaces present in the space. Because these surfaces potentially produce the same reflective speckle as a CCD or CMOS sensor, the system would target a non-existent camera.

False positives are not detrimental to the operation of the system. However, the superfluous projector light produced by the false positive may be distracting or even bothersome for users in the environment. The worst false positive situation occurs when the system incorrectly identifies a region near a person's face as a potential camera, irritating or even harming the person's vision.

We address these problems by further analyzing the potential camera speckles. For the case of a reflection caused by metallic or other lens-like surfaces we can determine a false positive by inspecting the suspected reflection from multiple vantage points. The reflection caused by the CCD or CMOS camera has a consistent appearance off its surface. If the reflection moves at a different vantage point views, then it is not a camera-based reflection. These other surfaces are imperfect reflectors, which is typically attributed to the surface curvature, such as eyeglasses or imperfect finishes like brushed metal. To reduce the number of false positives, our system uses two cameras spaced apart and pointed at the same region to detect when a reflection moves in different vantage view points. Another strategy is to place multiple illuminators on the same plane as the detector and then cycle between each light source. Reflected light that is not coaxial to the detector's view indicates that the reflector is an imperfect retro-reflective surface or not retro-reflective at all. Because eyes have a similar retro-reflective signature to cameras, they are likely to cause the most false positives. However, unlike camera lenses and CCD sensors, the human eye is not a perfect retro-reflector and thus we can employ this strategy to help guard against incorrectly detecting eyes as cameras (Fig. 7 shows an example of using two off axis illuminators).

Fig. 7 Anti-piracy prototype of the BlindSpot system being set in a movie theatre setting. The camera detection device is placed near the movie screen facing the audience

Handling False Negatives

Unlike false positives, false negatives are detrimental to the security of the space. One solution is to take a naïve approach and assume that any reflection is a potential camera. This may be appropriate when security is of utmost importance. However, this approach does not work when the CCD camera does not produce a reflection. Occlusion of the CCD from the camera detector is the primary reason for this, but typically an occlusion of the CCD inherently blocks a photograph from being taken in the first place. The camera can be angled sufficiently enough away that the incident light fails to reach the detector camera. In this case, the camera is already turned far enough away such that the capture-resistant space does not appear in its field of view. Thus, if there is no light reflection from the CCD, then the CCD camera cannot see the region around the detector.

We can place multiple pairs of camera detectors around a space for added security. From our experience, we have found one pair to be sufficient. A cheaper alternative is to place multiple IR light emitters throughout the space to increase the likelihood for a reflection. This solution may increase the number of false positives; however, its cost effectiveness outweighs those concerns.

We did not implement dead reckoning, but this approach would address the momentary loss of camera lens tracked by the system. By observing the trajectory of the cameras, the neutralizer continues to project the beam at the inferred path in hope of hitting the camera. This scheme works for very short-lived blips lasting a few seconds. Anything longer would likely make the dead reckoning ineffective.

5.1.2 Attacks and Workarounds

Aside from physical vandalism to the capture resistant environment, we identify some workarounds users may employ with their CCD or CMOS camera. We discuss how our system design addresses some of these attacks, explaining the non-obvious reasons behind why these attacks would not work. Where appropriate, we provide some theoretical justification.

Masks and Filters

An attacker may try to mask the camera lens with surfaces such as a lens from a pair of sunglasses. Typical sunglasses do not block IR light, and thus BlindSpot would still detect the CCD or CMOS sensor lens. Mirrored and even polarized sunglasses also fail to prevent the camera detector from finding the CCD. However, sunglasses are effective at mitigating the effects of the neutralizer on the camera. Sunglasses drastically reduce the intensity of the projected light. Despite this reduction, we have found that the light pattern and intensity we used in our system is still effective at neutralizing cameras from capture. A more intense and collimated neutralizing beam, such as from a laser, would certainly solve this problem.

IR filters pose the greatest problems for our particular system. In our current solution, we use pure IR light (880 nm) for CCD sensor detection. An 880 nm notch IR filter could be placed in front of a camera; this prevents IR light from reaching the CCD sensor while still allowing other visible light to pass. Because this is the greatest attack on our system, we can design our implementation to detect also IR filters in the environment and treat them as suspicious cameras. An IR filter reflection looks very similar to CCD sensor reflection to our camera detector (the only difference is a larger speckle size), thus making it a straightforward task to detect IR filters and treat them as a camera. However, this solution will result in more false positives. Because IR filters allow visible light to penetrate, the camera neutralizer is not affected by this attack.

Mirrors

A user can avoid pointing a camera at the capture-resistant region by using a mirror and taking a picture of the reflection on the mirror. However, our experience indicates that the camera detector can still clearly spot the CCD sensor in the mirror and the camera can be effectively neutralized by aiming back at the mirror. An attacker could hide a camera behind a one-way mirror to prevent it from being detected. Similar to the sunglass situation, IR light can still be detected appearing behind a one-way mirror, making it an ineffective attack. In addition, images taken from behind a one-way mirror tend to produce low quality images in the first place.

Modifying Camera Sample Rate

The camera could be pre-programmed to sample at the rate of the neutralizer pattern. We addressed this problem by interleaving random frequencies for each pixel in the neutralizing projection pattern. In this case, CCD or CMOS cameras would not be able to synchronize to the projected pattern and frequency because of its inability to sample each pixel at different rates. Although our solution does not implement this interleaving, it is a fairly straightforward extension to our system.

Another possible workaround is to evade the neutralizing beam by moving the camera faster than our detector tracks. There is a limit to how fast the camera can be moved when taking a picture because of motion blur. The 15 Hz tracking rate of our implementation is sufficient for all camera phones and most digital cameras. High-end cameras with extremely faster shutter speeds require faster tracking. Increasing the area of the neutralizing beam would address this problem because of the larger movement needed to move outside the beam of the light.

5.2 Limitations

Our current implementation is limited to indoor environments, although we have found success near widows and areas where there is significant amount of natural light. However, for settings such as an outdoor concert, this system would need to be modified extensively to accommodate for such a large distance.

This solution works well with traditional CCD and CMOS cameras, but may have problems with extremely high-end cameras that have very fast shutter speeds and frame rates such as SLR. Other capture technologies that do not employ CCD or CMOS sensors, such as thermal imaging, cannot be detected using our scheme. These cameras are still very hard to produce, and we do not expect to see such high-end components integrated into a mobile phone anytime soon. Although the quality and resolutions of camera phones will increase, they do not have a direct impact on the effectiveness of this system (our system performed well even on a 4 megapixel CCD digital camera). Capture technologies that do not employ CCD sensors, such as ordinary film cameras, cannot be detected nor neutralized by our system.

Most camera systems employ some type of optical system; by instrumenting the environment to locate any reflection from optical devices, it is possible to detect any camera, including SLRs and ordinary film cameras. However, this approach would increase the false positive rate.

The conical region of the camera detector poses a problem with "dead zones" close to the detector/neutralizer system. A "dead zone" exists a short distance in front of the protected surface, directly underneath the detector unit, and on the azimuth. A person standing in this dead zone will be able to take a picture, although the resulting image will be very warped. Placement of a physical barrier could limit proximity of users to the protected region and the "dead zone." Installation of another neutralizer at a lower level or different angle could cover the "dead zones" inherent to elevation and azimuth concerns.

Our system consists of three significant elements: a camera, a DLP projector, and a PC, costing a total of approximately $2500 USD. However, an actual implementation would be significantly cheaper. Video cameras are fairly affordable and will decrease in price with time. The PC is easily replaceable by a very inexpensive microcontroller. The projector is the most expensive of the three elements. We used a projector because of the ease in projecting concentrated light at very specific regions. Typical DLP projectors are designed to produce high-quality images at high resolutions, have tuner components, and incorporate sophisticated optical components. Our projection region is very small and does not require the level of optical precision and resolution available in typical DLP projectors. We can imagine a projector designed specifically for our application that is significantly cheaper. An even cheaper alternative and proper solution is to replace the projector with a scanning laser (similar to those found in laser light shows). By spinning a mirror and pulsing a laser at different rates, we can produce the same effect as we are creating with the DLP projector. This is not only a much cheaper solution, but also a more effective solution than a diffuse projector beam. Therefore, it becomes more practical to place many of these systems throughout a space for increased coverage.

6 Applying BlindSpot to Create Capture-Resistant Environments

Our original motivation for the design of BlindSpot was to build a system that would thwart picture taking of certain critical areas (inside of spaces such as office environments, conferences, tradeshows, and galleries) without having to confiscate recording devices from their owners. Within our research lab space, we often hang many posters that we created to present our project ideas internally amongst one another. In our initial demonstration of the system, we used BlindSpot to prevent the recording of one of our research posters. The poster was placed on one side of an 8-foot wide hallway. Although it was possible to take pictures at an angle up to 45° from 15 feet away on either side, the resulting pictures were usually extremely warped images of the poster. We used 2 sets of cameras and projectors to act as camera detectors and neutralizers. We instrumented these detectors and neutralizers above the poster to continuously monitor and protect a 90° sweep directly in front of it. When the system detected a camera, it neutralized it using the projectors. Both these steps happened automatically in the background without any manual intervention. Obviously, our approach did not prevent people from looking at the poster. Only when a user requested the right to take a picture did the owner of the space need to interact with the system to allow grant permission.

In this section, we present some interesting application ideas presented to us by others who have approached us during our development of this system, as well as the challenge of balancing against the lawless applications of this approach. The ideas presented to us by other interested parties include preventing the recording of copyrighted movies in theatres, protecting against industrial espionage, and using it as a part of an anti-paparazzi system. In addition to these applications of BlindSpot, we imagine obvious illegitimate uses of this system that may arise and must be addressed.

6.1 Anti-Piracy: Preventing Illegal Video Recordings in Movie Theatres

According to the Motion Picture Association of America (MPAA), the USA is the largest consumer of home entertainment products in the world, with consumer spend eclipsing $22.2 billion USD in 2002. In 2004, the US motion picture industry losses exceeded $3 billion USD in potential worldwide revenue due to piracy. The MPAA views optical disk piracy as the greatest threat to the audiovisual market in the USA, and the majority of all pirated products found in the USA is mastered from illegal camcording at theatrical screenings. Though movie piracy is an international problem, MPAA has spearheaded the worldwide effort to fight piracy, successfully lobbying Congress to introduce legislation and assisting in worldwide manhunts in pursuit of pirates around the globe. A sign of the MPAA's lobbying success was seen in early September 2005 when the Bush administration created the first Coordinator for International Intellectual Property Enforcement to help fight piracy. Though these efforts have made significant progress, movie piracy due to camcording continues to increase as box office numbers decline.

Simply delaying the release of pirated movies by just a few days can prevent the lost of hundreds of millions of dollars in revenues. Currently, a blockbuster takes just a few hours on average to go from full screening to illegal distribution over the Internet. There are over 30,000 screens in the USA, and one can imagine the logistical nightmare of guarding all of those, especially when theatre owners do not want to spend the money for extra security guards.

A potential application of the BlindSpot system is to actively prevent the illegal recording of movies. By no means would the system replace the security staff, but it would serve as a notifier for potential illicit activities. The BlindSpot system would be installed near the screens and directed towards the audience. Multiple units would need to be installed to cover large theatres, such as those with stadium style seating. During our development of this application, we quickly encountered concerns over the stigma of the "neutralizer" from the general public. Although the system is designed not to interfere with the viewing experience, the idea of a light beam being directed at the audience is not appealing from a marketing point of view. This is a tricky balance that must be solved. On one hand, the movie industry does not want to lose the revenues through piracy, but at the same time they also do not want to upset the people who are actually paying to watch the movie in theatres. A potential solution is to employ just the detection component, which would notify staff members of the seat with a clandestine camera. It would be the responsibility of the staff member to call the appropriate authorities to rectify the situation.

6.2 Preventing Industrial Espionage

By the last quarter of 2006, approximately 85% of mobile phones in Japan were camera phones; it is expected this number will saturate at 85–90% in 2006. By 2010, more than 95% of mobile phones shipped in the United States and Western Europe will have cameras. Camera phones, and related consumer technologies, make it extremely easy to capture still and moving images anywhere and anytime. Companies concerned that camera phones can compromise the security of their intellectual property often ban such devices from their facilities. However, banning is no longer desirable or nor practical, because of the growing number of such devices that people will likely have and their reliance on those devices. At the same time, any visitor or employee could be involved in a plot to compromise a company's trade secrets. Thus, industrial espionage, especially in the form of stealing company secrets is a growing concern, with claims that it causes billions of dollars of loss in intellectual property annually. Companies can install BlindSpot simply to detect cameras (as described in the previous section). Alternatively, the system also can be used to continuously monitor and protect areas of their buildings in a manner similar to our demonstrated application of the system within our own lab space.

6.3 Anti-Paparazzi: Preventing the Recording of People

With the increasing prevalence of consumer recording devices, there is a growing concern over unwanted recording of individuals in public and privates spaces. For example, gymnasium owners interested in protecting the privacy of their customers can install BlindSpot in locker rooms and bathrooms.

Interestingly, some of the early interest in this technology came from an anti-paparazzi firm in Hollywood interested in instrumenting celebrity homes and automobiles with BlindSpot. After the Princess Diana tragedy, there has been much interest in curtailing future problems with unsolicited photographers all trying to get their perfect shot of high-profile individuals. BlindSpot could play an instrumental role in helping to deter much of this activity, especially from the "stalkerazzi," who try to take candid pictures on private property.

It is important to recognize, however, that photographers imaginably will try to find counter measures. This could lead to a whole new set of problems, such as tampering or vandalism. The danger of employing this system must be considered, as counter measures could pose even more dangers than there are now for the people being recorded and the innocent bystanders.

6.4 Illegitimate Uses of BlindSpot as a Digital Cloak

We believe there is value in employing a technology like BlindSpot for the purposes of protecting one's privacy, especially during a time when recording devices have become so commonplace that everyone is likely to have one with them. With an almost impossible task of opting out of being recorded or confiscating every capture device from individuals who enter a private or semi-private space, an autonomous system can be employed to help against this growing concern. However, one major challenge that we faced while developing BlindSpot is the potential use of this system for illegitimate or illegal activities.

It will be years before BlindSpot can be miniaturized to a point where an individual could wear it as a digital clock. However, we can imagine legitimate concerns which arise from a wearable version of our camera detector and neutralizer which prevents the recording of individuals in public spaces. While intended to protect someone's privacy or a company's intellectual property, individuals also could use the system to hide or evade from security cameras when performing inappropriate activities, such as when robbing a bank.

With any technology, it is often difficult to prevent individuals from using it for illicit means. One way to curb the problem of this technology from getting into the wrong hands is to control it at the point of sale through a licensing scheme. Only authorized customers who can guarantee proper installation and security of the system itself would be allowed to purchase the system. In addition, areas requiring high levels of security would have to be alerted of the presence of this technology and employ alternative methods of surveillance and anomaly detection that do not rely on digital cameras.

7 Conclusions

In this chapter, we presented a proof of concept implementation of a system for creating capture-resistant environments which prevents the recording of still images and videos of regions within that physical space, called BlindSpot. The system actively seeks CCD and CMOS cameras in the environment and emits a strong localized light beam at each device to neutralize it from capturing. Although the directed light interferes with the camera's operation, it minimally impacts a human's vision in the environment. This approach also requires no cooperation on the part of the camera nor its owner. In addition, we discussed how this work can be extended to permit certain cameras to take pictures in the environment while preventing others. Although the proof of concept implementation effectively blocks cameras within its 45° field of view up to 5–10 meters away, we can easily add additional detector and neutralizer units to prevent capture within a larger sweep. This implementation provided a platform for investigation of the challenges inherent to producing a capture resistant environment. We explained how our approach resolves many of these challenges and described potential extensions to this work to address others.

This work presents an implementation that can be optimized in the future to detect and to neutralize camera recording for a wider variety of situations including large environments and mobile entities, such as a person. Finally, we discussed various applications of BlindSpot, such as protecting intellectual property in industry labs, curbing piracy in movie theatres, and preventing the recording of high-profile individuals. As we discussed, although this technology has interesting applications potential, there are an equal number of concerns with such a powerful technology.

References

1. Art. 29 Data Protection Working Party. (2004) Opinion 4/2004 on the Processing of Personal Data by means of Video Surveillance. Document 11750/02/EN WP89, European Commission, http://europa.eu.int/comm
2. Brassil J. (2005) Using Mobile Communications to Assert Privacy from Video Surveillance. Presented at the 1st International Workshop on Security in Systems and Networks 2005.
3. Chung J. (2004) Threat of Subway Photo Ban Riseth Again. Gothamist, November 30, 2004.
4. Eagle Eye. (1997) Bulletin of the Connecticut Academy of Science and Engineering. Vol. 12, No. 2.
5. Halderman J.A, Waters B. and Felten E.W. (2004) Privacy Management for Portable Recording Devices. In the Proceedings of WPES 2004: 16–24.
6. Haro, A., Flickner, M., Essa, I.A. (2000) Detecting and Tracking Eyes by Using Their Physiological Properties, Dynamics, and Appearance. In the proceedings of CVPR 2000: 1163–1168.
7. Iceberg's Safe Haven. http://www.iceberg-ip.com/index.htm
8. Pilu, M. (2007). Detector for Use with Data Encoding Pattern. United States Patent Application. 20070085842, April 19, 2007.
9. Video Voyeurism Prevention Act of 2004. (2004) 18 USC 1801.
10. Wagstaff J. (2004) Using Bluetooth to Disable Camera Phones, http://loosewire.typepad.com/blog/2004/09/using_bluetooth.html

Index